QUIET-TIME

MESSAGES

(Training for Believers)

Jere J. McBride

LPC PUBLISHING
P. O. BOX 725
ALPINE, TX 79831
A Division of Rancher's Supply, Inc.

©Jere Johnson McBride
LPC Publishing
P. O. Box 725
Alpine, Texas 79831

Copyright (©) 1994 by Jere J. McBride
All Rights Reserved

No portion of this book may be copied or reprinted without the express written permission of the LPC Publishing, Alpine, Texas, with the exception of a review of this book whereby brief passages may be quoted by the reviewer with proper credit line. Write for permission to the address above.

Printed in the United States of America

Library of Congress Card Number: 95-94044

ISBN Number: 0-9645310-0-3

FOREWORD

The messages in this book were recorded from April 1983 through March 1984. In April of that year, I found myself alone for the first time in my memory. I had married at 17, had 3 children, and finished my Master's Degree; by the time I was 43, all three of our children were in a university, far from home. I had resigned my job as a *special education counselor* to take over a family business while my husband was working on a special project in another state.

Since our business was at first very slow, I started spending more and more time with the Lord. Each morning, during my "quiet time", I began to receive prophesies from the Lord, which I wrote down and dated. After a few weeks, I noticed that these prophetic utterances were coming on a daily basis, so I began to record them in spiral notebooks. The messages would come as fast as I could write, and then, after a few minutes, they would end. I continued to record these messages daily, until they stopped----in April of 1984. Because they had been coming for such a long time, I did not realize that I had a year's worth of messages until I began to use them in my daily devotionals. For many years I only shared them with my immediate family and two close friends*.

In 1985 I recorded them on cassettes (4 in all) for a backup-copy, and then in 1994 I began to put them on my computer. While I was taping them, I realized that these messages could be useful to every believer. Then when I put the prophesies on computer

Foreword

as a whole, instead of individual daily devotionals), I discerned that God had used these messages to teach me about his character, his kingdom and spiritual warfare. He had used them to disciple and prepare me, as a believer. These Messages have blessed me more than I can relate, and I pray that they will bless every believer who reads them.

*Two of my closest Christian friends helped me with the scripture references and prayers at the end of each message. I would like to thank Faye Forgy and Sammie Lane for their support and assistance.

This book is dedicated to the following persons:

My husband and hero: Roy

My children: Rowdy, Randy, Rocky and Monica

My grandchildren: Cougar, Caleb and Micah

My parents: Mother and Bill

My special friends: Faye, Sammie, Astrid
Frances, Em and Margaret

Big Bend Women's Aglow

My sisters in Christ

QUIET-TIME MESSAGES

January 1

My people are the difference in the world today; they are the light. Their prayers, their influence, their stands on issues are the means I use to keep morality and righteousness before the people. You will see stronger and stronger people coming forth boldly to proclaim my gospel. You will see many lives harvested for the kingdom, even as evil ones wax worse and worse.

The battle has begun! Warriors must be trained and ready to attack and disperse the enemy, to bring relief to those in bondage. The task will not be easy, but it will be rewarding. Many listening ears will hear and obey. There are still so many who are longing to know the truth and these must be won. Be alert to signs of the end. Be aware of my leading and be quick to obey. A slothful servant I cannot use, but a ready hearer, a quick mind and a prepared spiritual man will not be conquered. I have seen to it!

Scriptures: Romans 8:35-39, Ephesians 6:10-20, I John 4:17

Prayer: Father, give me boldness. Give me your divine courage to stand for you. Give me listening ears and an understanding heart in this day. Help me to keep my eyes on Jesus and not be moved by circumstances. In Jesus' name I pray.

January 2
The time of redemption is near, for **Jesus Christ** the **Messiah** reigns. For aeons of time man did not have the privilege of coming to me. Now, not only can man come, but he can abide with me. When man fell, he removed himself from the umbrella of safety that had surrounded him. Through my covenant with Abraham, his seed gained the protection and benefits that keeping the law could bring. Now, through the shed blood of **Jesus**, all men have the opportunity to abide under my wings, to be truly united spiritually to **me**.

Many believers of **Jesus Christ** do not know or recognize the covenant-keeping power. They do not walk in its benefits nor benefit from its blessings. They have the covenant, but in name only. It is as if they've "received the diploma but never graduated." I am reviving the spirits of men to be partakers of the divine nature, the divine partnership, to walk in fullness of life. Knowledge of me is flowing like a river to those who have listening ears. Receive the covenant benefits by abiding in me.

Scriptures: John 15:4-5, Galatians 3:13-14.

Prayer: Father, I am so grateful for your keeping power. I ask that I might be aware of your protection----never let me forget it. I know that apart from you, I can do nothing. I thank you and praise you in Jesus' name.

January 3

The bread that you cast upon the water will always come back to you. Never be hesitant to give freely to others of your time, energy, prayers, money, talents. The only caution you need to take is that your deeds are done in the Spirit, not out of guilt, condemnation, or a need to be approved by men. I have anointed every work done from a pure heart, a heart that desires to please me and acts in love. Remember that I said to *do your good deed in secret and your Father would reward you openly.* Others may see your good works, but you do not do the good works to be seen of men.

I give my disciples many opportunities to serve, just as *Satan* gives many opportunities to fall. The power of discernment is always available to look into the spiritual realm to see whether the leading is of me. You can know how you are led, for *my sheep hear my voice.*

Scriptures: Matthew 10:42, Luke 6:30

Prayer: Father, help me to be sensitive to the needs of others. Help me to be a cheerful giver, the kind you delight in. Help me to be generous with my time and with my prayers, as well as with my money.

You have given me everything in Jesus. I thank you, Lord.

January 4
    I came to give you abundant life and you must receive it by faith. Life that I give touches every area of your being and causes no sorrow with it; the difficulty comes when you must yield your will to mine. Even yielding will be easy if you allow yourself to trust me and to walk out of fear into faith. The anguish you feel in trials and temptations comes from fear and unbelief. Put these aside and you walk on steady ground, surefooted and unafraid. You must choose to believe me and then to let my word renew your mind. This done, the rest is easy. I said that with faith, you could move mountains, and you can! I said to pray believing and you will have whatsoever you say. Order your conversation aright and see the glory of the Lord. I lie not!

Scriptures: Numbers 11:23, Matthew 17:20, Luke 17:6.

Prayer: Father, I thank you that you have given every man the measure of faith. You have equipped me with everything I need for abundant life. I praise you, and I thank you. I rest in you.

January 5
    Living in the Kingdom of God is more than a

January 5

commitment to **me**. It is a daily abiding in **me**, and **my word** abiding in you. To remain in my kingdom you must be in tune with **me** or you will find yourself thrust to the borders, where danger lurks. In the interior, you have the protection of the King (my provision, hospitality and good will). Failing to abide will carry you to the border areas where intense warfare reigns. The warfare is ever present, but deep inside the Kingdom there is a rest, a haven where the arrows of the enemy cannot reach. It is called *abiding under the shadow of the Almighty*. When you live on the border, you are still a citizen of the Kingdom, but you do not enjoy the immense benefits that life in the interior brings.

Come into deeper territory with **me**, so no harm touches you. Worry and fear cannot reach the life of one who lives in safety in the Kingdom of God.

Scriptures: Psalm 91, John 15:7-8, Hebrews 6:14-16.

Prayer: Father, I thank you for the secret place of the most high, under the shadow of the almighty. I thank you for your guarantee of abundant life. I thank you for your divine rest. I worship you, Father, I love you and I depend on you. I thank you, because in Christ, I have all provision. I thank you for taking away all my fears and for being my God.

January 6

I have forgiven you your trespasses, so be diligent to forgive others when they trespass against you. Have you ever thought of what that word means? When you trespass, you enter another's domain illegally. You are in places you have no right to be. When people trespasses against you, they are entering areas of your life where you did not bid them entrance and where their presence is unwanted. Trespassing may be done physically, emotionally, or spiritually.

You trespass on my love when you wound another, when you fail to show love or mercy, when you choose to follow your own will, instead of **mine**. You trespass on my grace when you fail to receive the freedom that **Jesus** bought. When you doubt **my** word, when you criticize others needlessly, when you utter words of fear, or hinder the work of the Kingdom, you trespass against me. I forgive your trespasses freely. Therefore,

You must refuse ------
to harbor a grudge,
to resent an ungrateful word or act,
to be bitter over an injury.

I forgive, and so can you. *To whom much is given, much is required.*

Scriptures: Psalm 103:3, Matthew 6:12-15, Matthew 18:21-22, Mark 11:25.

Prayer: Father, I appreciate your forgiveness so much! I thank you that when I stumble, you are faithful to forgive me (when I repent). Please keep me ever mindful of the fact that I must forgive. . . I cannot afford not to forgive others. Help me form the habit of forgiveness. Remind me that when I start to take offense, I lose my anointing. Oh God, I want to be like Jesus. He prayed, "Forgive them", even as they were crucifying him. I count on your forgiveness, Lord, and I thank you for it.

January 7

Be a ready learner, with eyes that see and ears that hear. You can open yourself to spiritual truths by thinking pure thoughts, meditating in **my word,** spending time with me, and choosing to learn of me. Remember, *as a man thinketh in his heart, so is he.* I will give you good things to hear and good things to see. Look for them, for the enemy is ready to tempt you with the lust of the eye, the lust of the flesh and the pride of life. He attempts to whisper deceitfulness to your heart. If you are unprepared to hear me, then you will hear him. If you choose his deceptions, you will not hear my truths. *He that hath an ear, let him hear.* You will not hear if your heart is full of darkness and evil thoughts.

Prepare yourself for **me**, for **my word**, for **my** voice, for **my** creative beauty in all you see. I have revealed myself to all men, so there will be none with excuse. Be ready to see my revelation and to hear the voice of your **Shepherd**. Be ready.

Scriptures: Joshua 1:3, Proverbs 4:20-23, Mark 4:24, Luke 8:13, John 10:3, Acts 13:44.

Prayer: Father, how exciting it is that I can hear the voice of the God of the universe! You are always with me. You said you would never leave me or forsake me. Father, I ask that I would never become so busy that I fail to hear your voice. I ask that I would learn to be selective in what I hear, always be ready for communion with you, and that I would tune out the voices of the world. I love you so much, Father. I can never express my appreciation enough. Sometimes I am so burdened, but you are always there.

January 8

The entrance into **my** kingdom is the real beginning of life. This is the life that counts for good and not for evil. It enhances all life and permeates into the very souls of men. Kingdom living brings the knowing of real peace. All attempts to obtain peace without Jesus fail. **Eyes are blinded and ears are deaf lest they should find it and be healed.....**There is no way to find it but through the door (**Jesus**). The thief cannot obtain this life.

Life lived in **my** kingdom gives you purpose and goals for life. It enables a man to see beyond himself and to live beyond selfishness. Life with **me** brings out the core of all that man was created to be and allows him to function without sin distorting his actions. It cleanses his soul and empowers him to love purely. I rescued man from his fallen state and his redemption becomes complete as he progressively matures in the kingdom of life. Man becomes whole again whole to serve, whole to create, whole to love and whole to reign. Life begins in the **Kingdom of God.**

Scriptures: I Peter 1:11, I John 5:1-5.

Prayer: Father, I believe that Jesus is the Christ, and through him, I have overcome all things. I thank you for your glorious salvation, Lord.

January 9

The ability to believe me has to be prompted by the Holy Spirit, so pray that the Holy Spirit would go before you to prepare the way. Then the seed of **my word** must be sown in prepared soil. Do not lament if the soil seems rocky or choked with thistles. Instead, pray again that the **Holy Spirit** would continue to prepare the soil.

The sowing and the nurturing are only part of the program. There must be a harvesting time. A crop left in the field does not benefit the kingdom. Pray that harvesters would be there to bring in the crops, and store them properly until they can be properly dispersed to feed many.

I have given you a task to do. It is to nurture and harvest, not just to plant. Look forward to life, to the days to come. There is much joy awaiting those who dwell with me, much joy in enjoying the fruits of your labor, long after the harvest time is over. *I came that they might have life, and that more abundantly.*

Scriptures: Matthew 9:37-38, John 6:44.

Prayer: Father, I pray that I might be a willing worker, prompt to do what you would have me to do Make me sensitive to the leading of the Holy Spirit. I pray that I might be ready to prepare the soil with prayer, water the soil with the word, and plant the seeds of the gospel in season. Father, I want to be part of the end-time harvest. I do not want to be lazy, Lord. I thank you and praise you for your divine provision. You have thought of everything, Lord. I pray that I will do my part.

January 10
Be wary as a serpent and gentle as a lamb. You should not be naive to the world's ways, but you do not have to indulge in them to know them. Remember that although *Satan* can seduce and corrupt, I am more than able to cleanse and purify. Do not see anyone as hopeless. Do not be unaware of lurking *evil*; allow the spirit of discernment to operate freely and combat evil on the spiritual plane.

Remember to bind the strongman. Then you can take his possessions and dismantle his abode.

Nothing is too corrupted for you to handle, but wait until **I** prompt you and go before you. **I** have given you power to tread on serpents and scorpions, but do not take them up without **me.** There is so much for you to learn, but **my Spirit** will lead you into all truth. **I** have not left you comfortless or defenseless. **I** have made provision for every situation, when you walk in the Spirit and in my will.

Be prepared spiritually with an informed and loving heart. You can deal with corruption without being corrupted. You can deal wisely and with good success. **I** have made all things possible.

Scriptures: Matthew 18:18-20, Luke 10:19-20.

Prayer: Father, I thank you for your leading and your protection. I pray that I may be discerning and diligent. I ask for wisdom in all things. I pray that I might always be strong in the Lord and of good courage. I thank you and praise you, Lord.

January 11

There is no lack in the kingdom of **God**----no lack of provision, no lack of love, no lack of power. Since the kingdom of **God** is within you, all these resources are there as well. **I** have given you the keys of the kingdom. You have keys to unlock all resources. One key is faith. This does not mean just listening to the **word.** It means <u>hearing</u> the **word.** *He that has ears, let him hear.* If you have a key, but do not use it, what good is the key? You must be a doer of the word, and the resources are there to use. The "binding and loosing" are the keys that enable the resources to flow. There are transferring keys that transport the necessary resource at the proper time. **My** kingdom is a storehouse of wealth that is found in the spiritual realm, but you must walk in the **Spirit** to operate in its realm.

Is it not all fascinating? As you mature, the mystery begins to unfold, and you begin to see more clearly. The resources are there. The keys are there. Accede to use them. **I** have given you the land.

Scriptures: Matthew 16:19, 2 Corinthians 9:8, James 2:20.

Prayer: Father, I thank you that you have provided me with everything I will ever need. I am so grateful, Lord, that in you I have every good thing. I repent, Lord, for the times I have failed to appropriate your blessings, and for the times I have failed to walk in the Spirit. I lift you up, Father, and I worship you. Help me always to have a listening ear.

January 12

Speak the truth in love. Do not be offended, nor offensive. If you walk in love, much is always accomplished. The truth you speak will open hearts. *If I be lifted up, I will draw all men unto me.* When you speak my words, do not be afraid. *Perfect love cast out fear. . . . I will send you as a lamb before wolves, but they will in no wise harm you.* I prepare the way before you, and the way will be amply lighted. Be steadfast and be not afraid. *Lo, I am with you alway.*

Scriptures: Psalm 119:165, I John 4:7-21.

Prayer: Father, help me to walk in love. I choose to love, Father. I choose not to be offended. Jesus has said that the second greatest commandment is to love my neighbor as myself. I confess that sometimes I find some people hard to love, but I choose to be obedient. I choose to love others in the love of Christ. Thank you for your wonderful provision and promise.

January 13

Carnal man is without hope in the world, but the regenerated man is at peace. If a man is not at peace, he is not walking in the light. *When the eye is full of light, then is the whole body.* Keep your eyes full of light. Look for the light and see the light. Where there is light, there is no darkness. So many stumble because they do not see the light. Yet the light is before them and they see it not.

How do you see the light? You search for it as

a man who is thirsty searches for water. You search for it as a man who is hungry searches for food. Do not rest until you find that which refreshes. Search for **me** with all your heart, and I will be found. You have my promise.....

I will be found!

Scriptures: Psalm 42:1-2, Isaiah 60:1, Amos 5:4.

Prayer: Father, I know that in Jesus I have light and peace. I pray that I might always walk in the light. I thank you for the light, Father.

January 14

The thoughts you receive in line with my will are the leading of the **Holy Spirit.** Learn to heed them and you will see more manifestations of power in your life. I desire obedience rather than sacrifice, and **I** need to be able to trust you to carry out my wishes. I am faithful to be a lamp unto your feet and a light unto your path, but you must choose to walk where I lead. Be ready to heed **my** voice, in season and out. You will not be deceived, for *my sheep know my voice.*

The acts of love, of kindness, of obedience that **I** bid you to do will become natural acts. Walking in the **Spirit** will seem normal. If you will learn to listen to me before you speak or act, then you will see my power. I give good thoughts and the one who wills to do **my** will, will receive from me. Stand ready, stand eagerly. Be anticipating good things. I have an exciting life planned for you.

Scriptures: I Samuel 15:22, John 10:1-4, Galatians 5:16.

Prayer: Father, help me always to hear your voice. I will to do your will. I thank you for your leading. Help me to walk in the Spirit so that I will not fulfill the lusts of the flesh.

January 15

Prepare yourself physically, emotionally and spiritual to walk in the paths where **I** lead. You have an obligation to make yourself a living stone that will fit in with the kingdom plan, a stone properly joined with others who love me. I am building a mighty kingdom whose foundation is **Jesus Christ** the **Messiah. He** is the author and finisher of your salvation. You have been bought with a <u>great</u> price.

The acts you do, the thoughts you think, the purposes of your heart----should be in line with my purposes. These purposes must become your goals. Prepare to be a fit soldier! Dedicate yourself to be enjoined with **Christ** in every area of your life. **He** has given you the power to overcome. He has opened the portals of heaven for you to see the light of the world, to have revelation knowledge of the word.

January 16

Let your heart and mind be set on heavenly goals and you will see the earthly goals diminish. **My kingdom is for those who are willing to serve unstintingly in victory and in power.** Those who overcome shall receive the crowns of life. You are one of these.

Scriptures: I Corinthians 6:20, Hebrews 12:2.

Prayer: Father, in the name of Jesus, I ask you to reign over every area of my life. I confess that I am an overcomer, and I thank you for it.

January 16

The way to **life** is through **my son**, Jesus, and to follow him brings peace. I have given you the blueprint of life in my word. There is nothing in life that can defeat you because **he** has overcome the world. Be diligent to keep your mind fixed on Heavenly goals, to keep the **word** before you night and day so that you cannot be moved. Many storms come in life, but there are none that can move the established heart. There is no enemy that can withstand the power **I** give and no obstacle that will be immovable.

You must share this new of victory. You must spread the gospel by the avenue of love. No one can resist a message of love. I prepare the soil with the fertilizer of your prayers. Be diligent to pray, be diligent to love, be diligent to obey and serve. I put men before you. Show them the way to **Jesus.**

Scriptures: Matthew 5:14-16, 28:19.

Prayer: Father, I ask for your strength and guidance in the assignment you have given me. I pray that you will help me to be diligent. Give me seeing eyes and hearing ears. Thank you.

January 17

The *enemy comes to steal, kill and destroy.* He is out to kill the body, the mind and the spirit. He will attack in any area in which a weakness exists. To defeat *him* you must have a hedge and you must use your shield. The hedge is built by prayer and the shield is wielded by faith. Once these are securely in place, you must stand in patience, not allowing fear to move the hedge or the shield.

Don't look at the operations of the *devil.* Don't look at *his* maneuvers against you. You will see vast armies arising to defeat you----armies of circumstances, evidence, words. The word-ruled mind will ignore these armies and will not be moved! You must learn to think **Godly** thoughts, thoughts that agree with **my word.** You must bring your thoughts into captivity, casting down vain imaginations.

Continue to pray positive prayers, stand in

January 18

unwavering faith and say words that confirm my word. Victory is inevitable! Nothing can defeat you when you operate in my power and love. Rejoice in the victory. It is done.

Scriptures: Job 1:10, II Corinthians 6:7, Ephesians 6:10-18.

Prayer: Father, in the name of Jesus I confess I am strong in the Lord! I have no fear for, I have the love of God. I confess that I am more than a conqueror, in Jesus. Thank you, Father.

January 18

Because you have chosen to follow me, and **I** have chosen to reveal **myself** to you, the kingdom of **God** dwells mightily within you. This kingdom is a living, vital organ of love that pulls down strongholds and defeats *Satanic* bulwarks. This kingdom is spreading like volcanic lava and is covering the whole earth with victory.

My Church, my people are coming into a unity of faith and purpose that will release captives. You will see many prisoners go free. You will see homes restored and children returned to security. There will be a haven of peace developed in places that now have storms of strife. The homes of my people will be a place of love and contentment. You will be a partner in the restoration of many. I will give you the means, the opportunity and the desire to serve.

I will work on your behalf to prepare the way.

Scriptures: Psalm 4:3, 140:13; Matthew 28:20.

Prayer: Father, I thank you for your presence. I thank you for your restoration and for your peace.

January 19

The ways of destruction are many, but the way to life is **One.** I have given the way to abundant life and you must walk in it. To those who can *see,* the decision is clear; it behooves you to lead others who may see things less clearly. In the *body* there are so many personalities; some are creators, some are steadfast doers, some are decision makers, some are those with vision. The desire of the **Father** is to see a unity of the faith in them all, and this unity will come about through love and commitment to **me.**

As you walk in the path of love, look around to see those who need to follow. If there is a willing heart among them, offer them the encouragement and guidance they need. Show them the path and strengthen them until they, too, can lead. I am building a kingdom of living stones, stones delicately hewed to desired specifications, hewed in love, paid for in sacrifice and obedience. These stones will stand forever and will be evidence of the **Father's** faithfulness in redeeming his people. Be looking for opportunities to gather, to lead, to encourage, to love. **I** have chosen you a special stone. **I** will use you to hew others to function in my kingdom.

Scriptures: Isaiah 50:4, 51:16; Matthew 4:19, I Peter 2:5.

Prayer: Father make me aware of the needs of those around me. Make me sensitive to the people you would have me minister to. Give me the courage and wisdom I will need. I thank you for it, in Jesus' name.

January 20

You are blessed. Daily rejoice in the blessings and let praise come forth. As you begin to praise in thankfulness and joy, the spirit within you begins to rise to release the worship it feels. Worship opens the way for freedom in the spiritual realm. Your spirit was meant to soar in freedom and power. Your spirit longs to commune with **me**. This is ecstasy in its highest form. As you learn to come into this state, you will seek it more fervently. This is learning to abide in me in the deepest way.

Praise starts with the choice to praise. Choose to come into *my gates with thanksgiving in your heart*, to come into *my courts with praise*. Begin to enter into the **Holy of Holies.** There will I be to bid you welcome and to lift you up in renewal and refreshing. You were created to fellowship with me. Choose to do so, and you will release the spirit that longs to come to the **Father.** The trip is worth the effort.

January 21

Scriptures: Deuteronomy 10:21, Psalm 100.

Prayer: Father, I praise you, I worship you. I am so grateful for all that you've done for me. Lord, I thank you. I choose to praise you. Teach me, so that I may be able to praise you more.

January 21

The time you spend with **me** is never time that is lost. You regain it minute for minute during the day. A refreshed mind and spirit function more effectively throughout the day. I have redeemed the time for you. The enemy would have you spend your time foolishly. He has trapped so many with his lies and deceits. When you spend the time in prayer and the **word,** you are being wise in all your affairs. Learn to release yourself during your prayer times. Refuse *Satan's* blockade attempts to bombard your mind with obligations, worries, chores and needs. You have but one need and that is to come into my presence for refreshing and life.

Choose to bless **me** and you will reap blessings. Choose to humble yourself before **me** and your status will be raised. I am the *giver* of all life. **I Am the I AM.** Come in, Come in. Your fears will be quenched and your petitions granted.

Scriptures: Exodus 3:14, Psalm 16:11, Luke 10:38-42.

Prayer: Father, thank you for redeeming the time.

January 22

Thank you for your presence. Thank you for your miracle-working power in my life. Thank you for your word, and most of all, thank you for Jesus.

January 22
When the temptations of life begin to assault you, turn immediately to me. Refuse to allow Satan a foothold! Temptations will come, but you do not have to receive them. If you fall (or fail), immediately repent. I am faithful to forgive you. Satan seeks to sift you. He is a destroyer, a killer, a thief. If you remember that greater is He who is in you than he that is in the world, you will always win. Rebuke Satan's attacks. Remember that he who is begotten of God keepeth himself, and the wicked one toucheth him not. These words are as true today as when they were written. You do not have to succumb to the wiles of the devil. You are an overcomer. I have declared it, and if you believe me, you will win!

I have given you power to tread on serpents and scorpions. You choose to use **my word**, and you will see the *enemy* flee. He cannot stand before the word. ***Resist the devil and he will flee***. You must store **the word** in your heart for the critical testing times. The **word** must be there in abundance in order to well up within you at the time you need it. The **word** will give you confidence, it will deliver you, it will save your life! Be not afraid; only believe.

January 23

Scriptures: Matthew 10:18-20, Romans 8:37.

Prayer: Father, thank you for your salvation and your keeping power. Help me always to turn to you. Help me to hide your words in my heart more and more, so that I will have strength in the hour of need. Thank you.

January 23

There is nothing impossible with **me**. Remember this in "impossible" situations! Remember the **word,** remember the acts and deeds done by those who accepted and acted on the **Word**. Were not the dead raised? Were not the blind given sight? Were not armies defeated and kingdoms restored? I have not changed, and **my word** has not changed. *To him who believes, all things are possible.*

Be prepared to go to the utmost of your faith, then see your faith go beyond that point. I don't tempt, I don't try, I overcome! (and so can you!) *Satan* would have it otherwise. *He* seeks to fill you with fear, so that you will fall back at obstacles and not be victorious. But I have overcome *him*, the world, and all that is in the world. I have overcome death, I have overcome sickness, I have overcome poverty and fear. You are sent, therefore, to overcome, too. Do all in my name, with pure motives. Where you see pain, rebuke it! When you see fear, speak faith! Nothing is impossible with me. Receive and believe!

January 24

Scriptures: Mark 5:36, Luke 8:50, Philippians 4:13.

Prayer: Lord, I <u>will</u> be strong in you. I <u>will</u> be an overcomer through Jesus who strengthens me. I am willing. Help me be better prepared to do your will.

January 24

My peace I give unto you, not as the world gives, but **my** peace. This is the peace that passes all understanding. There is a price for peace.

Peace comes through trust, trust in **my** ability
    to handle your cares.
Peace comes through love, your love for me and your
    confidence that **I** love you.
Peace comes through faith, faith in the **Father**
    bought by the **son**.
Peace comes though quietness, as you come into my
    presence and let **me** comfort you.

There is nothing that can forcibly take away your peace; you have to give it up. You can hold on to it by allowing the **Holy** Spirit to lead and direct you. **I** give peace freely. I have provided all things for you. Learn to accept them, to live in the kingdom of life and peace. I speak peace, and peace is.

Scriptures: John 14:27, Ephesians 2:14, Philippians 4:7.

Prayer: Lord, thank you for the peace that passes understanding. Help me always to live in your presence and your peace.

January 25

There are always those who are hungry for me. Look for them and then feed them. **I** sent my disciples into the world with the admonition to give peace to those households that accepted me. This is still the admonition of today. For whosoever will, let him come. Be alert to those whose hearts are open, so that you may supply the need. There are many who are hungry, but so few to feed them. **I** have given you bread unlimited to feed them. **I** have given the bread of life. So feed, feed, feed!

Scriptures: Mark 6:37, Luke 10:1-11, John 21:15

Prayer: Father, I ask your help in finding those souls who are hungry for you. Help me to feed those souls. Help me to hear you, Father, and to be quick to obey.

January 26

Because of the love **I** give, you can love, too. In your natural state, you are not able to love your neighbor. When you come to **me**, you are able to conquer all with love. **I** set the example for love, an unselfish love that never dies. You can love this way, too. You do it by dying to self. When you die to

January 27

self, you receive back so much more than you can possibly give. I gave one son out of love. I now have millions of sons who love out of a pure heart, and millions more to come!

Except a seed die in the earth, it cannot produce fruit. But when it dies, *it produces twenty, thirty, a hundred times as much.* Die to self and live to love. You will find it worthwhile to do so.

Scriptures: Matthew 13:3-9, John 4:7, I Corinthians 13:1-13.

Prayer: Thank you for your love. Father, I want to die to self. I choose to love, and I choose to walk in love. Thank you for loving us so much!

January 27

Unto those who believe are given the secrets of life, the power of life, the love of life. *Many are called but few are chosen,* because only a few are willing to see, are willing to be disciplined, are willing to obey. *He that has ears to hear, let him hear.*

Because you choose to come into the fullness of life, you will see the full salvation of my Son. You will experience the beauty and joy of abundant living. The grace that I have bestowed on all men is not received by all, but the grace is still given. Look for the beauty I give. Look for the joy that is for you. He that seeks will find. It is for you to seek, however. I am faithful to those who seek me.

January 28

Scriptures: Matthew 7:7, 21:6; John 10:10

Prayer: Lord, I am willing to seek the abundant life. Help me to see and seek your discipline for my life. Thank you, Father.

January 28

Begin each day with a new resolve to abide with me more. It is so easy to let your temperance slide; the evil of slovenliness ever lurks nearby. The *enemy* would have you think that a little slip will not matter. Then soon you find yourself in a landslide of spiritual apathy, with only rocky, shifting ground beneath you. Get a foothold each day by standing on the rock, ***Jesus Christ.*** Become steadfast and on solid ground daily, to keep the foundation of your faith secure.

Do not hesitate to begin anew, if necessary, going back to the beginning of your faith. If you gained strength from **me** once, you can again. The walk of faith is done purposely. It is not a happenstance! You must determine to come into my presence to learn of **me.** Choose daily to abide with me. Soon, abiding with me becomes as essential a part of your being as breathing. **I** am the breath of your spirit, and **I** invigorate you with life. *Neglect not so great a salvation.*

Scriptures: Luke 6:47-48, John 15:4-6, Hebrews 2:3.

January 29

Prayer: Help me, Father, to abide more and more in you. I want to be founded upon the rock of Jesus. Help me to avoid spiritual apathy. I love you, Father.

January 29

The place of functioning for you is wherever you are. I place you daily and you are in place spiritually. There is no fear in life when you know that wherever you are, **I am.** There is no place you can be where **I** am not. There is never a time that you will fail to hear **me** unless fear blocks the channel. A heart of fear hears only the *enemy* (that vile creature *Satan*). He inhabits fearful, worry-filled hearts and shuts a mind to faith. However, a steadfast believer will not hear *him*. Be secure in that wherever you are, **I** have a reason for you to be there. I will lead you safely to the good pastures, the cool water, to the place of rest.

You belong to me and **I** will never forget you. Your name is written on the palm of my hand. I am faithful to those who trust in me. Function wherever you are. Show forth my character, my heart-cry, my love. You are my disciple and **I** live in you.

Scriptures: Exodus 33:14, II Chronicles 15:2, Matthew 28:20.

Prayer: Father, thank you for your presence. Thank you for always being with me in every circumstance, in every place.

January 30

The *God* of this world has deceived man into worshiping himself. Man considers only his wants, his desires, his health, his future. But to those who have heard the news of the gospel of **Jesus Christ**, there is another way. The one who has made **Jesus lord** and has had the mystery of Christ revealed to him is no longer controlled by the *evil one.* That person no longer has to obey circumstances, emotions and fear. He is free to rise above his own greed and needs. He is thus free to live life unselfishly. He can now know that the things he once worshiped in the flesh have been made new and are now provided by the **Father of Love.**

I am the Father of all men who call upon my name. **I** have given unto you, who believe, the very things you once exalted and made a god over your life. Through my son, **I** have provided health, well-being and a glorious future in the heavenly realm to which you are raised and now can call home. You are now totally free to pursue **my** great commission, knowing that if you seek first the kingdom of God, *then all these things shall be added unto you.*

Scriptures: Psalm 34:10, 63:1; Matthew 6:33; Romans 8:1-18.

Prayer: You are my Lord. I praise you and thank

you. I know, Father, that you have given me life, that in you, I have every good thing. Thank you. Help me always to seek you first.

January 31
The warfare is real and the needs are without number. You are beginning to see how essential it is to have a trained, disciplined army who can fight the *enemy* effectively and without mercy. I have no mercy on *evil* and you must not either. You have prepared yourself. Prepare others.

You must learn not to waste yourself on scattered skirmishes, no matter how much the need, but to join and train others so that you fight not in vain. The *enemy* comes with guerilla warfare to wear you down and keep you scattered. You concentrate on training others, who will train others, who will train others. Soon the *enemy* will meet a spiritual giant at every step. *He* will run into overpowering forces at every turn. *He* will be defeated on the right and on the left.

I am preparing many to train more. The **army of God** cannot be defeated, but you must be ready to fight effectively. To do this, open the training ground to all who will join. This is the fastest way to win.

Scriptures: II Corinthians 10:4, I Timothy 6:12, II Timothy 2:3.

January 31

Prayer: Father, help me to welcome your discipline and training. Make me ever willing to do your will. Keep me alert to carry out your divine orders. Give me courage. Help me to do what you would have me do at all times. Thank you, Father.

FEBRUARY

February 1

In order to see the hope that **I** give, you must look always beyond the present circumstances. Always consider what is **my** best for any situation and believe for that. You will know what is best because **my word** will confirm it.

If the circumstances are in conflict with the **word,** then the circumstances will have to change, for the **word** will never change. Set your eyes on the **word,** on the redeeming power of **Jesus,** on the hope that never fails. **I** have already given the power and authority to tread on every serpent and scorpion. **I** have already given the weapons of warfare and the promises of victory. There is nothing more to give! Go, using the authority invested in you, as you have believed. There is nothing impossible with **me.**

Scriptures: Malachi 3:6, Luke 1:37, Luke 10:19, II Corinthians 10:4.

Prayer: Father, thank you for your Word. Help me always to make your word the final authority in my life. Help me always to remember that you never change.

February 2

The command *to rejoice in the Lord always* is not based on feelings, but on choice. There is a power in the act of rejoicing that begins to move

February 2

circumstances and paves the way for the miraculous.

Rejoicing in **me** acknowledges the reality of me.

Rejoicing in **me** reinforces the hope of your faith.

Rejoicing in **me** brings peace of mind and comfort to the heart.

Rejoicing in **me** floods your being with a covering of security.

Rejoicing in me brings an inner consciousness of my presence.

Choose to rejoice that *this is the day that the Lord hath made.* **I** am the **God** who hath made all things, and shall not this day also bring forth good? Open your spirit up to the power, the might, the authority that has been given you. Open your spirit up with acts of praise and worship, acts of thanksgiving and adoration. Then see my glory fall upon you as you submit unto me with joy. Remember, **I** am your benefactor, your source of good. Is it not worth rejoicing over?

Scriptures: Psalm 34:1-4, Psalm 99:1, Isaiah 29:19, Luke 10:20.

Prayer: Lord, I rejoice in you. I thank you for your provision for me. I praise you and worship you. Thank you Father.

February 3

The wages of sin are death. This is a statement of fact, but there are many ways to die. First, there is a physical death which will come to all. This is a vicious sting to the sinful man, but not to the redeemed. There is a mental death that comes to an unrenewed mind. The unbeliever has no idea of the creative, illuminating aspect of a mind that has been freed from sin. Then, of course, there is a spiritual death that lasts throughout eternity. The unbeliever is never to know his creator.

The sinful state is a tormenting one: physically, mentally, spiritually. But **I** have given **my** only begotten **Son** that man should not perish, but have everlasting life. Is not life the opposite of death? This means a new physical life, a new mental life, a new spiritual life. **Jesus** said, *I came that they might have life, and that more abundantly.* Heed these words and be free from the wages of sin. Life abundant belongs to you. Receive it!

Scriptures: John 3:16, John 3:17, John 10:10.

Prayer: Father, I am so grateful for life. Help me not only to receive your precious promise of life everlasting, but to share that promise with all who need to hear it. Thank you for taking away the sting of death, Lord. Thank you.

February 4

He that is greatest must be the servant . . . . Greater love hath no man but that he would lay down his life for his brother. These words are incomprehensible to the carnal mind, because that mind rebels against both servanthood and pure love. A man who is a servant in the kingdom of God is one who denies himself daily.

He denies the urge to sleep instead of pray.
He denies the urge to put off his meditation and Bible-reading time.
He denies the desire to stay away from people who need his counsel or support.
He lays down his life by giving his life to serve others.

He does this, not as a chore, but because he loves the **Father** first, and he also loves the brethren. He delights in his family and enjoys the fellowship of believers. He wants to mingle his faith with their faith. He abhors evil and chooses to fight it wherever it appears. He is sensitive to the **Father's** wishes and obeys the prompting of the **Holy Spirit** in serving his fellow man. He has seen the perfect example of unfeigned love in his **Savior, Jesus Christ.** He has chosen to imitate **Christ's** life and love. He is great in the kingdom of **God.**

Scriptures: Matthew 5:46, Matthew 16:24-25, Matthew 23:11.

Prayer: Lord, I want to be pleasing to you. I ask that I might be willing always to do what you want me to do . Make me sensitive, Lord, to the promp- ting of your Holy Spirit. Help me to be more like Jesus. Thank you Father.

February 5

There is no obstacle, no temptation, no circumstance that is beyond your power to remove, for I have given the authority and power over it. Keep the **word** active and foremost in your mind. Do not give in to fear, despondency, depression, anguish, heaviness. Draw on resources, bought and provided through the blood of the lamb. Do not give the evil one a foothold in your mind, body or actions.

You can stand firm, you can assert yourself against the enemy in power and might. Use the weapons of warfare to tear down strongholds and to set captives free. Let not vain imaginations rule your mind and actions. Bring every thought that disagrees with the **word into captivity.** You have the power to do so! Choose to hear the **word.** Choose to believe the word. Choose to act on the **word.** You have the victory and the strength. Cast off those things that would hinder you, and go forward unafraid. Many giants will fall at your feet because you have believed the **word.**

February 6

Scriptures: John 14:12, I Corinthians 1:19-20, Galatians 5:1.

Prayer: Father, I choose the Word! I thank you for the power of the blood of the lamb. Thank you, Father, for you Holy Spirit's teaching me and reminding me what the Word says in every situation. Thank you.

February 6

When you share **me,** you bring good news to those who have no hope. You bring an answer to a longing that has been heretofore unnamed and unanswered. Never be ashamed of the gospel. The good news is more valuable than rubies or the gifts of kings. I will open doors and hearts before you so the flow of power can go forth unhindered. I make a way where there is no way. I put down, and I raise up. Be prepared to go in where I have opened the way. Be ready to answer the call to arms. Be instant with words of truth, of love, of hope, of faith. And most of all, be not afraid. What can flesh do to you?

Scriptures: Psalms 19:9-10. Psalm 56:4; Isaiah 41:11-13.

Prayer: Father, I thank you for the good news of the gospel. Help me to be diligent to share it where you would have me to share it. Make me sensitive to your Spirit, to speak where the door has been opened.

Thank you for courage, Lord.

February 7

Redeem the time, for the days are evil. The time you spend in preparing yourself for warfare will be the time you will save by not having to war. When temptations come, you will defeat them with the word, and will not have to spend time in great warfare. You never waste the time spent with **me.** You sow it to reap it abundantly, later.

Never feel that you do not have time to pray, to meditate, to read the word. You make time for these, and I'll make time for you in other areas. I am the creator of time. You use your time wisely, and I'll give you time back in abundance to do all the things that need to be done. The time you spend with me is the time you will not have to spend apart from me. I will give you time in abundance.

Scriptures: Psalm 37:4-5, Mark 1:15, Galatians 4:3-5, Ephesians 5:15-17.

Prayer: Father, I thank you for time. Forgive me for being careless with my time, Lord. Help me use well the time you have given me. Help me not to waste time any more, but to prepare myself for spiritual warfare. Help me to seek you more, pray more, study your word more, and love you more.

February 8

The weapons of our warfare are not carnal; they are mighty through God to the pulling down of strongholds. You have mighty, powerful weapons. Learn to use them. You have weapons of love, of faith, of power. You have weapons of hope, weapons of trust. These are mighty weapons that come through the **word,** your sword. These weapons come as the **word** begins to speak to your heart. As you see the might and power behind these words, begin to hide them away in your heart.

You can call upon reinforced faith that can be mustered at any alarm. You have a mighty arsenal of weapons stored for use at a moment's notice. **I** put the desire in your heart for the **word,** but you must put the **word** in you for use. Determine to do so. Let **my word** flow in and out of you as the tide flows---just as persistently, just as irrevocably. Many battles are fought, but you are a victor in them all, through the mighty power of the **word, Jesus Christ.**

Scriptures: Psalm 119:11, John 1:1-2, I Corinthians 3:19-20.

Prayer: Father, thank you for providing everything I'll ever need through your word. Help me to hide your word in my heart that I might not sin against you.

February 9

The name of **Jesus** is above all names, all principalities, all power. Learn to use that name in faith. Then you will see mountains fall and crumble as dust. Circumstances will hasten to change, wrongs will be righted and demons will flee. The name of **Jesus** will bring peace and calm to a troubled heart. But more than this, every power will bow to this name. Meditate on the use of this name. Let the words, *ask anything in my name,* be imprinted on your heart. Learn to heed the voice of the **Holy Spirit** and to use the name of Jesus to the glory of the **Father.** At my name, every knee shall bow. Learn to love the name of **Jesus.**

Scriptures: Isaiah 9:6, Joel 2:32, John 16:23-24, Philippians 2:10.

Prayer: Father, I thank you for the name of Jesus. Help me to realize the awesome power of that name, the precious provision of it. Help me to keep the name of Jesus in my prayers and on my lips. Thank you.

February 10

The way to abundant life is in the **Holy Spirit**. As the **Spirit** in you increases, the old man decreases. This enables the *Lord of Hosts* to work mightily on your behalf, because you become caught -up in doing my will. I have given many directions instructions and promises. They are constant, without change. If these are heeded, they will bring harmony, peace, prosperity, health and safety. I am your refuge, your strength. Allow your spirit to grow and develop by prayer, meditation and knowledge of the **Word.** Then you are open to hearing my voice because you are abiding in me.

I have nothing hidden from those who seek **me.** I reveal **my** will, **my** plans, myself to those whose hearts are pure toward **me.** Choose to walk in the **Spirit.** Choose to be a victor and obtain my full salvation. It is your inheritance.

Scriptures: Psalm 18:1-3, Luke 12:31-32, John 10:4-5, Galatians 5:16, III John 1:4.

Prayer: Father, I pray I will always seek you and be caught up in your Spirit. Reveal yourself, Lord. Help me to walk in the spirit, so that I will not fulfill the lusts of their flesh. Thank you for your inheritance, Father.

February 11

Draw nigh unto me and I will draw nigh unto you. I am always waiting for you to come near. I am always ready, always there. Only your will will block you from coming to **me.** Choose to order your life aright so that you have time for me.

Choose to place a priority on our abiding. I

have much to share, and you have much to learn. There are untold blessings awaiting the hungry heart, so choose to be filled with **me**.

Satan would hinder you if *he* could, but he cannot! He has no ground unless it is given. *He cannot stay apart from fear, unbelief, or doubt filling your mind.* These are *his* welcome mats. When you operate in these areas, you invite him to enter. You can *resist the devil and he will flee.* You need not be bothered with *his* lies, deception, and terrors.

Choose to trust **me** in everything. Heed my voice in every area. I will always lead, *if* you will follow. I am always there, ever ready to comfort, guide, fellowship and love you. I am the best friend you will ever have. I am your all in all. I am **Jesus.**

Scriptures: Matthew 6:33, James 4:7-8, Revelations 3:20.

Prayer: Father, I come into your presence with love and gratitude. I thank you for loving me. Help me to do my part in the divine friendship. A friend loveth at all times. I love you, Lord.

February 12

As you come into a deeper union with me and **my body,** you will begin to see areas of service and concern that you did not heretofore see. Your love for the **body** is steadily growing stronger, and you are more aware of the needs of others. You are

February 13

learning to serve physically, emotionally and spiritually. I am giving you a clearer insight into areas of prayer, areas of love, areas of assistance.

I am giving you, also, a new attitude concerning these. You will serve, not because you have to, but because you want to. You will love, not out of a sense of guilt, but because you cannot help yourself. You will genuinely love the brethren. You will fellowship with others, supporting them with your friendship, not because you should, but because it blesses and pleases you. You are finding that you abound in all things. You are full of peace and joy perpetually. These are fruits being made manifest in your life. Enjoy the produce of kingdom living. I have given it, and you can receive it.

Scriptures: Matthew 10:7-8, John 15:17, Hebrews 13:16, James 2:14-26, I Timothy 6:17-18.

Prayer: Lord help me be ready for "divine appointments". Help me be quick to carry out your instructions. Thank you for the divine adventure of serving you!

February 13

I have given you discernment to recognize seducing spirits, for my sheep know my voice and the voice of another they will not follow. You can always tell who is speaking to your heart and mind. You know when it is I, and you know when it is not.

February 14

When you listen to *Satan's* lies and deceits, you are *drawn away of your own lusts and enticed.* Refuse to hear him! Stop *him* immediately with the power of the **word.** Satan is allowed to talk, but you do not have to listen. You speak **my** word and he must flee. Do not *give him* a foothold, and *he* cannot stay.

Satan brings fear to torment, but perfect love casts out fear. That is perfect love of **me** and in **me.** No fear can stay when you allow **my** love to overcome the fear. As you realize the depth of **my** love and the rewards it brings, there is no room for fear. Refuse *Satan!* Give *him* no room and show *him* no mercy. *He* is a defeated foe.

Scriptures: Psalm 46:10, John 10:27, James 1:14, I John 4:18.

Prayer: Lord, thank you for your perfect love that casteth out fear. Thank you for your voice in my spirit. Thank you, father, for your divine leadership and protection.

February 14

The words that I speak unto you are life. They will give you life and they will keep the life of **God** alive within you. There is no real life outside of **my** protection and scope. There is only a semblance to life, all counterfeit, and a mockery of truth and beauty. The life in the Spirit is *eternal* life that prepares and enhances the believer for humanity. It gives dignity

February 15

and worth to your purpose in life.

I have a purpose for your life. You choose the measure of **me** that you allow to come in. If you heed the words that I speak, you will see the glory that comes to one committed to **me**. You will experience the abundance in living meant for the children of men. You will have **my** love flowing through you to others who are desperate for a holy touch. I will give *rivers of living water to flow out of your belly,* rivers of water that bring life, the life of one who abides with **me. I am** the source. You be the vessel.

Scriptures: Isaiah 55:11, Jeremiah 1:5, Matthew 24:35, John 14:15, Romans 8:6.

Prayer: Lord, thank you for your life. Thank you for the abundance. Help me to live in constant connection to you. Help me to hear you at all times. Help me to be a ready vessel. Thank you, Father, for your living word.

February 15

I have given you words of victory, words of conquest, words of power. These are just words unless they are heeded and believed. My word is truth, and he that heeds and believes it shall see the salvation of the **Lord**. In believing **my word**, begin with a choice to do so. As you walk on with **me**, the word will loom larger and larger until you cannot see defeat any longer. You only see victory, you only see the **word**. **My** overcoming power will rise within you until it will flow out to change circumstances, change evidence, change events.

Walk faithfully on toward the goal, the goal of victory. **I** have overcome the *devil* and all *his* evil strategies. He cannot defeat the word-ruled mind with his *lies* and deceits. *He* may put up shallow defenses to hinder your walk, but they fall at the feet of an armored believer. You will tread over each hindrance as **I** light your pathway. As **I** told Joshua, *Be strong and courageous, do not tremble or be afraid. The Lord your God is with you, wherever you go.* These **words** are forever true to him that believes.

Scriptures: Joshua 1:8-9, Isaiah 50:7.

Prayer: Thank you, Father, for your words of victory. Help me to set my face like a flint toward the goal, as Jesus did. Help me not to be side-tracked in any way.

February 16

With blessings I will bless you. The blessings from me are without repentance and come with joy. Look forward to the days ahead as a small child

February 17

anticipates Christmas. This is the attitude of one who really trusts me to do good toward him, one who believes my **word**, one who heeds my voice. *I came that you might have life, and that more abundantly.* Is abundant life filled with doubt and worry? Choose to be happy, choose to allow my Spirit of gladness and praise to well up within you, knowing that I keep watch over **my word** to perform it.

The gloomy heart has no faith. The worry-filled mind is not trusting. The heavy heart has not the joy of the Lord. I gave **my** kingdom to **my** children, those whose child-like faith enable them to accept **me** wholly. I said to such belongs the kingdom of God. Stay in the kingdom. Let your joy be made full! That is **my** wish and my command.

Scriptures: Genesis 12:1-3, Nehemiah 8:10, II Thessalonians 3:3.

Prayer: Father, thank you for the joy of the lord, my strength. Thank you for the assurance that everything will be all right. Father, I rejoice in you.

February 17

My peace **I** give unto you, not as the world gives. **My** sheep hear my voice, and because of this, you have peace. You have learned to identify the voice that speaks to you. You can tell when I speak or when it is the voice of a deceiver. Do not listen to seducing or lying spirits! Their intentions are to kill, steal and destroy all men. Do not let them fill you with doubt, despair or despondency. You are under **my** protection if you have received **my son**; you are in **my** dominion since you hear **my voice**, and the voice of another you will not follow. Rejoice in the truth that I give. Rejoice in the peace that **I** give. Rejoice in the **Lord** always, always! You are free, so rejoice!

Scriptures: John 14:27, Ephesians 2:14-22, 6:23-24.

Prayer: Oh, Father, I am so grateful to you for the peace you have given me through Jesus. No matter what the circumstances, I choose to live in peace. I choose to tune out the voices of the world and rejoice in your peace.

February 18

Let your heart rejoice in me. Allow your spirit to soar. Release all tensions, all anxieties, all fears to me. Allow **me** to take your burdens and cares. Can any man add a single cubit to his height by worry? You give Satan a foothold when you fear. *Cast all your care on **me** for **I** care for you.* This is the greatest gift **I** give (that peace that passes understanding), when you put all things into my keeping. It sets you free spiritually, mentally and physically. **I said** to come as a little child. A child has peace. He trusts in those who care for him. You do the same. There is no fear **I** cannot handle. Refuse to let the cares of this

February 19

world rob you. Refuse to dwell on negative fears that rise to haunt you.

I am capable, and yea, ready to handle any problem, any task, any situation. You can trust me to do it best. **I** am the **Lord God.** I do not fail.

Scriptures: Philippians 2:16-18, I Peter 5:6-7.

Prayer: Father, I rejoice in you. I thank you for taking all my cares. I give them to you, Lord. I thank you and praise you. I know that you are working every problem out for my good. Thank you.

February 19

Bring a cheerful, happy countenance into my presence and rejoice in **me.** Think on the things **I** have done and will do for you. *Happy is that people whose God is the Lord.* Count your blessings daily. Recount the joys of victory often, and keep hope alive and active. Go forward unafraid, singing glad songs of victory, for **I** have given you the land. No enemy can stand before you; no demon can with-stand **my word.** **I** have given you authority and you are free to walk in faith and love.

These tidings bring hope to those who have no hope. These evidences lift hearts who are downcast and fearful. You are blessed beyond measure and you will bless, because of **me.** You are light in a dark, scared world----a world scarred with hate, fear and anger. Your light will reveal the love, hope and joy that are accessible to whosoever will believe. Be glad—be very glad, for you carry the good news of the gospel of peace. What a heavenly message you bring, a message of hope and forgiveness. Rejoice in this day and be glad. Your **God** reigns!

Scripture: Psalm 9:2, Psalm 144:15, Psalm 146:5.

Prayer: Father, I thank you for taking care of everything. I will not fear or worry or doubt. I rejoice in you. I love you, Father. You are my God and I will declare it. Help me to rejoice in you all this day.

February 20

If you will choose to believe **my word** under all circumstances, you will see **my glory** manifested in your life. I can only work where unconditional faith abides and operates. Satan will seek to hinder, but then, he always does. He has sought to hinder the children of man since the beginning of time. He has no effect, however, on the one who refuses to doubt and chooses to believe.

Faith is an unnatural act to the carnal man, but it is a force that reigns in the spiritual realm. If you will walk in the spiritual realm as directed, you will enjoy the fruits thereof. Choose not to fear and you will not, if your mind is renewed in **my word.** If you will trust me to deliver you, **I will!** I am moved by faith, and **I** never fail. Fear not. Only believe.

Scriptures: Deuteronomy 32:10; Psalm 32:7, Psalm 91:1-16, 103:11-12, 121:4-5; II Thessalonians 3:3.

Prayer: Father, thank you for your protection over my life (and over the lives of those I love). I am so grateful for your mighty power in my life. Father, you protect me as you would protect the apple of your eye. Thank you.

February 21

The **Holy Spirit** quickens you and intercedes for you as you yield yourself to him. **Jesus** gives you power and authority to operate in his name, and ever makes intercession for you. **I,** the **Father,** hear you and move according to your faith in **me. We** are your all-in-all, singularly and in unison. This mystery of the **Godhead** will become more and more evident to you as you mature into the perfect man. *Be ye perfect as I am perfect.*

There will be those who scoff at revelation knowledge, those who would doubt and deride your relationship with **me.** But it is of no consequence, when compared to the beauty of knowing **me,** of hearing me, of walking with me. **I** made you to fellowship with **me.** The fact that you do is the pearl of great price. You have discovered the eternal treasure and no man can take it from you. Never fear man. Only fear **me,** the giver of all life. What is man in comparison with **me?**

Scriptures: Psalm 103:17-18, Proverbs 7:1-5, II Timothy 1:12.

Prayer: Father, Noah's neighbors laughed at him, but he did not let it bother him. He knew his instructions came from you. Elijah faced opposition when he took his stand for you. Jezebel even wanted to kill Elijah over it! Moses faced derision, as did so many of your servants, but they knew your voice. I thank you for knowing your voice. You are the most important one in my life. I choose to be obedient.

February 22

The *wisdom from above is pure and peaceable and easy to be entreated.* Seek wisdom in all your affairs. Discover the timeless knowledge that comes from abiding in **me.** I have promised wisdom to him who asks in faith. Therefore, there is nothing that can hinder its reception except the receiver. You have learned a great secret by choosing to obey **my** will, choosing to receive **my word,** choosing to believe by faith. You can choose to have wisdom, too. I left the initiative with the seeker. **I** withhold no good thing.

You can make right choices. You can operate in wisdom. You can choose to believe and nothing will hinder you. It rests in your will, in your choice. Is it not wonderful? Because of your faith, nothing is impossible.

February 23

Scriptures: Proverbs 2:6-7, Proverbs 4:20-23, Ecclesiastes 2:26; Isaiah 2:3.

Prayer: Father, thank you for guiding my choices and giving me wisdom in all my ways. You are my provider of every good thing. Thank you.

February 23

There is now no condemnation in **Jesus Christ**. This is such a difficult concept for many to grasp. I came, not to condemn the world, but that the world might be saved. Because of **my saving grace**, you are free from condemnation. Refuse to operate from condemnation. Ask for mercy, believe you receive, and accept righteousness.

The effectual, fervent prayer of a righteous man availeth much. Believe you are righteous! I paid the price that bought it. You have been redeemed and, therefore, are now an inheritor of the promises, through faith in my Son. **Jesus** does not have to pay the price again and again. In a moment of time, it was done. He said, *It is finished,* and finished it is! Receive your righteousness. Receive your inheritance. Receive your justification. Believe and receive.

Scriptures: John 3:17, Romans 8:1-4, James 5:16.

Prayer: Father, I thank you for Jesus' sacrifice on the cross. I thank you for the righteousness of Christ that has now become mine. I receive by faith that sacrifice and that righteousness, and I thank you for it.

February 24

As you freely give of your time, your prayers, your gifts, your prosperity, **I** return to you a hundred fold. Time is given back to you, prayers are answered and blessings given. You receive abun-dantly from the **God** above all gods. Never feel used, never feel beggarly. You are serving the Most High **God**, and **I** reward you openly and with pleasure. Your giving is an extension of **my** giving. *Freely you have received, freely give.*

Scriptures: Proverbs 11:25, 28:27; Daniel 2:47; Matthew 10:8; Luke 6:38.

Prayer: Father, thank you for your bountiful blessings to me. Thank you for the abundant return on every gift. Thank you.

February 25

As you take the time to abide in **me**, you will hear the voice of the one who loves you most. You will hear words of encouragement, words of promise, words of victory, words of truth, words that will lead you in straight paths. **My word** must be stored in your heart. You must have made provision to meditate in **my word** or else you will not be able to bring these words up from your heart. **I** speak to you out of the abundance of your heart. The things of the spirit are a mystery to the natural mind, but the spirit man knows the truth that **I** speak, and he understands by the Spirit. *If you abide in me and my words abide in you . . . .* this *is spiritual truth.* Heed it! It never fails.

Scriptures: Psalm 119:105, John 15:7, Hebrews 11:6.

Prayer: Father, your presence is so precious. I thank you so much for your care for me. Thank you for your company, Lord. I delight in you. You are my hope, my security, my guide, my treasure. Thank you for being my Lord.

February 26

Remember to praise me in all things. **I** inhabit the praises of **my** people, and praise enables **me** to move in your life. Praise is an expression of faith. As faith rises to belief in **my** ability to carry out **my word,** praise comes forth praise to thank me for the answer, praise to magnify **my** wondrous power, and praise to glorify **my** name. It is the **Spirit** within you that reacts to praise, the **Spirit** that I breathed into you. **I** react to your praise towards **me.** Praise expresses confidence in **me.**

Neglect not to praise **me.** Remind **me** of **my** promises and thank **me** for the answers to prayer before you have the physical evidence. Praise is the expression of believed prayer.

Scriptures: Genesis 2:7, Psalm 33:1, John 20:22, Acts 2:18.

Prayer: Father, I praise you. I glorify your holy name. You are worthy to be praised. I want to praise you; I choose to praise you. We are your people, made for your glory. There is no other God before you. You are the mighty one, the delivering God. Praise you, Father. You are my source, my provider, and I worship and praise you.

February 27

There is not time spent with **me** that does not become special. Just as you enjoy those precious, intimate moments with a child, a parent, a lover, or friend, so do **I** enjoy our special time. **I** made you to fellowship with me, and as you do, a special need in you is satisfied. **I**, too, enjoy fellowshipping with my creation. **I** made you in my image for that purpose.

You must take time to spend with **me**. Make a place for **me** in your life. Determine that your spiritual development is of enough importance to make sacrifices in your schedule. When you do, you enable **me** to abide with you. The resulting strengthening of your spirit will affect not only your life, but every life you touch.

Scriptures: Genesis 1:26, II Chronicles 15:2, Psalm 63.

Prayer: Father, you are with me always. Help me to be diligent in taking time to enjoy your fellowship. Help me always to be aware of your sweet presence. I love you, father. I know beyond all doubt that you love me. Your companionship is the sweetest thing in my life.

February 28

You are being prepared to change many lives, not by coercion, but by example. Because you are allowing me to transform you, others will desire to imitate you. Your transformation stems from obedience and a desire to please **me**. As this obedience is tempered by discipline and love, it becomes an object of great beauty and respect. Obedience is not a negative concept as many perceive it to be. Obedience is a lovely expression of training, as is fine-tuning a splendid instrument. The instrument may be excellent in workmanship and skillfully made, but until fine-tuned, its great potential will not be reached.

By obedience you are being transformed into a useful and lovely function in the body of **Christ**. Obedience will knit you firmly to the rest of the body. Thus, the flow of action within the body will be done smoothly and fluidly, a bride without spot or wrinkle.

Scriptures: Psalm 106:3, Psalm 119:2; I Samuel 15:22; John 17:11.

Prayer: Father, above all things I want to be obedient to you and to be pleasing to you. Help me to be the finely-tuned instrument for your use. I thank you so much for being my God.

February 29

The effectual, fervent prayer of a righteous man availeth much. You need to realize that heart-felt, fervent payers carry great weight and overcome seemingly immovable obstacles. Be ready to pray with fervor. Pray whole-heartedly and diligently. Satan has sown abroad the lying ideas that prayers are a useless waste of time and that you cannot expect to be heard. This is a lie from the pit. This lie must not be heeded!

Pray with emotion, pray with faith, pray without ceasing. You will see wonders unfold before you. **I** initiated the act of prayer. **I** hear every whisper uttered to **me**. Say aloud your prayers, so

Februray 29

that the universe can bear witness to my faithfulness. Pray in faith and according to **my word**. If you pray according to **my** will, you know that **I** hear you, and if you know that **I** hear you, you know you have the petitions you have asked for. So ask, and keep on asking. Seek, and keep on seeking. Knock, and keep on knocking. To him who asks, receives; he who seeks, finds; and to him who knocks, the door will be opened.

Scripture: John 15:4, I Thessalonians 5:17, James 5:16.

Prayer: Father, I glorify your name. I thank you for hearing my prayer. I praise you and I adore you. You have given me all things.

MARCH

March 1

I always bring a message of hope: hope for a better tomorrow, for a better future. Hope keeps man alive for where there is life, there is hope. Hope is the image that man perceives in his mind. There is often much difficulty in turning from hope to faith. Faith comes by hearing, and you must choose to hear. *He that hath an ear, let him hear.* Many believe in the possibility of the miraculous, but few have the faith to see it come into being.

I have given to each man a measure of faith, so everyone has a basis for faith. Choose to let faith grow. You must choose to have hope turn into faith, which will cause events and hearts to change; then the miraculous can occur. Learn to operate effectively in the spirit world. The alternative to having hope and using faith is to live in despair, controlled by circumstances, and to fear life. I came to give abundant life. Choose to have that abundance by believing **my word** and acting in faith.

Scriptures: Psalm 31:24, 33:18; Romans 8:24; Hebrews 10:22-23.

Prayer: Father, I believe your word. I acknowledge you as the only hope for a dying world. I hope in you, Father. I put my faith in you and you only. I love you, Lord.

March 2

The heart of a man is exceedingly evil until cleansed and purified by the blood of the lamb. Then the heart can receive the message of the **Spirit,** which is the **word of God**. Renew your mind daily and keep it with all diligence, for out of the heart flow the issues of life. Your mind must receive and store the things of the **Holy Spirit** before the fruit of the **Spirit** can appear. There will be no fruits until seed is planted, which is the **word.** Water and cultivate your mind with the **word.** Think and meditate deeply on the things of the Spirit. Your spirit man must be renewed day by day.

Then, as you go forth prepared by the **word,** you will have the abundance of life being manifested to you. You will overcome the tests of life, because greater is **he** who is in you than *he* who is in the world. *Satan* cannot defeat the **word**-ruled mind that refuses to heed the signals of fear, doubt and unbelief that he sends. Your heart is made righteous by the blood, and your mind is being renewed by *the washing of water by the* **word.** Rejoice ----be exceedingly glad----and go forward unafraid!

Scriptures: Matthew 7:16-19, II Timothy 3:16, I John 1:8-9.

Prayer: Father, I choose to renew my mind with the washing by water of the word. I thank you for the blood of Jesus and for your word. Help me always to choose to put your word first place in my life in order to pass the tests of life.

March 3

You have begun to deal with trials effectively, now learn to receive blessings graciously. Do not fear blessings! Do you think you are unworthy or undeserving. Just be grateful that a loving **Father** wants to bless you. Do not put strings on blessings. Do you fear enjoying your blessings because you think evil days may lie ahead? Come as a little child, delighted in all you see or hear. Enjoy the moment, and all that it brings. Be delighted and relish each moment. **I** love to see my children happy and full of joy. Live life to the fullest. Be free in **me**. Remember, *whom the Son sets free, is free indeed.* You are free! Enjoy **my** Creation, enjoy your health, enjoy your loved ones, enjoy **my** gifts. You show your appreciation to **me** by being delighted.

Scriptures: Psalm 67:4-7, Psalm 68:19, Luke 12:32.

Prayer: Father I receive your blessing. Thank you for health, joy, my home, my family. Thank you most of all for saving me and loving me.

March 4

When you find a door closed to you, do not despair. Simply pray that the best door would be - opened. **I** want your best, always. Be ready to ask for the best. Be diligent to **seek me** for true guidance. Once it is given, be diligent to persevere faithfully until the requests are granted. It is to the overcomer that the prize is given. He who holds on in faith never loses. Give **me** the opportunity to expand your faith! Do not waver in your faith. Be faithful, as **I** am faithful.

Scriptures: II Chronicles 20:20, Psalm 138:2, Jeremiah 1:12, Hebrews 11:1.

Prayer: Father, I thank you for opening the <u>best</u> door. I thank you for your faithfulness in giving me your best always. Help me always to be an overcomer. I thank you.

March 5

The events that take place in your life may not always seem pleasant to you, but if you have faith in me, those events will work to your good. I will change circumstances to benefit you if you believe in me and in **my power.** It takes much chiseling to make marble flawless. In order to get the best grain to show, sometimes the sculptor must make deep cuts. Often much polishing is needed to let the beauty shine forth.

The events in your life will make you stronger if you are a victor through the power of **Jesus**. The enemy has no power to do evil unto you if you just believe that *greater he that is in you, than he that is in the world.* Rejoice always in the victorious life you can lead in **me**.

Scriptures: Deuteronomy 28:13, John 15:16, Romans 8:28, Romans 8:37-39, I John 4:4.

Prayer: Father, I believe that all things work together for my good because I love you, Father, and I am called according to your purpose. I thank you for the refining you do in my life. I praise you and I declare my victory over circumstances through Jesus.

March 6

Be steadfast and patient, never wavering in your petitions. I have granted all things that are necessary, according to **my will.** This is the confidence that you have in me, that if you ask anything according to **my will**, you know that **I** hear you. And if **I** hear you, you have the petitions that you have asked.

Keep your confidence unspotted, unspoiled and unpolluted. Do not let vain imaginations, self-pity or doubt rob you of your victory through **Christ**. Your faith has carried you far, and will carry you farther. Do not waver in your convictions. I have not changed. Only circumstances change, and they can change again. Be of good cheer. I have overcome the world.

Scriptures: Psalm 50:14-15, Mark 11:24, John 14:14, I John 5:14.

Prayer: Father, you are the unchanging one. You are the only one in the world who doesn't change. I thank you for your steadfastness. I praise you for your absolute love, your absolute authority in the world and in my life. Thank you for hearing my prayers.

March 7

I have given you the land, but that does not mean there are not giants to slay, cities to conquer, fields to plant or crops to harvest. You have received the ability and the knowledge to conquer, but conquer you must! The *enemy* never sleeps; neither do **I**. *He* is roaming about, seeking whom he may devour. However, **I** have said that you are more than a conqueror. You must constantly choose whom you will believe, my word or *Satan's* lies. As you trust **my word** and ignore circumstances (difficult though it may be), you will always see victory. The harder the testing, the sweeter the victory!

In the trying times, you may only feel pain, you may only reason negatively, you may see no possibility of escape. If you will choose to trust **me,** choose not to doubt, choose to believe **my word**, the victory will come. It has to come, because I am faithful to my word. I sent it and it will not return void. Remember these words, "let us hold fast the profession of our faith without wavering, for he is faithful that promised." I am **"He"**.

Scriptures: Isaiah 54:17, Romans 1:5-6, Colossians 2:10, Colossians 3:17, Hebrews 4:14-15.

Prayer: Father, I acknowledge the truth of your word. Let God be true and every man a liar. I speak your word boldly in the face of circumstances. I choose to look to you for success. I thank you for the victory in Jesus.

March 8

Be open to guidance and closed to vain imaginations. Learn to sift your thoughts and cast down those destructive ones. The enemy would cause you to fear; fear is how you recognize him. He would bring temptations to you to keep you sidetracked from seeking **me.** Learn to discern your thoughts. As you do, you will find yourself listening more to me and less to him.

When you allow **my words** to abide in your heart, you override Satan's voice. **My word** will defeat him every time. **My word** will give you life and hope. **It** will soothe the weary spirit and bring joy to the brokenhearted. The **word** will give your mind

March 9

new energy and change your attitude. Remember to wash your mind with the water by the **word** and to meditate in **my word** day and night. The newness of heart you receive will reward the effort expended. There is no other way.

Scriptures: Psalm 119:105, II Corinthians 10:5, II Timothy 3:16, James 4:7.

Prayer: Thank you, Father, for your word. I choose to base my life's decisions on your word. Help me always to hold fast to your word. Thank you.

March 9

Just as the sunshine warms the earth and brings newness of life to every creature, so does **my Spirit** invigorate and refresh the soul. Your soul has need of me. It has need of the cleansing that **I** give, just as the earth receives the cleansing rain. As the cool breeze refreshes the body, so your soul needs **me**. Your soul has need of the spiritual food and wholeness that only **I** can bring. **I** provide completeness to the soul; **I** fill every void and need. There is no lack in **me**.

Rejoice in the knowledge that your soul needs never to experience the hollowness of life again. Rejoice that you can rely on **my** support and strength. Rejoice that pain can be rebuked and overcome, because of the joy **I** bring to your soul. Say often, *Bless the Lord, Oh my soul*, because you are truly blessed.

Scriptures: Psalm 34:1, Psalm 103:1-5, John 15:26.

Prayer: Father, I rejoice in you! You have given me everything I will ever need for peace, joy, health----everything. Thank you, Lord.

March 10

My word brings the good news that man is no longer condemned. He has the choice of eternity in his mouth. Because you have experienced the "new birth" and the awakening of your spiritual senses, you are indeed a new creation. You have been bought and paid for by Jesus. Your redemption is complete. You are in right standing with the **Creator** of all things. Let this awakening penetrate every fiber of your being so that you learn to respond positively to the affairs of life.

As the realization of the divine **Spirit** within you unfolds, you will begin to recognize your authority and role upon the earth. You have a purpose in the kingdom and are being aptly trained for it. You are in right standing because of **Jesus**, and you are renewing your mind so that you can recognize spiritual guidance and leadership. You have a dual role. You are to humble yourself, and you are to take authority. **Jesus** said, *I am meek and lowly in heart, and, all power and authority has been given unto* **me**.

March 11

He is your role model. Think on this and act accordingly. There is much to learn.

Scriptures: Matthew 11:29, Luke 10:19, Romans 10:10, I Corinthians 6:20.

Prayer: Father, thank you for giving us Jesus, our divine role model. Thank you for the Holy Spirit who is our teacher and guide. Thank you for helping us to do your will and be in your blessed will.

March 11

Contemplation is for the natural mind, and meditation is for the spiritually-minded. One thinks on things that he knows, the other on things that he knows not. Man should evaluate his experiences, but he should only do it in the light of the **word**. Much of the muddle in the human mind comes from dwelling on events that are insignificant to eternity. These are events that hinder kingdom precepts from forming in you.

Meditation in **my word** changes events and ideas into opportunities for growth. As the mixing of chemicals can change the inherent structure of a substance, so can the **word** change past events into an opportunity for the future. You were given a mind with which to reason, contemplate and study. It is a mind that must be renewed, however, to see events, ideas and circumstances in the true light of eternity---- past, present and future.

Scriptures: Joshua 1:8, Psalm 32:8, Psalm 119:111, Romans 4:18-21, Hebrews 4:12.

Prayer: Father, I choose to meditate on your word. I choose to let the word renew my mind. I choose to think on things of eternal significance. I ask your help, Lord, in this---and I thank you for it!

March 12

Your words should always be an extension of **my words**. Then your words will have power. When you agree with the **Holy Spirit**, you are in a position to believe and receive. The **Holy Spirit** leads you into all truth. Jesus is the **truth**, the **way**, the **life** and the **light**. **He** is the **word.** Therefore, you must make your words agree with **Jesus.**

Renew your mind to speak the **word,** think the **word**, pray the **word.** I promised to confirm my word with signs following. Let no man deceive you. Words have power, and **my words** lead from darkness into light. Be not dismayed. Only believe.

Scriptures: John 1:7-14, Romans 3:22-24, Romans 5:2.

Prayer: Father, I ask your help in reminding me of your words, that I might speak them. I thank you for your word.

March 13

When you are in the spirit, there is no room for doubt. How do you get in the spirit? You abide in me. This abiding is a choice, an arrangement of priorities, a commitment of time. You choose to come into **my** presence and you open your heart and spirit to **my voice**. You begin to trust the promptings of the **Spirit**. You learn to listen to the inner man speaking the **word of God**. You learn to believe that the **words** you hear are from above and not from your natural mind. As you do these things, your confidence begins to grow and you learn to accept **my words**.

The *enemy* speaks also. You have listened to *him* for years. You can discern my voice. **My** sheep hear **my voice** and the voice of another they will not follow. Listen to **my** voice and heed it.

Scriptures: Ezekiel 36:27, John 10:3-5, John 14:23.

Prayer: Father, help me to abide in you. Remind me, Father. Quicken my spirit to spend my time with you instead of attending to the things of the world. I choose to spend my time in the spirit and I choose to heed your voice.

March 14

I am training men and women who can stand the test of faith----men and women of courage, and full of the **word**. In training, often obstacles are met, and are not overcome. However, through perseverance and proper instruction, obstacles are brought under submission. You have much to learn. You have decided to enter the training, but the discipline will be rigorous. Prepare yourself well that you may learn quickly.

You will not go through impossible instruction, for nothing is impossible with me. Do not fear the obstacles. Learn from them! Draw strength from the **word** and try again. You will overcome by your faith. This is the victory that overcometh the world, even our faith.

Scriptures: Psalm 119:17-18, Proverbs 2:6, Isaiah 30:21, Jeremiah 9:10, Jeremiah 32:38-41, Romans 3:3.

Prayer: Thank you, Father, for your training. Help me to have the courage and dedication I need. Give me your grace, Lord. I want to succeed.

March 15

The hindrances in life will make or break you. If you yield to them, you will fall back defeated. If you yield to **me** and let them teach you, you will arise a victor. Let nothing hinder your instruction, your discipline, or your walk with me. The cares of this world will try to choke the **word** in the believer. The

March 16

enemy sends hindrances to block your progress. But to him that overcometh will the crown be given. **My word** says a good man may fall down seven times, but will arise each time. **I** will give you strength to arise. You will find courage if you look to **me.**

Refuse to allow circumstances to put fear into your heart. Refuse to believe evidence that is contrary to your faith. Faith is the proof, faith is the evidence---not the things you see! The just *shall live by faith.* You are made just by me.

Scriptures: Micah 7:8, Habakkuk 2:4, Hebrews 11:1, James 1:2-3.

Prayer: Father, thank you for giving me the power to overcome the hindrances of life. Thank you for the courage to overcome the stumbling blocks of the enemy. Thank you for your instruction, your promise and for your word.

March 16

Be of good cheer. . . . I have overcome the world. . . . Let not your heart be troubled, neither let it be afraid. Notice that I said, "let". You have authority over your heart. You must choose what you will believe. Your mind must be renewed by the **word**. The **word** must be in your heart in abundance before it can be used. Out of the abundance of your heart, your mouth will speak the **word.**

As you grow in knowledge of my **word,** your heart will be strengthened. *Fear* cannot be cast out of your heart unless your heart abounds in faith. *Faith cometh by hearing and hearing by the word of God.* You have the hope that you will be a victor, because **I** have overcome the world. Build yourself up in the most holy faith and you will not falter (or fail).

Scriptures: Matthew 12:34, John 14:1, John 16:33, Romans 10:17.

Prayer: Father I choose to put your word in my heart in abundance---and to believe it! Thank you for the victory, Lord.

March 17

There is no fear in the perfect love of **God**. This is because *perfect* love casts out fear. If you truly believe **I** love you, then you can believe in my power to heal, save, prosper, deliver and bless. The torments of the mind are aimed at demeaning my love, making my love of little effect. Satan would have you believe that circumstances will not change to benefit you, and that your worst fears will come to pass.

Refuse to dwell on his thoughts. Replace those thoughts with **my word**, my promises of deliverance. I am not a man that I should lie, and **I** change not. You must examine the alternatives----to believe me or to believe Satan's lies. Choose whom you will believe!

March 18

I am faithful. I will not fail those who trust in me.

Scriptures: Numbers 23:19, I John 4:7-8, I John 4:18.

Prayer: Father, thank you for loving me. I believe that your love can take care of every problem and every lack in my life. I believe you want to take care of me and that you will do it! Thank you for blessing me, Lord.

March 18

My grace is sufficient for you. No temptation or trial is impossible for you. You are capable of victory in them all. **I** have made you a way of escape through every trial, if you choose to take it. The way of escape is the way of faith. You must train yourself in faith until you only respond to stress by faith. You must have your mind ruled by the **word** so that the **word** fills your mind before fear appears.

Remember, fear is doubt of **my word.** Fear is doubt that **I** will answer your petitions or fulfill **my word.** The *enemy* uses such tactics to inject fear. *He* dares not contradict my word directly. *He* injects fear of **my** willingness, rather than of fear of **my** ability to answer your prayers. *He*'ll use anything to make you doubt the outcome of your petitions.

Train yourself to listen to my **word**. Let **my word** so richly dwell in you that *Satan's* lies are drowned in a sea of faith. If faith is filling your mind, if **my words** are imprinted upon your heart, then *Satan's* lies are lost in your trust. The *deceiver's* voice will be a small one, shouted against a hurricane of love. Develop your mind to receive only the **word.** It is life to you.

Scriptures: Deuteronomy 26:8, Psalm 84:11, Psalm 106:9-12; Isaiah 41:10, Mark 9:23, II Timothy 1:7.

Prayer: Father, I repent of the times I have given in to fear. I ask your forgiveness, Lord. I choose your way out of fear and trouble. Thank you for your grace, which is sufficient for me.

March 19

When you stand in faith, you have made the decision to believe. Now you must let patience have her perfect work. Patience is believing under trial. So many lose the victory here. The only way to sure victory is to believe **me** more than you believe circumstances. The natural mind rejects this stand, and says, "you're not facing reality." But **I** say, *Let God be true and every man a liar!* If you can only stand for what you can see, you are not operating by faith, or by the **Spirit.**

Think of each trial as a *testing time*, just as if you were in school. You are having to prove that you really know the material without the aid of evidence. But **I** do not leave you helpless. **I** give you the solid

March 20

rock of **my word** and the comfort of the **Holy Spirit**. These aides will defeat any enemy when used in conjunction with your will. Determine to win every trial, every testing. If you stand firmly on the foundation of **Jesus** (the **word**) and are quickened by the **Holy Spirit**, you cannot lose! The victory belongs to you. Take it!

Scriptures: Numbers 11:23, Psalm 32:8, Romans 3:3, Romans 12:12, James 1:4, Revelation 1:18.

Prayer: Father, thank you for your word and the assurance of victory in the trials of my life. Help me to have the patience to stand until the victory is manifested.

March 20

My peace I give unto you, not as the world gives. The heart that has accepted the Son has opened the way for *peace. Peace* has a price, however. It is the price of confidence in **me.** Often, in **my** mercy, **I** anoint one in distress with my peace, unexplainable in the circumstances. But the real peace that comes and prevails, comes as a fruit to the confident believer. This is one who has learned of my character, **my** faithfulness. This is the state of mind that all men should seek. The knowing that **I** am always near, that **I** will never leave or forsake you brings peace.

Because peace is a fruit, it can---and must---be cultivated. Doubts must be pruned away. Your mind must be watered with the **word**, and fertilized with meditation on **my word**. The storms of worry and fear may come to take the fruit, but the warmth of **my** love and protection will nourish the fruit to maturity.

Peace is sought by all men. It is the natural state of mind for the reborn spirit. I created man to live in peace with me. The world gives an absence of conflict and calls it peace. I give peace in spite of conflict, *the peace that passes understanding.*

Scriptures: Psalm 29:11, John 14:27, Galatians 5:22-23, Philippians 4:7, II Timothy 1:7.

Prayer: Father, thank you for the peace that passes understanding. I refuse to listen to anything that upsets my inner-man and my God-given peace. Thank you for the fruit of your spirit, peace.

March 21

Jesus is ever before the throne, making intercession for the **body**. If **he** is your example, do not neglect the time of your intercession. *The effectual, fervent prayer of a righteous man avails much.* If only the church would realize the power of prayer, the necessity of prayer, the purpose of prayer. To pray without ceasing and in everything give thanks are commandments. When you discipline yourself to spend time in prayer, you will begin to crave the time alone with me and see its benefits. You have heard the

March 22

old proverb, a "stitch in time saves nine". Well, a prayer in time saves nine. So much evil, so much heartache, so much pain and distress could be avoided by prayer.

Pray prayers of intercession over situations, people and circumstances before the enemy takes control. You must pray before the situation looks hopeless, before your faith has to confront impossible situations.

Intercession may not seem exciting in the natural world, but in the spiritual realm, great battles are waged----and won----due to the intercession of the saints of **God**. Faint not! Be diligent in season and out. Build yourself up in the most holy faith through prayer. Prayer moves mountains.

Scriptures: I Thessalonians 5:17-18, James 5:16, Jude 20.

Prayer: Father, help me never to neglect my prayer time. Help me to know how best to pray in each situation. Give me the stamina and determination to pray without ceasing! Thank you for Jesus, who ever makes intercession for me.

March 22

The world is looking for a savior. The reasons people do not recognize **Jesus** are that they have hardness of heart, or they have not heard. We must pray for prayers can soften the hardest of hearts so that the good news may be heard. Every member of the **body** can pray. Every member can tell of **Jesus**. Let your light so shine before men that the **Father** may be glorified.

Being a witness is a **24**-hour-a-day job. Being an intercessor is a very high calling. It is not difficult to tell what you have seen and heard. If you yield your members to me , I will make opportunities for you.

If you will yield your prayer time and your willingness to talk of my wondrous, saving power, you will be amazed at whom **I** place in your path. **I** promise.....

You will only have to walk where **I** have prepared the way.

You will only have to talk where **I** have opened the door.

You will only have to pray for those **I** lay upon your heart.

You will only have to learn to be sensitive to the leading of my **Holy Spirit**.

Yours is an easy task. Take **my** yoke. It is easy and its burdens are light. **I** have plans for your life. Believe **me** and enjoy the benefits. This easy task will cost you, but **I** reward abundantly.

Scriptures: Proverbs 22:4. Matthew 5:14-16, Matthew 11:29, Acts 1:8; Galatians 5:18,25.

March 23

Prayer: Father, I yield myself and my time to you. Lead me, Holy Spirit, to those who need Jesus in their lives. Jesus, place on my heart those you would have me pray for. Give me the opportunities and the words, Lord.

March 23

Every step you take can be lighted, for that is my promise. I said that I would be a lamp unto your feet and a light unto your path. However, you choose the path on which you tread. The path of righteousness and peace is yours when you follow my leading. The path of briars, thorns, stones and cavities is the path of self-will and deception, a dark pathway whose end is death. *The thief cometh to kill, steal, and destroy.* If *he* can keep you in darkness, fear, in torment of body and soul, he will!

On **my** path there is abundance of life. This is life that brings joy to the soul, peace to the mind, health to the body and rest for the weary. The trials and tribulations of life may loom large before you, but **my** path will take you securely through the storms of life and the pitfalls of the enemy. To stay on my path, you must have confidence in **me**. You must believe that **I** am leading you, and you must trust the way that **I** show. This way may not always seem the easiest, safest way----but it is. **I** would not deceive you.

Scriptures: Psalm 37:5, Psalm 37:23, Psalm 119:105, Proverbs 3:6, Isaiah 42:16.

Prayer: Thank you for your leading, Lord. Thank you for the safety of your path. Thank you for your word, which lights your path so that I will not stumble. I choose your ways, Lord. Help me never to leave your precious presence.

March 24

I created a world of order out of chaos, and I can change a life of sin into something of beauty and harmony. Before I set the sun and moon, the earth and stars, there was no order in the universe. Now the order is so predictable that men can figure, years in advance, the course of the planets. Your life can be that way. You may not be able to predict events in your life, but you can determine how steadfast, faithful, and involved you will be in the body of **Christ**.

Out of the fear and conflict of human existence, I sent the **Savior** to guarantee redemption and resurrection. You now have tangible evidence of eternal life, and of your kingdom inheritance. You can now live in harmony with **my** purposes for your life. You are no longer separated from **me**, but can work with me for eternity. You are now able to move into the wonderful order of **my** kingdom, a kingdom of peace, joy and rest. **My** kingdom of order contains life, activity and purpose. You are now in position to further my will upon the earth. You can flow and move with the children of light into the glorious plan I have for eternity.

March 25

Scriptures: Genesis 1:1-31, Psalm 112:6, Isaiah 32:17, II Peter 1:10-11.

Prayer: Lord, I love your order. Thank you for the order of your creation. Thank you for giving me more order every day. Thank you for the order and serenity of your kingdom.

March 25

Even if you do not realize it, your prayers carry weight in the kingdom. *The effectual, fervent prayer of a righteous man availeth much.* **My** kingdom is not of the world, nor does it operate as do the kingdoms of the world. In the world's kingdoms, it is the loudest voice that is heard. In **my** kingdom, the smallest prayer is heard. **I** hear the humble, the weak, and the feeble.

Speak often to **me**, making intercession for all men, building yourself up in the most holy faith. Pray my will into the earth and watch the marvels unfold. Take part in the kingdom. I want you as a participant, not a spectator. Be a good kingdom citizen. When active, you care for the business of the kingdom. He who would be greatest must be the servant. Serve your fellow man with prayer for him. Your service may be in secret, but **I** reward you openly.

Scriptures: Psalm 9:12, Psalm 37:4, Isaiah 65:24, Zechariah 12:8, Matthew 6:6.

Prayer: Thank you, Lord, for the joy of prayer----for the answers to prayer in the lives of others, as well as my own. I am so grateful to be allowed into your holy presence. Thank you, Father.

March 26

Do not sink when you can swim. Do not go down in defeat when **I** have given you talents, resources and power to be an overcoming victor. The parallel comes to mind of a car manufacturer urging passengers to wear seat belts. All of the safety features matter for nought if unused. It is the same in the spirit world. **I** have given you authority to tread on serpents and scorpions, but tread you must! If you refuse to submit to **me** and to resist the devil, he does not have to flee. The spiritual laws will work for you or against you.

I have given authority, **I** have given victory, but the battles must still take place for you to be victorious. If you cringe back in fear, **I** have no pleasure in you. You will lead a life filled with terror and defeat, if you refuse to act and live according to **my word**. Refuse to give in to the temptation to yield to *Satan*. Gird up your loins and fight to victory! Hold yourself calm in the day of adversity and see the glorious victory given. There is no fear in **my** perfect love, and you do not have to fear, either. Just strengthen yourself in **me** and go on to win. **I** am with you. Do not tremble or be afraid.

March 27

Scriptures: Leviticus 26:3-8, Joshua 4:24, I Chronicles 29:11-12, II Thessalonians 2:8,15.

Prayer: Thank you, Father, for giving me courage, power, and victory over evil. Because of Jesus, I do not have to yield to Satan's pressures. I do not tremble with fear any longer. The Holy Spirit is leading me into all truth.

March 27

Refuse to be robbed of your faith. **I** came to give life, and that more abundantly. When *Satan* fills your mind with lies, fears, doubt or unbelief, refuse to heed them. Think on **my word** and submit to them. Receive **my word** into your heart and you will find that *his* words leave. This involves an act of your will. It is a choice you make. Choose you this day whom you will serve. Will you believe *Satan's* lies or **my word?** *Satan* can make circumstances seem convincing to prove *his* case, but **my word** is higher than any other.

Yield to me, not to *Satan*. Heed **my word**, not *his*. As you choose to believe the truth, you will find *his* tactics ineffective. *He* cannot operate in your life unless you given *him* entrance. Give no place to the devil. Give *him* no foothold. **My** power is greater than *his*, and you do not have to yield to *him!*

Scriptures: Joshua 24:15, John 8:36, John 10:10, Hebrews 10:35-36, I John 4:13-17.

Prayer: Father, help me to keep my faith strong. I want to recognize your voice in every situation. I resist the devil and stand firm in the assurance of victory in Jesus. I choose life, I choose health, I choose prosperity, I choose victory.

March 28

Go forth strong in the purpose and in the power of the **word**. This is a combination that cannot be defeated. "Purpose" involves your will. Power is given by **me** to whoever will receive it, and the preparation of the **word** in your heart must be ongoing. *Satan* cannot stand against this combination. Make the *enemy* tremble at the thought of you. Make *him* back away when you approach. **I** have defeated *him* and made a show of *him* openly. *He* cannot stand against a **word**-ruled mind that refuses to fear *him*. Be aware of **his** deceits and stand ready to defeat *him*.

I gave charge to cast out devils, to heal the sick, to preach the gospel. You cast *him* out wherever you find *him*. Backed by **my** power and **word**, there is no trick to it. **I** have given you the keys to the kingdom. Use them!

Scriptures: Matthew 10:7-8, Matthew 16:19, John 4:33-36.

Prayer: Father, I purpose, I determine to do your will. I thank you for the mighty power of your word. The purpose and the power together form an unbeatable union, a winning team. Thank you.

March 29

If you can believe when circumstances are adverse....
If you will choose **my word** over things you feel.....
If you will hear **my voice** over that of the enemy....
You will always be the victor.

Never did I say in **my word** that trials and temptations would not come. But you can count them all joy. The victory is so sweet, though it is human nature to want the victory without the battle. In the spiritual realm, as in the natural realm, growth is often painful and requires discipline. Always seek my best. Never settle for mediocrity, when the best is available to him who perseveres. It is far better to have the crown of victory than to lose the race.

Scriptures: II Chronicles 20:3-30, I Corinthians 15:58.

Prayer: Father, I choose to keep my faith-level high, so that when I am faced with adverse circumstances, I will be able to believe your word, as did Jehoshaphat. Thank you for being the God who is faithful and the God who cannot lie.

March 30

Sing forth **my** praises, rejoice in me, for **I** reign in your life. **I** am the **God** above all gods, and **I** fail not.

- Rejoice that you know **me** and are known by **me**.
- Rejoice that the kingdoms of the earth are under **my** feet and you shall see the day when every knee shall bow to the **King of Glory.**
- Rejoice that you, who have been born twice, will not die twice.
- Rejoice that the kingdom of **God** is a very real place and that your name is written in the **Lamb's** *Book of Life*.
- Rejoice that I am the alpha *and omega*, the *King of kings* and the *Lord of lords*.

It is **my will** that all who know **me** rejoice in **me,** rejoice for **me**, rejoice with **me**. You make it your *will* to do so.

Scriptures: Deuteronomy 26:11, I Samuel 2:1-10, Psalm 97:1, Isaiah 66:14, Revelation 5:11-12.

Prayer: Father, I rejoice in you. You are the King of Kings, the Lord of Lords, the Holy One of Israel. You are glorious, wonderful and mighty! I worship you and I love you.

March 31

Whoever seeks the higher life will lose the lower life, but whoever seeks to save the lower life will lose the higher life. Look always at my best for every situation, and then persevere until you have it. So often my children live beneath the best and settle for the mediocre. I still love them, but there is a loss of pleasure in them. Nothing can separate you from **my** love, but aim for the higher life. Choose not to allow *Satan's* hindrances, deceits, confusion and hurts to hinder your success. Determine to overcome and you will! You have the weapons available, and the victory has been won. I have given the land to you, so take it!

Look not at the giants or the fortified cities. Look not at the number of the *enemy*. Heed only **my** word and believe that I have granted the requests you've made. *Fear not. Only believe.*

Scriptures: II Samuel 22:18-22, Luke 8:50, John 12:24-26, John 14:12-14.

Prayer: Father, I choose the higher way. Help me always to discern the difference. I no longer choose to be satisfied with less than your best for me. I thank you, Lord, that you want what is best for me in every facet of my life.

APRIL

April 1

The road to victory is fraught with many detours and pitfalls. Only the heart that is in tune with **me**, that has the *ear* to hear what the **Holy Spirit** is revealing, can successfully traverse these grounds unhindered. Strengthen yourself in me constantly. Be eagerly listening to **my** voice, ready to obey, ready to heed any change of direction. The long walk to victory is a walk in the spiritual realm. It requires a stalwart, well trained heart to withstand the strenuous pressure placed on it by the enemy.

I am the trainer, the healer and the maker of your heart. If victory were not possible, **I** would not lead you this way. Have faith in **my** guidance. Trust **me** to guide you safely and securely to complete victory, past all the wiles of the *devil*. The crown is worth the training, the hardships and the effort necessary to win the race.

Scriptures: Psalm 32:8, Matthew ll:15, John 16:33, I Corinthians 9:24-27, Galatians 5:16.

Prayer: Father, I want very much to tune my heart to your voice. I want to walk in your spirit. I **choose** to hear your voice and to tune out the voices of the world. I thank you for leading me safely to victory.

April 2

When the road seems steep, look up. When the way seems dim and distorted, look up. Look up April at **me** and see the salvation of **God**, for **I** am ready to deliver you out of every peril. Be not deceived by temporary setbacks, be not dismayed at the strength of the *enemy*. Temporal circumstances can be easily changed; **I** deal in eternity.

The heart who chooses to rely on **me** will always see the ultimate success of eternal goals. *Choose you this day whom you will serve*----and see the might and power of the only true **God** deliver you from the snares prepared by the enemy. Look up at **Jesus**. Look to the only true **God** for help, and you will surely find it!

Scriptures: Genesis 28:15, Joshua 24:15, Psalm 27:1, Psalm 91:11.

Prayer: Father, thank you for the assurance of your protection. I choose to rely on you. I decide right now, with your help, to look to Jesus for his help in every situation. I absolutely deny the right of anything to be a threat to me. I set eternal goals, Lord, and I thank you for them.

April 3

. . . And David strengthened himself in the Lord. At the time when the cause seemed hopeless, David chose to turn to **me**, and received strength. Because he knew his **source**, he received back what was lost and won the victory. David was unique in that he put **me** <u>first.</u> He was a man after **my** own heart. **I**

respond likewise to all who do the same. David's strength and courage were renewed when he chose to seek me, the source of all things. Because he knew **me**, he had no hesitancy about where to turn. This relationship took time to develop, but David had spent time with me. He abided in **me**, and **I** abided in him. He did not seek other sources of aid, no other god, no king, no army. He sought **me!**

You do likewise. Seek **me** first, not as the last resort. Seek **me** with all your heart and you will not be disappointed. Remember, **I** am your shield, your abundant compensation. Your **reward** shall be exceedingly great.

Scriptures: Genesis 15;1, I Samuel 30:6, Psalm 28:7, Matthew 6:33, John 15:5.

Prayer: Thank you, Father, for the example of David. I choose to seek you <u>first.</u> I abide in you, Lord. Help me to love you and seek you more. I want your companionship above all things. Then I know I will have good success.

April 4

To be truly free, you must totally rely on **me**. There is no freedom in anyone or anything else. No one can acquire freedom by demanding it; only by receiving the restrictions of obedience and love can true freedom begin.

Begin to desire obedience to rule you. Let love

April 5

operate without fear of rejection. Love and obedience are the tracks on which the freedom train moves. Be obedient and believe that **my** perfect love enfolds you. Be truly free.

Scriptures: Psalm 106:3, John 8:32-36, John 16:13, II Corinthians 3:17, Philippians 4:9.

Prayer: Father, I truly want to walk in obedience and love. Thank you for your blessed freedom.

April 5

Count your blessings daily. When you begin to realize how blessed you are, then you can push back the tendrils of self-pity that try to trap your inner man. Allow gratefulness to change your attitude and appreciation to well up within you. Open your heart for new blessings. Look forward to tomorrow on which the sun of fulfillment will shine. Choose to be happy. Choose to have a right attitude. Choose to overcome. Fight the giants and take the land!

Scriptures: 4:40, Proverbs 11:25, Proverbs 20:7, Matthew 5:8, John 13:17.

Prayer: Father, thank you for your blessings. I choose to trust in you, Lord, to refrain from worry, to keep my heart thankful and appreciative at all times. I choose to take the land.

April 6

Be not discouraged or dismayed, for the Lord your God is with you, wherever you go. Never feel that you are leaving **me** behind. I dwell in you, if you abide in me. I said that I would make **my** abode with you, and I have. Great opportunities for faith await the one who will venture forward, unafraid. Fear may attack, but it does not have to defeat!

If you will trust me through the darkest hour, I will bring you through. I recognize your frailties, but I know that faith untested is not faith. True faith must stand under adversity. *Blessed is the man who can hold himself calm in the day of adversity.* I will always bring you out of adversity.

Wonders unfold before you. Go forward unafraid. Put your trust in **me**. Do not fear change. Allow **me** to direct your life. I care for you. Use your authority, and nothing shall by any means hurt you.

Scriptures: Joshua 1:9, Isaiah 41:10, John 15:10, I Peter 1:18, I John 5:4.

Prayer: Father, I am so grateful for your strength, power and protection. I know, Father, that you are watching out for me at all times. Thank you for your voice of encouragement, Lord. I am so grateful for you.

April 7

I came to console you, to give you comfort and peace. **My** light and my love are within you. The **Spirit** of the **Lord** is enough. When obstacles stand in the way, remember **my** love and concern. Things are working on your behalf. The times of testing are necessary. Glory in them, because triumphs follow.

Remember the saying, *it is darkest before the dawn.* When troubles come, be lifted up and draw comfort from **me**. You must rebuke the despair, cast out the doubt, seize hold of faith, and hold on!
Your redemption does draw nigh. Glorious things are coming on the morrow. Gird up your loins and speak things of faith. Testing makes for purer gold. The refining and pruning of **my** workers are a necessary part of the training and must be endured. But what a glorious product results. If there were a shorter, easier route to perfection, **I** would take you on it. Do not fear. Guard your thoughts and rest in me. **My** grace is sufficient. It is only necessary to seek me, and you will know that all is well. **I am** full of power and strength. I can handle it all! Give your troubles to **me**, and remember them no more. **I** don't. Refuse to dwell on negative things. **I** have washed your mind with the **word**. Now you choose to keep it clean! **My word** cleanses. The *fear of the* **Lord** *is clean.*

Scriptures: Psalm 19:9, Psalm 34;19, Psalm 138:7, Proverbs 1:33, Zechariah 13:9, I Peter 5:7.

April 8

Prayer: Father, I cast all my care on you, because you care for me. Thank you for your help, protection and consolation. I will meditate on your word and your love, Lord. I have great peace because I love your law.

April 8

Behold, I send you tidings of great joy!. . . . The joy of the Lord is your strength. If you can discipline your emotions and react in joy, you will always have the strength you need. Remember, happiness depends on circumstances, joy depends on attitude. **I** have told you to rejoice in the Lord, always. To "re"joice means to come into joy again. Joy is a state of mind. It is the mental condition of one secure in **my** love and faithfulness. When you know and trust **my word**, you can live in joy.

Seek this condition! Joy will change your life; it will change circumstances in your life. You will then change and influence the lives of others.

Scriptures: Nehemiah 8:10, Proverbs 16:20, Habakkuk 3:18-19, Romans 14;17.

Prayer: Father, I rejoice in you. I praise you and worship you. I give you thanks, glory and honor. Your joy is so wonderful. Your peace is so satisfying. Thank you for the joy of the Lord.

April 9

Remember to walk in love. *Greater love hath no man but that he lay down his life for his friends.* Laying down your life is difficult, but you must do so to gain the higher life. Laying down your life is to love your neighbor as yourself, and fulfills all the other commandments.

Is your desire to please me? Can you trust me enough to deliver you? Do you believe that love never fails? Decide to look for ways to show love. You will find, as you yield to **my will** for your life, that love is a fruit that blossoms and **grows.** It matures into seed producing thirty, sixty, or one hundred times as much. This is the higher life of love.

Scriptures: John 15:11-17, I Corinthians 13:13, I John 4:20-21.

Prayer: Father, help me to love you more. Help me to love others more. Thank you for your perfect love. Help me to be a vessel of your love.

April 10

*I will keep him in perfect peace, whose mind is stayed on **me**.* Comfort others with this news and make sure you keep peace within your **heart**. There is so much to fear in the natural world, but you belong to another kingdom, and therefore can *abide under the shadow of the Almighty.* The enemy would April 11 give you cause to fear if you would allow it. He would rob you of the *peace* that comforts spirit, soul, and body-----peace that gives life to all your flesh.

Peace is a state of mind that comes through trust in **my word**, in **my** ability to answer prayer and to grant your petitions. Remember always, that **I** am able, **I** am faithful, **I** am trustworthy. **I am the I am.** If you believe, all things are possible.

Scriptures: Psalm 91:1, Isaiah 26:3, Mark 9:23, II Timothy 1:12.

Prayer: Father, I thank you for peace. Thank you for your great promises and for your faithfulness to keep your promises.

April 11

Be ye perfect, even as I am perfect. The path to perfection is one primarily of love-----love for the **Father, Son,** and **Holy Spirit.** (I look on the heart.) The path is also one of obedience, for obedience is better than sacrifice. With these two forces working within, the rest of perfection will come. When love and obedience are in operation, patience is brought forth to have her perfect work. This fruit enriches perfection in every saint of mine.

The tests and trials of life are traps, planned by *Satan* for your destruction. However, **I am** using them to perfect you. *He* brings a chisel to cut into your heart. I take that same instrument and lovingly cut away any flaws in your character. This is only possible when you choose to let love reign instead of fear. Perfect love casts out fear and opens the door to give opportunity for further perfection.

I am perfecting you through your interaction with the **body of Christ**. As you love one another and submit to one another in love, the perfecting process continues. Perfection is the action of love and obedience in the heart of every believer.

Scriptures: I Samuel 15:22, Matthew 5:48, James 1:2-4, I John 2:5.

Prayer: Lord, Thank you for perfecting me. I choose to thank even you for the pain I endure while perfection is taking place. Help me to grow in patience and obedience, so that I may be pleasing to you.

April 12

As you enter **my** gates with thanksgiving in your heart, you are opening your spirit to receive from **me.** You are allowing your faith to reawaken to my saving grace. As **my** faithfulness and love are brought into remembrances, it is like warm-up exercise to the spirit. Can a runner run a 100 yard dash with no warming of the muscles? Can an opera star sing a solo without first exercising his voice? It is possible, but with poor effect. Thanksgiving leads the spirit into praise; it warms the spirit so that it can receive from **me**. These exercises in the spiritual realm are as necessary as any physical or mental exercise if your spirit is to grow and develop to its potential.

Thanksgiving starts with an act of your will, as does all exercise. As the spiritual muscles are warmed, soaring to praise and worship becomes a fluid motion. This is a natural result of entering into the **holy** places. Prepare your spirit as you prepare your mind and body. Thanksgiving, praise and worship are natural functions of the spirit, but they must be trained to reach their full potential. This preparation and development of the spirit will bless you. It is a state in which your spirit was meant to soar.

Scriptures: I Samuel 2:1-2, II Samuel 29:10-12, Psalm 9:1-3, Ephesians 1:3, Revelation 4:10-11.

Prayer: Father, I exercise the spiritual muscles with thanksgiving right now! Thank you for Jesus, thank you for my family, my home, our country, and this day. I am so grateful for your blessings. Thank you for empowering us to prosper in every good thing.

April 13

Do not lose sight of the promises **I** have given, and the answers to your prayers of petition. Do not allow the *cares of this world* to choke the **word** in your heart. It is easy to lose sight of your heavenly

April 14

calling, to allow circumstances to cloud your vision. You must determine to believe until victory is accomplished. Do not lose heart or faith! You can choose, you know, whether you will stand or not. You decide whether you will believe the **word** or not. Store the **word** deep in your heart so that you have a solid foundation on which to stand.

With this foundation of power----and patience to gird you up---you will overcome all things. You will see my will accomplished in your life, and in the lives of those for whom you pray. This is a spiritual reality, as sure as the dawn each morning. **I** never fail and you do not need to fail. Do you dare to believe it?

Scriptures: Psalm 119:37-40, Psalm 77, Matthew 13:18-23, Mark 11:24.

Prayer: Father, I am determined to stand in faith, believing, until all prayers are accomplished. I choose the word. I choose to be patient and not doubt. I believe your word is true. I praise your name, Lord.

April 14

Be ye not a hearer only, but a doer of the Word. It is easy to hear. But to do the word requires much faith. The enemy goes about as a roaring lion, looking for whom he may devour. So many are being devoured for lack of faith, for lack of knowledge.

They may hear, but they have failed to act on the **word**.

You must not be discouraged or lose confidence in **me**. Although you may see much failure, **I** have not failed, nor will **I** fail those who do **my word**. You must learn to guard your faith with all vigilance so that you will be able to stand until the inevitable pit of corruption is dug for the wicked. When your faith is ready, you can move mountains of doubt, mountains of despair, mountains of fear. Not only <u>can</u> you do these things, you will do these things. **I** am preparing a faithful people, people who hear and do **my word**.

Scriptures: Isaiah 38:17, Romans 12:1, James 1:22-25, James 2:14-26, I Peter 5:6-10.

Prayer: Father, my prayer is that I and those for whom I pray will stand, will hear, will be doers of the word and not hearers only. I believe with your help, that we will.

April 15

Just begin, and **I** will lead you. It takes much faith to start on a journey with **me**, but if you will just start, **I** will show you the way. In the natural, before you journey, you plan your strategy, your goals, your way. However, in the spiritual realm, you must come as a little child, trusting the **Father** to lead surely, safely, securely. Fear will interfere with **my** leading.

April 16

It will make you impetuous, impatient, and demanding. When fear takes over, **I** withdraw, for you become, spiritually, as an uncontrollable, spoiled child. When faith returns, your spirit comes into rest, with the assurance that all is well. **I** can then begin to lead you again.

My word says above all, to guard you inner self. You must guard your heart so that it does not fail for fear, that it does not fail to follow **me**. I have promised never to leave nor forsake you, that **I** will be with you always. **I** will be there, ready to take your hand and lead. Step out in faith.

Scriptures: Psalm 19:14, Proverbs 4:23, Zachariah 4:6, Mark 14:38, Luke 18:1, Luke 22:46.

Prayer: Father, thank you for your promise to lead me if I step out in faith to do your will. Give me the strength to act on faith in the assurance that you are there. I purpose to guard my heart and thoughts, that I might not fear.

April 16

The world is seeking solutions to satisfy a spiritual hunger that only **I** can satisfy. I sent **Jesus** into the world to reconcile the world to **me**, but how few recognized him at the time. Spiritual revelation often comes slowly. If built upon consistently, it will come as the light of dawn----dimly at first, but then bright as noon day.

Do not be discouraged at apathy or disinterest. I am patient for I know the end of it. If you have prayed in faith, you also know the end of it. There will come a dawning of revelation in others, and you will see the seed spring forth eventually to bear much fruit. Let patience have her perfect work in others as well as in yourself. I am long suffering. Be ye likewise.

Scriptures: Proverbs 4:18, Isaiah 53: 2-6, John 6:45, Galatians 5:22-23.

Prayer: Father, I choose to be longsuffering and leave the details to you. Thank you for the harvest.

April 17

All the talent, ability, or resources that a man possesses or acquires are as nothing if his heart is not in tune with **me**. I created him to glorify **me**. If he lacks a spiritual union with **me**, he is empty, naked and ashamed. **My** Spirit was meant to infuse life to him so that his natural abilities could flourish under **my** anointing and inspiration. Youngsters with ability are destroyed as they use their talents for the god of this world. *Satan* takes all they have and destroys them. Lovely artisans, composers, and writers are doomed in this life, and hereafter. With wasted lives they serve a *god* whose aim is to destroy them.

I came to give life, and that more abundantly. A creative mind, in conjunction with a pure heart, a

April 18

new spirit and renewed mind, produces loveliness in music, art, literature and architecture. Man was meant to glorify **my** name. **I** lifted him up out of the miry clay and set his feet upon the rock, **Jesus Christ**, the foundation of my church. Man was to be free to create with the inspiration and anointing of the **Holy Spirit.**

Scriptures: John 10:10, Romans 8:6, Galatians 5:13-17.

Prayer: Father, I pray for all talented people, young and old, that their talents be used to glorify your name. I pray that I might glorify your name with every shred of talent I possess.

April 18

Have you learned to see the beauty in my creation? There is always the obvious beauty: a sunset, a moonlit night, a lovely rose. There is also a beauty that is hidden, that awaits to delight the adventuresome, the searcher. The beauty of the spiritual realm awaits the seeker of me. **I** enhance every physical sense so that beauty is more evident. **I** give insight into the hidden beauty of the soul.

With this insight, you have a deeper appreciation of beauty that is touched, tasted, smelled and perceived. You learn to discern the beauty in spirits that will delight your heart. You will come into a deeper awareness of all my creation as you learn more of **me**. **I** will lead you into delightful paths and **I** will reveal vistas that a carnal man cannot experience. Trust the creator of all life to reveal the creation to you. This is the beauty that only the **master** of beauty can reveal.

Scriptures: Psalm 48:1-3, Romans 1:20, Philippians 4:8, I Peter 3:4.

Prayer: Lord, I love the beauty of your creation. Lead me into a deeper awareness of the hidden beauty of your world. I long to be led into a greater appreciation of the beauty you have created. Help me to appreciate it more, Lord.

April 19

Keep your heart with all diligence for out of it flow the issues of life. When you guard what enters your heart, being careful how you hear, you are keeping your heart. What goes into your heart is what will come out of it, *for out of the abundance of the heart, the mouth speaketh.* This abundance also flows throughout your body. It carries life, if you feed your spirit good things. It carries death, if hatred, resentment, unforgiveness, and fear have been the fare on which you have feasted.

My word gives healing and health to all your flesh. It keeps your body at rest, not anxious or nervous. Trust **my word** to bring life to your members. Trust **my word** to give healing and health to your flesh. I am not a man that I should lie. Trust in **me.**

Scriptures: Numbers 23:19, Proverbs 4:23, Matthew 12:34.

Prayer: Lord, I desire above all things, to please you. I will feed my spirit good things so that my heart might be full of your word. I do trust your word to bring life to me.

April 20
Beneath you are the sheltering arms of love. You will never fall as long as you trust in **me.** I have made provision for **my** children, those who hear and do my **word,** to be held in times of stress. Be not afraid. I have overcome the world with its problems, its difficulties, its circumstances. The storms may come to you, but you will not fall.

My word says, *Submit yourself to God, resist the devil and he will flee.* These words should give you confidence and make your faith rise to new heights. Every man and woman of faith must encounter trying times. Indeed, the whole world is under attack. You will overcome! You are acquainted with the **God** above all gods, the **maker** of the universe, the great **I am.** Do not be discouraged at Satan's hindrances. Rise up, count your blessings, and go forward in confidence to overthrow and conquer *him!* I have given you the land. Receive it.

April 21

Scriptures: Joshua 1:13, Job 11:15, John 16:33, I Cor-inthians 15:57, James 4:7.

Prayer: Thank you, Father, for your protection and love. Thank you for the assurance of victory. I submit myself wholly to you, Lord, and I am so grateful that there is nothing to fear.

April 21

Do not hesitate to do good work. This makes being a doer of the **word** so much easier. **I** give good thoughts and promptings by the **Holy** Spirit. Immediately *Satan* comes with procrastination, vain imaginations and human reasonings to steal the seed that **I** planted. You will recognize a deed inspired by me. If you are diligent to respond, much is accomplished for the kingdom of **God.**

Be not slothful or double-minded. Heed these promptings. You can recognize **my voice,** and the voice of another you will not follow. If you are hesitant about what kind of spirit is speaking, ask if it is **I**, or the voice of a *deceiver.* Does the voice line up with **my word**? Being a *doer of the word* means the **word** is being made real in your life. It is allowing **me** to be manifested in your life, and to your being able to minister *life* to others.

April 22

Scriptures: Mark 4:13-20, James 1:22, I John 4:1-3.

Prayer: Father, make me diligent to hear and to obey your voice. I want to be faithful, Lord, and prompt to do your bidding. I will heed the leading of the Holy Spirit.

April 22

Rejoice, for **He** is risen! The event that seemed to be such a tragedy became the most glorious event for mankind. Out of sorrow, **I** brought new life, hope and joy. **I** am still doing it today. What Satan means for evil, **I** work for good. To those who heed **my word** and act on **my word,** the kingdom of **God** shall be manifested. There are no circumstances which cannot be changed, for **I** am **Lord** over all. With man, circumstances may be impossible, but with me, all things are possible.

Come into my presence with thanksgiving and into my courts with praise. **I** have redeemed you. **I** know your name, and **I** know the number of hairs on your head. **I** have known you from your mother's womb. Rejoice in my redeeming power. Rejoice that **He** is risen! Rejoice that **I am Lord** over all! Rejoice! Rejoice! Rejoice!

Scriptures: Jeremiah 15:16, Psalm 97:1, Matthew 28:6, Acts 1:1-3, Acts 1:29-32, Romans 10:9.

Prayer: Father, I do rejoice! I rejoice in you! Thank you for the resurrection and redeeming power of Christ, your anointed Son. Thank you for working all things to my good. I love you, Lord.

April 23

They that wait upon the Lord shall renew their strength. Waiting upon me means many things. It is abiding in **me** and coming into **my** presence for renewal and strength. Waiting upon **me** is to trust me for results during the passage of time, so that patience is gained and strengthened. It is also serving **me**, as a waiter serves a table. To wait upon **me** involves spiritual, emotional and physical action.

Your whole man must be strengthened daily, or you will falter and stumble in your walk with **me**. He who is diligent to wait upon **me** *shall mount up with wings as an eagle. He shall run and not be weary, he shall walk and not faint.* **I** will teach you to wait upon me if you will be diligent to seek **my** presence, learn of **my word** and act in obedience to **my** commandments. It is a wonderful thing to run and not be weary, to **walk** and not faint. You can learn to live in this state.

Scriptures: Psalm 27:14, Psalm 103:5; Isaiah 40:31, Zechariah 10:12, Matthew 11:28.

Prayer: Father, I know I can do nothing worthwhile

without you. I will gladly wait upon you, Lord. Thank you so much for your strength and guidance. Thank you for renewing my body, soul and spirit.

April 24

I give new life, renewed life, to each person who receives **me**. There is no abundance of life outside my kingdom. **I**, alone, can heal the hurts of life. **I** am the source of all life. If you are obedient to live **my way**, you become immune to the *destroyer* of life. **I** vaccinate you with joy unspeakable and full of glory. You are then able to overcome all obstacles in strength, without the mental anguish of fear. You are confident of victory and can joy in the results of prayer before they are seen.

This attitude enables you to rise in victory over all of *Satan's* hindrances. The **word** begins to work mightily within you, to bring power to overcome and be optimistic in the face of adversity to your life. You are immunized against depression, despondency and fear----*Satan's* major weapons. You are resilient when attacks come and do not succumb to pressure, for you are confident of every outcome. **I** make a way for victory.

Enjoy the life **I** give you. Be determined to receive the most that life offers, a life filled with expectancy, joy and hope. This life is for all who call upon the **name** of the **Lord**.

Scriptures: Psalm 27:1-3. Proverbs 8:35, John 1:4,

April 25

I Peter 1:7-9.

Prayer: Father, I choose life. I choose to live in abundant life through Jesus. I make a solemn choice to abandon all fear and worry and to accept the joy of the Lord.

April 25

I made the **gospel** so simple that little children could understand it, but it confounds the wise. One can only come as a little child, humbly and meekly. Those who are wise in their own sight refuse to acknowledge their need of a **savior**. They fail to see that there is one **greater** than themselves. Pride looms up to trap tender thoughts of submission. Reasonings and vain imaginations steal the seed of faith, planted in mercy and forgiveness. Just as **Jesus** lamented over the hardness of hearts in Jerusalem, so the **Holy Spirit** grieves over the rejection of **His** love by suffering mankind.

As **I** am merciful and long suffering with the children of men, be ye also merciful, kind and patient. Many a child was won to **me** because he saw **my** likeness in human form. **I** said that if **I** be lifted up, **I** will draw all men unto me. Lift **me** up in your actions, thoughts and words. Scatter seeds of **me**. Much of the seed will be wasted, scorched, choked or scattered. But some will take root and flourish to enhance the world. This good seed will give back more than you can imagine. Tiny little seeds will take

April 26

root in humble hearts, bringing in the kingdom of God.

Scriptures: Proverbs 10:13,23; Matthew 18:2-4; Mark 4:31-32; John 12:32; II Corinthians 10:5.

Prayer: Father, help me to plant good seed. Help me to be merciful and kind. Help me to show Jesus to the world. Father, I thank you for making the gospel simple and understandable. I pray that it will be received in the hearts of men more and more.

April 26
Believe that *whatsoever ye desire, when you pray, believe that ye receive them and ye shall have them.* Then continue to thank **me** for answered prayer. Continue to acknowledge before **me** and before men that you have received those things for which you prayed. Continue to submit to **me** in order to resist *Satan's* lies, deceits, doubts, and to rebuke *his* attacks against you.

Do not allow fear to hamper your praise, to rule your thought-life. When you consider the **word**, your prayers and **my** faithfulness more than you consider circumstances or evidence, you are beginning to trust me. **I** am faithful and **I** lie not. Consider **me** first, and the hindrances will begin to fade from importance.

Say often, "**God** is faithful", and "**He** answers prayers". Then you will have the peace that passes understanding.

April 27

Scriptures:Deuteronomy 7:9, Mark 11:23-24, I John 3:22.

Prayer: Father, help me consider the word instead of the circumstances. I choose to disregard all fear. I choose to speak only those words that are in line with the word.

April 27

I have provided for man in every way. I have provided for his spiritual rebirth, his mental renewal his physical resurrection. I have provided for prosperity, health and abundant life. Yet, so many are perishing. They perish physically and go to an early grave. They perish emotionally, bringing havoc to themselves and their loved ones. They perish spiritually and end in hell. They perish for a lack of knowledge. Put yourself in a position to hear the word, and having heard, to act on the **word.** *He that hath an ear to hear, let him hear.*

My covenant is with those who believe. Search the scriptures and receive the **word** into your heart. Meditate on it day and night. There is no other way to make your way prosperous and to have good success in every area of your life. I came to give life, and that more abundantly. Receive **my word**, act on

April 28

my word and enjoy the abundance that was meant for you from the beginning.

Scriptures: Psalm 1, Hosea 4:6, Matthew 11:15, ITimothy 4:15-16.

Prayer: Father, thank you for your glorious provision for me. I want your blessing, Lord, and I choose to meditate on the things of God. Help me to attend to your word.

April 28

Man has a way that seemeth right, but the end thereof is death. You must do things **my** way. Often that seems to be the longer, more difficult way, but it is not. **My** way is the sure way----the only path that will lead to success, permanently. **My** way involves humbling yourself, being single-minded, determining to stay the course until victory is won. My way means ignoring and resisting Satan's lies and traps. You must allow the word to become reality to you. You must abide in me.

My way is too hard for many, but it is the only way to win. Along the way you will encounter many others who are also going **my** way. You need them, and they need you! There is no acceptable alternative to **my** way. Other ways are temporary and will not succeed. Do it my way. I win.

Scriptures: Psalm 25:10, Proverbs 14:12, Proverbs

21:2, Isaiah 1:19, Hosea 14:9, Luke 16:15, John 13:17.

Prayer: Father, I ask your help as I continue to try to be faithful to your word. I choose your way and to resist all other ways. I know there is victory in your word, and <u>only</u> in your word.

April 29
Be strong and courageous; do not tremble or be afraid for the **Lord** *thy* **God** *is with you, wherever you go.* Being strong and courageous is an attitude that can only come to the trusting heart.

The natural mind will faint at circumstances that deny victory. The trusting heart remains steadfast and secure, trusting in the **Lord.**

When you put your faith in **me**, you are humbling yourself and are coming as a little child. I will not fail you! You may go forward, unafraid, knowing that I go before you, preparing the way before you.

Scriptures: Joshua 1:9, Acts 18:9-10, Romans 2:6-7.

Prayer: Father, I take you at your word. I trust you. I know you are faithful, and regardless of the circumstances, I know I will be victorious. Thank you for the victory, Lord.

April 30

The battles are not over until absolute victory is won. This will be when **I** reign as **King** of the Earth. Then I will have other tasks for you. Therefore, do not allow weariness or despondency to set in. You have much to do! Satan would have you give up and fall down in defeat. You will not, you cannot, as long as you trust in **me**.

Do not tremble or **be** afraid. I have given you the land. Stand firm, march forward, receive it!

Scriptures: Joshua 1:13, Mathew 25:23, Revelation 2:10, Revelation 21:7.

Prayer: Father, I will be faithful to Jesus, in whom there is no failure. I thank you for the victory. I look forward to the prize.

MAY

May 1

When you walk in the valleys, **I** am there. When you go through trials, **I** am there. When you need me most, **I** am there. **I** am also there in the times of pleasure, in times of joy, in times of peace. Learn to seek me early, before trials and temptations come. Come into **my** presence with praise and thanksgiving so there will be no break in our fellowship, no dissolution of our relationship. Then when trials and temptations come, you are prepared----prepared to fight, prepared to stand, prepared to win. **The King of Glory** will then shine in you and through you.

For those who seek **me** last---after they have tried the doctors, the lawyers, the counselors, the bankers----much pain could be avoided by having a constant relationship with me. **I** give fortitude and strength to your spirit, which gives you stamina and staying-power. You then have the will to *stay the course,* to fight until you win!

You must build up a trust in **me**, a confidence in my faithfulness. This cannot be developed in a time of stress. It only comes with an abiding relationship over a period of time. Choose to come into **my** presence daily. Choose to seek **me** early and often. You need **my** abiding presence constantly------not just during emergencies.

Scriptures: Psalm 27:8, Psalm 63:1 Proverbs 8:17

May 2

Amos 5:4, Matthew 6:33.

Prayer: Father, I thank you for being my God. Thank you for being the answer for all problems, for being the comfort for all hurts, the provider for all needs. Thank you for the peace that passes understanding.

May 2

...great is thy faith. Be it unto thee even as thy will. The things of this world would be far different if man would only believe **my word.** You must choose to believe and stand on **my word,** regardless of the pressures and circumstances that come to bear. Is not faith the evidence of things not seen? Establish yourself firmly on the **word** and see **my** glory manifested. Believe and receive! This is the only way to abundant life. You must let the **word** dwell in you richly. Choose to let the word permeate your thought life. Cast down fearful thoughts and go forward, unafraid. Trust my faithfulness, trust in **my** power. Trust **my** willingness to act on your behalf. Faith moves mountains and faith moves **me!** Be exceedingly glad.

Scriptures: Mark 5:36, Mark 9:23, John 6:29.

Prayer: Father, I believe your word. I stand on your word and I will not be moved by circumstances. I thank you, Lord, that you are able to keep that which

I've committed unto thee against that day.

May 3

There is no one who escapes from life. Life was meant to be lived, and in life, you should have dominion. Escape is a temporary measure of relief that more often brings a greater measure of stress. It is procrastination in the emotional realm, and its results are the devastation of lives.

There is one escape, however, that is beneficial. Escape unto **me!** Come into my presence and cast your cares upon me. **I** will give you rest. From this escape you grow victorious over the trials of life. When you escape unto **me,** you are abiding under the shadow of the **almighty.** Escaping this way means rescue from trouble. **Man** has sought refuge in addictions, in imaginations, in adulteries, in physical hideaways, in institutions. But when you escape unto **me, I** strengthen you, and you are then able to conquer the trials of life. Then you are actually entering into real life, the life of the **Spirit.**

This is the life that has dominion over circumstances, over physical difficulties, over mental stress and pain. Escaping unto **me** means entering into the realm of victory and abundant life. If you can see the truth in this, and will act upon this truth, you will have dominion over life, instead of being defeated and destroyed by life. You choose.

Scriptures: Psalm 91, Matthew 11:28, I Thessa-

May 4

lonians 1:9-10,13, I Peter 5:6-10.

Prayer: Father, I choose to escape from the stress of life by coming into your presence. There is true rest, peace and safety in you. Thank you for the safety, Lord, and the refreshing, strengthening inspiration found in your presence. Thank you, Lord.

May 4

Have no preconceived notions on how **I** will answer prayer or how **I** will perform my **word**. Be open to creative acts and unexpected events, so that you will recognize my moving on your behalf. So often my children are prepared for **me** to answer prayer in the ways they expect. Many missed the coming of the **Messiah** because I sent him not as a king, but as a servant. Many will miss **His** second coming because they will not expect him to appear as he does. I will fulfill all prophesy, so be open to **my** quickening of your spirit, and see **me** moving in the earth.

Learn to trust your spiritual discernment and to believe in **my** operation in your life. I am not limited to what man may think. I do more than you can ask or think. *Eye hath not seen nor ear heard the things that I have in store for those who love* **me**. Be ready to receive and be open to **my** ways. He who looks for me will find **me**, and you will see the wondrous acts **I** perform.

May 5

Scriptures: Psalm 31:19, Isaiah 64:4, I Corinthians 2:9, Ephesians 1:17-23.

Prayer: Father, I repent of every time I have tried to work out my own problems, or have failed to look to you for help. I want to be open to your leading, Lord. I trust you and you alone. Thank you for moving in my life.

May 5

Life's real journey starts with the *new birth*, because before that, you were on a journey to *death*. If you will renew your mind to see this journey as the sure way to abundant life, it will change your whole attitude toward the trip. This journey is not a 100-yard dash. It is long, hazardous, and filled with perils. It is also filled with wonder and victory, and, it is the only alternative you have to death.

You must realize that there are no acceptable alternatives to this journey. When you reach the end of this journey, you will have won the *crown of life*. Keep this goal firmly fixed in your mind, and the way will seem far less weary. Learn to enjoy the beauty presented along the way. True, there will be times of testing, but there would be bad times even if you were not traveling at all. Remember **who** goes with you, showing the way. I give aid, comfort, support and delight to you. You will never have to travel alone, unless you stray from the main path.

Look for the good along the way. Enjoy the

beauty, knowing that you'll only pass this way once. If you will partake of the heavenly food **I** give, you will not famish or grow faint. When you reach the end of life's journey, you will hear those lovely words that will make it all worthwhile. *Well done, thy good and faithful servant.*

Scriptures: Matthew 25:21, Matthew 28:19-20, James 1:25, Revelation 2:7.

Prayer: Father, life seems so exciting when I think about traveling the road accompanied by you. Help me to be aware of your presence. I want to enjoy the beauty along the way, instead of being caught up in worrying about the next step. Thank you for going with me.

May 6

Rejoice and be exceedingly glad, for **I** am the **King** of Glory. Very few recognized **my** kingship while **I** dwelt among men. This knowledge can only be revealed by the **Father** through the **Holy Spirit**. Pray often that men's hearts would be softened to receive knowledge of **me**. I have given you the keys of the kingdom, keys to bind and loose. Use your authority to set men free, free to accept **me** without hindering spirits blinding their eyes. Come into agreement with others whose desire is towards **me**. Remember that I said, *if two of you agree as touching anything. . . . .* Stand on your agreement. Bring it to

my remembrance. Do you believe that **I** would neglect the cries of my elect?

Pray without ceasing, and in everything give thanks, for it is already done, if you believe. This is the rejoicing that you have, it is already done! *It is finished.*

Scriptures: Psalm 68:3, Matthew 18:18-20, John 19:30, I Thessalonians 5:16-18.

Prayer: Father, when Jesus said, "It is finished," he meant his work was done. He freed me from sin, death, emotional pain and bondage, from sickness and disease, from poverty and lack! When I agree with another believer, when we bind and loose, and when we ask in Jesus' name, we can have whatever we say according to the will of God-----because it is finished! I rejoice in this, Father.

May 7

Let no man or thought deceive you concerning my will and purpose. As **I** have thought, so will it come to pass----not as the world thinks, not as the enemy thinks. Line up your will with **my will** and you shall have blessings instead of curses. **I** made provision for you to be redeemed from the curse, but it is provision to be acted upon rigorously, not passively. You are to be a doer of the **word**----not a hearer only. Renew your mind to reject thoughts or values that contradict my **word. My** purpose for your

May 8

life is revealed in **my word**. If you act rebelliously to my word, you deny yourself the blessings.

Make the **word** and your will to be in alignment. This is a choice, not a feeling. Do not allow self-pity, circumstances or pride to influence your affairs. **I** cannot use anyone who refuses to obey **me**. Rebellion is not part of **my** kingdom. A willful heart will not succeed.

Saul was disobedient and he lost his kingdom. Learn from him and submit yourself to **me**. Submission is a sacrifice, but **I** receive sacrifices. They are pleasing to **me**. Put *self* on the *altar* and receive the blessings. You will never be sorry that you did!

Scriptures: I Samuel 15:23, Isaiah 1:19, James 1:22, Hebrews 10:36.

Prayer: Father, I choose to die to self. I choose to line up with the word. I choose to be obedient. I refuse to let self-pity, circumstances or pride influence me in any way. Thank you, father, for the victory I have in you!

May 8

When you pray, believe you receive, and you shall have what you say. When you pray, I hear. If your faith is even that of a mustard seed, you will see results. A little faith, held onto and believed, is all it takes. If you will not let go, if you will only stand steadfast and hold on, you shall have what you say. It does not take great faith to move **me;** it only takes a little. A few words, taken literally, will bring results. Force yourself to think on the *rhema* that you have received. Go over and over and over those **words**. You are casting down vain imaginations when you do. The **word**-results spring forth. You are bringing your thoughts into captivity. This takes some mental exercise, but it is a possible task. In fact, it is a necessary task for spiritual growth and success. You are in spiritual warfare and you must fight or fall back defeated, wounded and despondent.

    The alternative to defeat is victory. With just a small amount of faith, properly applied, you can win every battle. Choose to believe. Choose to fight. Choose to win!

Scriptures: Psalm 112:7-8, Mark 11:22-24, II Corinthians 10:5.

Prayer: Father, I make the decision to bring every thought into the captivity of Christ. I choose to believe, to fight and to win! Help me to put the word first in every situation.

May 9

    The way of the overcomer is bright. Expectancy brings many rewards. **My** children are above the fears of the **earth** because they trust in **me**. All could have this trust, this faith, this reliance on

May 9

me if they would allow themselves. Faith cometh. The perilous times of the world's ways will destroy and wreck many, but not **mine.** They are founded upon the rock of **Jesus**, and the storms affect them not. They see the storms, they hear the storms, they feel the storms, but their security is in me. They say, what time I am afraid, I will trust the **Lord**, and **my** rest comes to them.

The peace **I** give comes through faith in me and is far above rubies or riches. I give freely and my children must receive freely. Testings and trials are part of the universe but the conquering power is only of me. I give the power to conquer and defeat. **My** way is sure and steadfast; no one needs to stumble or fall.

The ways of the wicked are not so-----they are snared and trapped all along the way. Evil confronts them on every side, and fear is their companion. The way of the righteous is the way of peace and joy. I shield **mine** from the evils of the day, and even though my children may see the *evil, the wicked one* touches them not. Rest in **my** love, **my** protection, **my** care. Let ease and comfort be your attitude, because all is well.

Scriptures: Psalm 84:7-8, Psalm 112:10, Romans 10:17, Titus 3:5, Hebrews 10:38-39, I John 5:18.

Prayer: Father, thank you for your overcoming power through Jesus. Thank you for the Light. Thank you for the assurance that I do not have to fear anything----not even death! Thank you for giving me the power to overcome fear and every other hinderance through Jesus.

May 10

Each day, wipe the slate clean and begin anew. **I** keep my **word**, and no one need carry the burdens of yesterday's failures to tomorrow, or even today. The past is forgotten when it has been repented. **I** do not need to remember, nor do you. So many are troubled and tormented by yesterday's failures, but this need not be. **I** am the **God** of all, and **I** choose to forget. You must keep charge over each thought you let dwell in your mind. Permit no evil to enter. Dwell on the good, the hope **I** give you, and the **word** of faith. These will keep you in the peace that is your inheritance, and no evil can damage that peace.

I want **my** children to dwell in love and safety. By guarding your thoughts, no evil can disturb that peace, or disrupt **my** best. Because you have control over your mind, you have to act, to initiate. This causes many to fall, because they simply do not want to act.

Scriptures: Psalm 103:12, Matthew 11:28-30, ICorinthians 3:19, Romans 2:13.

May 11

May 11

Prayer: Father, your mercy is so great. Help me this day to put the past behind me and go on in faith, trust and joy. I repent of every failure, Lord. I believe, and thank you, that I am forgiven. Thank you for your mercy and love.

May 11

The heavens are not as brass when you speak, because you ask according to **my** will. In order to feed others, you must be prepared. Know that **I** hear all who call, but they must be robed properly and ask appropriately. I allowed **my Son** to die so that **my** people would be properly attired, and in right relationship to ask of me. The people who neglect to "line-up" with **my word** have no excuse. They are ignorant and they perish because of it. Ignorance and rebellion are killing them. They want the blessings, but they do not want the **blesser!** It will never work that way.

*All who call upon the **name of the Lord** shall be saved,* if they believe on **my Son**, and doubt not. I have an ordered universe, and an ordered kingdom. This is what gives man freedom in them both. Because **my** truths and blessings are everlasting, man is comfortable in life. He can see **my** faithfulness, and know that **I** change not! I love **my** children----all of them, but they must line-up with **my word** and yield to **my** order of things. They remove themselves from **my** blessings when they heed not **my word.** I do not remove them; they remove themselves. Only a pure and obedient heart that loves me can move and operate in **my** kingdom. **I** cannot look on impurity or rebelliousness. Rest assured your prayers are answered, all according to my **word** and **will**. **I** do not fail. **I** am trustworthy. Be ye likewise.

Scriptures: II Samuel 22:4, Hosea 4:6, Acts 2:21.

Prayer: I thank you, Father, for being trustworthy. I repent for being rebellious in any way. I will line up with your word and be faithful. I want to be pleasing to you, Lord.

May 12

I have given you the land. Believe and you shall receive. **My words** are as true today as they were when **I** first uttered them to (and through) my prophets of old. They believed and so shall you! The things of **God** seem strange to those who are not heavenly minded. But to **my own,** they are life and light. Keep your heart pure and clean, and **my** thoughts will be your thoughts. Let nothing bother or upset the relationship between you and me, you and **my body**, you and **my kingdom.** You do always have a choice in what you hear, how you listen, what you say. It may not seem so, but <u>you do</u>.

Days of great stress are coming on the earth, but my people will not know it as the world does.

May 12

They are to be carried along on a cushion of love. The ones who love **me** will only see **me,** and they are as protected as a babe in the womb.

Keep your time apart with me, that your heart will not quake in fear. **I** will insulate you as you give me leave to enter. The strength you draw from me will strengthen many. You can trust **me**. **I** am faithful.

My followers must discipline themselves so that they are unencumbered by the world. You must not let the world's woes drag you down. You have the power to be in command of your life; you do not have to yield to the pressures. **I** am stronger than any pressure that can be brought to bear on you. Stand strong in **my word**, stand firm on **my word.** Live and love as **my word** indicates, and no harm can come nigh your dwelling.

My peace is priceless and **I** give it freely to all who will partake of it. It is a gift to **my** people and it is manifested in the lives of those who yield themselves to **me**. It comes without beckoning and lasts without season. It is priceless, but free. To whosoever yields will it come.

These **words** are to be stored in yielded hearts, as food for the hungry. They will feed the spirit for all time, because **my words** never die. As **my** people are washed in **my word**, their hearts become clean and their minds are renewed. Truly, nothing shall offend them or make them stumble.

Scriptures: Numbers 33:53, Psalm 101:1-4, Micah 6:8, Philippians 4:7.

Prayer: Father, I choose to be strong in the word. I will not heed the loud voices of the world with its dire predictions. I will shut my mind to them, but open my mind to you. I rely on your strength to keep me. Thank you for the gift of your peace. I love you, Lord.

May 13

Be prepared to go through many changes, many trials, much distress, but <u>always</u> with the sure knowledge that **I** *am* **Lord** *over all*. Do not shrinkback, do not fear, do not despair. **I** am **Lord** of every circumstance, and **I** prepare the way. Nothing is too hard for me to overcome or disannul. As my Spirit leads, so you must follow. **I** will only tolerate strict obedience----that obedience which allows my power to flow.

As you yield, then can my wonder-working power take control. Circumstances are always in the physical realm. **I** am not! Be sure of **my** control and **my** power. Do not allow your natural mind to rebel or lack faith.   You have the choice. Cling to your confession of faith and see **me** work. I do not change and **my** power is from everlasting to everlasting.

The days of the earth are numbered, but **my**

May 14

people prevail. They are not subject to the distresses that the unprepared are. Their reliance must be in me. Distress may come, but not defeat. Do not give in, do not give up! I am **Lord.**

Scriptures: Isaiah 1:19, II Corinthians 12:10, Ephesians 6:10.

Prayer: I praise you, Lord, that my steps are ordered by you. Sometimes I don't feel strong, but I believe your word more than my feelings. I choose to be obedient, strong and to let your power flow. Thank you that you are the unchanging one. I thank you for your outcomes; I know I can rely on you.

May 14

My word never fails. He who is faithful to believe me never loses. I reward those who diligently seek me. Look always to me and to **my word.** I will do what I have promised. The enemy comes to rob, kill and destroy, but his power is limited to deceit. Deceit is given to *Satan* until the day of the **Lord's** coming, but because **Jesus** reigns in the hearts of **his** own, *Satan* has no authority there. *He* cannot defeat a **word**-filled, a **word**-acting, a **word**-believing Christian. *His* weapons are puny and futile against the **word**; *he* cannot penetrate the armor I have given **my** children.

Rest in this knowledge. Be joyful, be glad, rejoice always, and you will see **my word** performed gloriously! Refuse emotions, actions or thoughts that would keep you from victory. I have given you the power of patience and faith----they are abundantly ample to defeat all the tactics of *Satan*.

Scriptures: Matthew 7:7-8, Romans 13:14, Ephesians 6:13-18, II Timothy 3:15-16, Hebrews 11:6.

Prayer: Father, I rejoice in you, your word and your victory over the world. I put on the whole armor of God and rejoice in its strength and invulnerability. Praise you, Father!

May 15

Trust **me.** Each day's coming brings new challenges and opportunities for **my** kingdom. Think of what that first daybreak meant to those who saw it. Look at your day with the same kind of enthusiasm and awe. Life is meant to be lived in full measure, not in some humdrum, dull way. I provide much adventure in **my** kingdom for those who follow and obey.

My followers have often been thought of as weak, dull, introverts-----this is indeed a picture painted by *Satan!* I am life, so how can **my** people lack life? **My** ways are not only exciting and challenging, but they are also fulfilling and full of power. I am creative; so are those who imitate me. I am exciting and full of joy! So are **my** disciples. To live life in its fullest measure, one must be **mine.**

May 16

The enemy comes to take life. **I** offer it abundantly. In my kingdom, there are no dullards. Only quick minds, ready hearts and lively bodies inhabit me. **I** renew the mind. **I** renew the youth. **I** quicken the spirit. Does that sound like death that *Satan* offers?

Life in my camp is full of pleasure. No false stimulus is needed to spur mine own to victory. **My** followers are full of the **Holy Spirit**, joy and gladness. As they look to **me** for guidance and confidence, it flows like heavy streams to invigorate their every cell. When eyes are upon **me,** no foot fails or loses its way.

My way is sure. It is fun. It is full of joy. It is full of challenges and victories. **My** way is the way, and **I** give it to you.

Scriptures: Psalm 18:30, Psalm 118:24, Isaiah 14:28, John 14:6.

Prayer: Father, how exciting it is to be in your kingdom! How glorious your promises are! Thank you for each new day. I will be conscious of your presence and live this day to the fullest! I am so glad that Christ has redeemed me from fear, sickness, lack, and evil. Thank you, Lord!

May 16

The preparation of **my** body is not an easy task, because **I** have so much flesh with which to contend.

May 16

But it is not impossible, either. With **me**, nothing is impossible. As **my** people voluntarily begin to obliterate the flesh, kill the self and lay down their lives, the forming of the **body** comes. It is an inherent desire in each of **my** children to be part of me, part of **my** leadership, part of **my** goals. So often they miss the mark, because they fail to heed me, to listen to **my** direction. They are more concerned with their own wants and needs than with my kingdom.

My yoke is easy. **I** lead gently; **I** cause no sores on the necks of obedient children. Those who fail to heed **my** commands, those who run wild and come out from under **my** protection, suffer until they docilely again return to **my** gentle yoke. I force no one. It is always a voluntary decision to come under the yoke. What peace is there, what joy; plenty of provision and comfort. When you feel the chaffing of **my** yoke----- stop, until you see which way **I** am leading. If you again find yourself pulling away, you must be sure to follow **me**. If you will but listen, you can hear my voice, even though the way seems dark to you. A light will guide your every step, until you are again walking step-in-step with **me**. When one goes aright, it is so much easier for others to follow my paths. Only follow where **I** lead. You know **my** voice. You will find **me**.

Scriptures: Psalm 119:105, Isaiah 30:21, I John 5:3.

May 17

Prayer: Your guidance is so wonderful, Father. When I remember your word, I can put flesh behind me and can resist the gravitational pull of the world. Your word is life to me, Father. Thank you for your abundant provision.

May 17

As long as your heart is pure towards me, and you examine your heart, there are no closed doors. Be of an humble and submissive attitude. **I** use people like that. **I** only withdraw **my** permission when it is dangerous for you. Keep your heart and mind clean by the washing of the water in the **word.** **I** pose no obstacles for **my** own, and **I** keep **my** own from harm.

Seek always **my** will, **my** kingdom. Cast down a haughty spirit. My Spirit is always there to check your spirit, if you will but yield to **him.** You will be victorious in all areas, because your heart yields to **me**, and loves **me**. Do not fear failure. **I** will not let you fail, as long as you yield to **me.** Do not fear temptation; you are stronger than any temptation which might come, because of **my word** in you.

Discipline yourself in **my word**, and the rest is easy. Yes, **I** said "easy"! As your mind becomes renewed, **Satan** becomes no more than a pesky fly, and you hold the fly swatter. **He** is not able to torment you, unless you allow it! You have much to learn and the **way** is exciting. Look forward to life with me. **I** am the **Lord**, and **I** have ordered the way.

May 18

It is a joyful life, to live in **me.** You shall see! **My** paths are full of light, joy, peace and gladness. You shall see!

Scriptures: II Chronicles 16:9, Psalm 5:2-3, Proverbs 21:21, Ephesians 5:26, I Peter 5:5-6.

Prayer: Father, I choose to humble myself and to keep my heart pure. I yield myself to your Spirit and choose you, and you alone. I empty myself of all worldly desires that do not line-up with your desires for me. I thank you for crowning my efforts with success.

May 18

Be not discouraged when you fail to see evidence of your prayers. **I** am moving and working on your behalf. Stand steadfast on the **word**, and there shall be a performance of those things which were told you. Let **me** be your shield of protection. Do not try to protect yourself with carnal weapons; they will fail. When you turn to the world's ways, you have to live with the world's results----and they are woefully inadequate to meet your needs.

The mystery of the kingdom is revealed to stout hearted men and women, those who trust and stand. The rewards will never go to the fainthearted or the fearful. You choose to be an inheritor of the promise when you refuse to let evidence, circumstances or people move you off of your confession of faith. Out of the abundance of the heart, the mouth will speak, so fill your heart with the **word**. Meditate on the **word** day and night, so you can run the race and win the prize. The victory is yours. I have promised it----but you must still run and win to obtain it.

Scriptures: Matthew 12:34, Romans 12:2, Hebrews 4:14, 10:23, 12:3-6.

Prayer: Father, Forgive me for being faint-hearted when I should have been brave. I truly desire to be brave. Thank you for the evidence of my prayers. With your word behind me, I will run the next race much better than I did the last. Thank you for the word, the renewing of my mind, and the victory.

May 19

I am giving you many things; keep yourself clean: mentally, spiritually, physically. Your mind must be stayed on me. I am a jealous God, and I suffer not transgression. Repentance is there, but I demand more of the leaders in **my** kingdom. I am using you in many areas of warfare, but you must be ready. No *enemy* must be allowed in the camp.

What would be innocent to others is sin to you, for you have been called out to serve **me.** I am enough for you. You do not need other diversions. **My** love, **my** joy, **my** interests will occupy your life. You are often suddenly tempted, but do not yield.

May 20

You do not have to. **I** am sufficient for all your needs. **My** work is to build a kingdom, and the few who will give themselves wholly shall help others to build, also. Great things, great miracles are wrought in single-mindedness. Stand firm. It is not as hard as you think. **My** power and strength are ever- present, as well as **my** peace and **my** joy. The fear of the **Lord** is clean. Be clean.

Scriptures: Deuteronomy 5:9, Psalm 19:9, I Corinthians 15:57-58.

Prayer: Father, I will keep my mind on you, so that I will be clean. Help me to realize that you are more than enough for me. Thank you for being sufficient for all my needs, and thank you for your power and strength. I need all the help I can get.

May 20

My child, **my** child, you must believe on **my** word and doubt not. You must teach others to fight, so they will not be destroyed. I do not tolerate fear in **my** kingdom. Only faith moves **me**. Fear has to flee at **my** word; I am **Lord** over it and over all. Do not let circumstances sway you, or make you doubt. I am **Lord** over all! When **my** children stand, and then march, all of *hell* quakes----and with good reason. **My** Son moves against *Satan* and the *evil ones*. They are defeated, and they know it! **My** army is coming in

May 20

great power to heal, deliver and save. The forces of *hell* are scared. *They* are bluffing when they attack. *They* are scared! *They* are hoping **my** children will be influenced by what they see, but **my** army is steadfast, unmovable, obedient.

My people know **my** word, and they are strong! They are impregnable and cannot be defeated. It is an accomplished fact, because **I** do not lose!

I am **Jehovah, God Almighty.** **My** people abide in **me**, and **my word** gives them strength, victory, conquering power! The might and power are mine to give, and **I** have given it! See victory coming upon the earth. See *Satan's* stronghold's defeated. It is already a fact, and *he* knows it. *He* has no power against **me,** and **I** have no mercy on *him.* Is it not awesome to be in the victory corner? Rejoice and be glad that you can share in the victory over the *enemy.* **My** power is everlasting! There is none greater than **I** and those to whom **I** give authority. Rejoice and go forward unafraid. The enemy is afraid because the **God of Glory** leads you.

Scriptures: Deuteronomy 28:7, Psalm 60:12, Psalm 112:4, I Peter 3:13.

Prayer: Father, you are mighty in pulling down the strongholds of Satan and his forces. No one can stand against you, Lord. I am so grateful to be on the winning side; that I no longer have to "win a few, lose a few". Now I can "win a few, win a few more."

Thank you, Lord, for enlisting me in your army.

May 21

The days are shortened until the time of **my** return, and then all the world will surely see **my** glory. Many will be grieved because they neglected **me**, but oh, the joy of those who were faithful. I am a just **God**, and **I** alone know the heart of man. No one needs fear another's judgement. (Only **mine**). As your thoughts and actions are pure with me, you shall have your reward. You do not have to worry what your neighbor, or even your brother, thinks----- only what **I** think!

No one will be able to escape my scrutiny; **I** see through all. For you who truly love **me**, this will be the time of fulfilled expectancy. No one knows when **I** will come, but the days are shortened. Be ready to share me. Be ready to let **my** Spirit flow through you. These are the demands **I** make on **my** children. <u>Be ready!</u> The **Lord** of **Hosts** leads, and you who follow **me** must be ready!

Scriptures: Matthew 24:1-27, Matthew 1:44, Matthew 25:14-30, John 14:28-29, Titus 2:13.

Prayer: Father, because of Jesus, I am ready for the Lord's return. Because of him, I can count myself faithful, for he has paid for my sins. Thank you for Jesus. Thank you so much for Jesus!

May 22

The church is coming together, never fear. **My** body is an extension of **me** and it will obey **my** wooing. **I** am leading the body of **Christ** into areas never transversed by human hearts. The way shall be abundantly lighted. As **my** people yield more of themselves, they will see **my** glory coming in greater and greater measure. **I** am going to do mighty and glorious works among men. The prophets of old foretold these events, and they will come to pass. **My word** does not fail.

Becoming a member of action in the body requires obedience and sensitivity. Yielded hearts meet this criteria. The working of **my Spirit** is a mystery to man, but the plan has been drawn to perfection. Many may miss major battles because they are unprepared, but **I** have enough, always. Just as in days of old, **I** weed out the ones whose hearts are not ready, so that men cannot say, "We did it, in all our strength." **I** do not share **my glory**, except with **my son** and with, of course, **his** body.

Scriptures: Judges 7:2-7, Psalm 57:5, Ephesians 5:25-27.

Prayer: Father, it is exciting to be on the side of the Living God! It is so wonderful to be in your glorious army. I am so grateful to be a part of the church and be triumphant over all of the works of hell. Thank you, Father, for preparing me to be a soldier.

May 23

I do not measure you as the world does. You are a unique individual to **me**, and **I** alone, read your heart. The things in your heart are often hidden, even from yourself. As you let the light of my glory shine in, **I** reveal the hidden things of the heart. You can choose what your mind thinks, and, in a measure, regulate the purpose of your heart.

However, only as your spirit is aligned with me can your heart become pure. I purify and cleanse the heart so that its motives will be pleasing to me and will edify you. If your heart is deceitful, it is because you have failed to yield your will to **my will**. Such a heart is in rebellion, and is full of lies and guile. You cannot right this until the rebellion is quenched and your will is yielded unequivocally. I will not accept rebellion in **my** kingdom. Only obedient, yielded hearts dwell with **me**, and they dwell in love, rest, joy and abundance.

Scriptures: I Samuel 16:7, Psalm 19:14, Isaiah 30:1, Hebrews 12:11.

Prayer: Lord, I yield my heart to you. I want to be pleasing to you. I want to do your will. I want to have clean hands and a pure heart. Thank you,

Father, for accepting me in every way.

May 24

The length of time necessary to reach spiritual maturity varies directly with the amount of time given to the **word**, meditation, and prayer. There is no easy route to maturity in any area, whether it be spiritual, mental or physical. That is why Paul wrote that we must buffet the body,. . . run the race,. . . be instant in season and out. Only the persistent get the prize and acclaim. Others participate, but do not receive the honor, or the victory, that winners do. What a thrill of victory----to be victorious over the enemy, over the world, over self! The confidence and peace that come are indescribable. Nothing is without cost, but the prize is worth all the cost. In fact, just the training, the discipline and the denial of self reaps great rewards.

To dwell with me and see my handiwork is prize enough, but that is only the beginning. Eye, truly, has not seen nor ear heard what **I** have in store for **my** faithful ones. Is it not exciting?

Scriptures: Matthew 6:33, Romans 12:1, I Corinthians 2:9, Ephesians 1:17-20, Hebrews 12:1-2.

Prayer: Father, I eagerly submit to the discipline and training you have for me. Thank you for providing the way to victory. I will put the word first place so that I will be a victor in Jesus.

May 25

The sands of time are eternal, but man's life on earth is but a vapor. His spirit, however, lives forever. This is what men do not see, cannot comprehend; the life man leads on earth is as nothing, but it is here he decides his fate for eternity. A man cannot grasp the significance of this, unless he yields to the **Spirit of God** within him. I have so many who need to hear the gospel, so that their spirits may be awakened. The **Holy Spirit** has to woo and draw, but a man's spirit must be open to **my** calling. Flesh calling to flesh is vain.

My chosen ones will wait for **me** to prepare a heart before they confront or invite a lost one. You are sensitive to **my** leading, and listen when **I** direct. The joy that **I** have in a yielded spirit who will let me lead, or recognize when **I** lead a lost one to them, is immeasurable.

This is what **I** have trained you, my disciples, for. You do not have to work for **me**; you just have to let **me** work through you. However, to find yielded, obedient spirits is rare.

Scriptures: Psalm 103:15-56, Luke 12:12, Luke 21:13-14, John 8:31-32.

Prayer: Lord, I want to be yielded and obedient so that you may work through me. Help me to be what I should be in order to be used for your kingdom.

May 26

Have faith always. As you move in the realm of faith, you will see more and more of me. I am a faith being, and I operate in that area. All who are of me, must also operate in faith. No miracles, no changes are wrought, apart from faith. It is a commodity, something tangible, but only in the spirit world.

No one can understand this with the natural mind; only the spiritual man can comprehend. Faith, like maturity, comes. It must be developed like a muscle, to be strong. I give a measure of faith, but you, my disciples, must do the rest. There is no limit as to how much faith can develop or grow. It is not so in the natural world----all things have limits. But in the spiritual realms, natural laws do not reign.

As faith develops, miracles occur. Natural things are changed by faith. If you learn this principle and what its implications are, you will seek to exercise and develop faith more.

Scriptures: Habakkuk 2:4, Matthew 17:20, Romans 12:3, Ephesians 6:16, I Peter 1:7, I John 5:4.

Prayer: Father, thank you for the faith you have given me, and for the way you have honored my faith. I choose to develop my faith more and more. I know that without faith, it is impossible to please you. I do want so much to please you, Lord.

May 27

My children are growing up. Heretofore, the *body of Christ* has consisted of spiritual babes. The time of maturity is at hand. **I** am giving a spirit of nurturing to those who seek **me,** and they in turn, are producing fruit. **Many** are seeking with a new intensity, as **my Spirit** draws. Many are learning obedience, that, until now, was practiced by only a faithful few. The *enemy* is frightened, and *he* knows the time of **my** coming grows near. *He* can see the fig leaves sprouting and understands that the time of fulfillment is drawing nearer.

I am preparing mighty men and women to go into spiritual warfare, and they are armed with weapons of warfare. They are leaving basic training, prepared to do great battles----and to win! The army is coming together in full power and regalia. They are assembling under the banner of **Jesus** and they are awesome! **As** the world sees them forming, they become eager to enlist. **A** mighty force is awakening, and **my son** leads it. The lines of battle are becoming clearly established. The *enemy* is preparing, too, but *he* knows *he* cannot win. *He* has played a game of guerilla warfare long enough, and now *he* is being routed out of every dark corner in each heart. *He* cannot stand the light, and it is coming in full glory. The times of battle are hard, but when victory is assured, the battle goes quickly. Excitement and expectancy are penetrating the hearts of **my** warriors. They are lifting the banners of **my** Son for the world to see, and the world is excited!

My Son leads a mighty army, not a rag-tag bunch of misfits. They are fully clothed, royally garbed, strong-limbed warriors who know how to lead and to obey commands. The war is coming and my people are prepared. More will join as they see the victories and hear the conquering cries.

Scriptures: Psalm 18:39-40, Psalm 18:48, Psalm 27:14, Isaiah 40:28-29, II Corinthians 10:4.

Prayer: Father, I choose to build myself up on your word and to become a mature soldier, strong enough for your army. I choose to be a brave warrior, and not a coward. I believe that I will serve you faithfully.

May 28

Though the way seems weary, take heart. There are many beautiful glades that lie ahead for you. There are many fretful times, too, but the beauty of life far outweighs the ugliness. Without me, you cannot possibly appreciate the afflictions of life. Appreciate afflictions? Afflictions are the character building blocks that make you whole. Without afflictions, you are shallow, narrow and dull. Life is filled with the interesting, the humorous and the delightful. After character is formed, these form the "icing on the cake."

May 29

Rejoice! Be glad! Look up!. Today and tomorrow are rich in adventure. I have prepared a feast of life for those who love me and I prepare it in the presence of your enemies. The enemies (those of dullness, despair and boredom) weep in sorrow, because they have lost another victim to abundant life. Take courage. The life I give will bring fullness of joy. Look forward to life, unafraid.

Scriptures: Psalm 16:11, Psalm 23:5, Psalm 32:18, Psalm 34:7-9, Psalm 34:17-19, Psalm 37:23-24.

Prayer: Father, I rejoice that the beauty of life outweighs the ugliness. I rejoice that you have made all the provisions and plans for an exciting, adventurous journey. I look forward with anticipation to my life with you, Lord.

May 29

The storm clouds gather in the heavenlies, but the battle has been won. The natural mind cannot understand the predetermined mind of **God**, only the spiritual can understand. I have revealed **myself** to my disciples, and they can read the signs. The signs will not be evident to the unprepared or the unspiritual, but will be clear to those who diligently seek me.

My Holy Spirit quickens the hearts of the faithful; they see **my** plans and purposes. They recognize **my** leading, **my** guiding and hear **my** voice.

May 30

The stranger will not understand the mysteries of **my** kingdom, but my children comprehend easily. Knowledge and wisdom begin when a soul accepts **me**.

The rate of understanding then grows as much as the individual permits **me** to influence his life. To whom much is given, much is required. **I** expect **my** captains, majors and generals to respond differently from the privates. The officers know the war plans. The private only knows his duty. Accede to be an officer, a confidant, a *son*.

Scriptures: I Samuel 17:47, Luke 12:42-48, John 10:1-4.

Prayer: I seek your understanding, Father. I really want to be faithful and sensitive to the quickening of the Holy Spirit. I want to recognize your voice and to be aware of your presence. I want your blessings and gifts, Father. Help me to please you.

May 30

I have often told you of **my** love and concern for **my** children. The thread of love that unites **me** and **mine** is stronger than any force on earth. It cannot be broken. Because it is not a visible sign, those to whom the spiritual life is not alive, do not believe this thread to be real. However, the spiritual world is infinitely more real than the physical world, and it always will be.

May 31

The intangible forces of the universe are the most powerful----the positive (love, faith, hope) and the negative (hate, doubt and fear). Man lives in these realms and his life is governed by them----whether he recognizes them or not. When a man opens himself to the **God** of the Universe, he is able to receive the positive power of the universe.

When he lives selfishly and sinfully, he is open to the negative *Satanic* forces that dominate the earth. *Satan* does not rule in the universe; *he* only has earth, and that for a short while. *His* power is so limited!

Scriptures: Job 1:7-8, Proverbs 8:17-19, John 3:16, John 10:10.

Prayer: Father, thank you for loving and blessing me. Thank you for the positive power of the universe. Thank you for wooing and drawing me to you. I praise you that I have been spared from Satan's negative forces. I do not have words to express the gratitude I feel *when I survey the wondrous cross on which the Prince of Glory died.*

May 31
The door of life is open and no man can shut it, except for himself. A man has the power to refuse what **I** offer, but oh, the tragedy of that man. One who lives with **me** has abundance in all things---health, wealth, wisdom. This abundance does not

May 31

come automatically. It comes through the exercise of spiritual muscles. I have given you the land and the weapons of warfare to take it, but you have the option of using the weapons or not. The battle, however, is assuredly won.

It is difficult to see needless suffering heaped on my children; it does not have to be so. I have given you power to fling away anything that hinders or slows you down. The exercise of the will is necessary; you must decide who will control your will---your body, your mind, or your spirit.

The times of trials give you an opportunity to develop spiritual might, which is the inheritance of the Saints of **God**. Development cannot be hindered in you, except by your will. Choose to win, to dwell securely and confidently in **my** kingdom. You will see, then, that you will!

Scriptures: Psalm 48:14, 89:34; Luke 10:19; Philippians 1:9; James 1:2-4; Revelation 3:20-22.

Prayer: Father, help me to use the power you have given me, and to fling away anything that hinders my spiritual development. Help me to use your weapons skillfully. Thank you for your overcoming power and for your abundant life in Christ.

JUNE

He that believes on **my** name shall be saved. I have declared that in **my word** and it is true. Salvation is not just a release of the spirit from the body, to dwell with **me** throughout eternity. Salvation covers the mind and body, as well as the spirit.

Man is saved daily. His mind is saved from corrupting influences, evil intents and destructive thoughts. His mind is delivered and conforms to the mind of **Christ.** **Man** must yield his thoughts to my thoughts, so that **my** will and purposes are released into the earth.

Man's body is delivered from sinful gratification, excesses of the flesh, from disease and from corruption by evil. His youth is renewed so that he functions in accord with **my word.** His body is a blessing to him, and glorifies **my work in** his life.

As the **Spirit** of man grows, the mind and body come into the order of the universe. The mind and body are set free to do my work, and thus he is saved.

Scriptures: Psalm 103:2-5, John 5:24, Romans 12:2.
Prayer: Father, you are so good to us. I praise you and thank you for your blessings----mental, physical and spiritual. Father, help me to share this Good

News with those who need to hear it. Thank you for salvation----complete salvation.

June 2

The relationship that comes through abiding with me is a treasure beyond measure. Only the heart who has experienced my love and faithfulness can truly appreciate the comfort abiding brings. I am always there. **My** comfort never leaves. You can always depend on me. What a joy that is!

In a world where nothing lasts, nothing is stable and everything fails, **I** alone stand as the anchor. In the final analysis, you can only rely on **me.** As you grow ever more like **me,** your faithfulness and steadfastness will become as a light to lead the world toward **me.** The world is looking for **me,** although blindly. It gropes futilely toward this god and that, never satisfied because of deception.

I am truth and light. When a soul truly seeks me, **I** will be found. No power on earth can hinder my coming. As you draw near to **me, I** draw near to you. Oh, the satisfaction of your spirit as it unites with **mine.** A feeling of coming home after a long, weary journey could best describe the union of a seeking soul finding **me**----a soul that has found rest.

Scriptures: Joshua 1:13, Psalm 91, Isaiah 32:17, Malachi 3:6, Matthew 11:28.

Prayer: Father, your faithfulness is so great. I count

on you, Lord. Thank you for always being with me to guide, counsel and comfort. Thank you for your fellowship, instruction and encouragement, Lord. Thank you for your divine rest.

June 3

My *peace* is not the peace of this world. Peace is not just a quietness, but a rest of the soul. **I** give a tranquility to the spirit and relaxation to the body. You can be in a quiet place and have no peace. Ask prisoners in solitary confinement if they have peace. The *peace* that comes from **me** brings the whole man into rest. You lose the anxiety, the **fear**, the torment that drives you. It is the *peace that passes understanding*. A soul apart from me will never know this peace. It is the peace I give, through **Jesus.**

You were made to be in communion with **me. I** communed with Adam and made him complete. **My Son** knew the power that comes from communing with me. **He** drew strength and peace from **his** time with me. As you come into contact with **my Spirit**, your strength is renewed. If you meditate on **my word,** your mind is renewed, and if you spend time with me, your spirit is renewed.

Scriptures: Psalm 29:11, Psalm 119:165; Proverbs 3:24; Isaiah 26:3; John 14:27.

June 4

Prayer: Father, thank you for rest and peace. The assurance of your love, provision and protection is the greatest gift in a troubled, noisy world. The noises of the world are so annoyingly constant; the fear is ever present to those who do not know your peace. Help us, Lord, to know your peace. Help me never to forget the peace that is available for me at all times.

June 4

*My sheep hear **my** voice and the voice of a stranger they will not follow.* Never be afraid of deception. It is a ploy of the *enemy* to keep **my** children from acting boldly. As your heart attempts to be in tune with **my Spirit**, and is pure towards me, you will not be deceived. If you ask your **Father** for the leading of the **Holy Spirit,** in truth and without guile, you will get it. The *enemy* wants **my** disciples to be afraid to act boldly on **my word**, to refrain from my leading and guidance. He wants you to fear following in wrong paths. *I am a lamp unto your feet and a light unto your path.* **Satan** would like to deceive you, but he cannot----as long as the **Spirit** leads and you follow.

I am leading many into unchartered areas of service, warfare and discipline. The leaders will open the way and chart the course for many to follow. You can be sure that you will not deceive yourself or others, as you seek **me** in faith and with a spirit of truth. Trust in **my** leadership. **I** would not deceive you.

Scriptures: Psalm 48:14, Psalm 119:105, Proverbs 3:6, Isaiah 30:21, John 10:14.

Prayer: I want to be very consistent in asking for and accepting your guidance, Father. I desire to be very bold. I trust you, Father, to give me courage to act on your truth, your divine wisdom. Your sheep know your voice. I am one of your sheep, and I know your voice. Thank you for helping me to listen only to your voice.

June 5

The reasons to rejoice in **my** love are always present, as a redeemed soul realizes what **I** have done. **He is free,** after countless ages of bondage, because his spirit can now receive **me.** As he comes into realization of this freedom, his mind begins to comprehend what the **Spirit** knows. As his mind and spirit work in harmony, his body begins to line up. The body is always the last to obey; the spirit is always the first. The spiritual part of man is hardest for carnal man to comprehend, because it is least evident to the triune man. When the spirit is given an opportunity to grow and develop as it should, the spiritual will take precedence and dominion over the carnal. He will then see a whole person, complete in **Jesus,** emerge to govern him.

June 6

Scriptures: Deuteronomy 26:11, Matthew 26:41, Galatians 3:13-14, Ephesians 4:15.

Prayer: Father, I rejoice in you! I rejoice in freedom from bondage. I rejoice in your love and am comforted that my body can get in line with my spirit and the Word.

June 6

The children in **my** kingdom have to **be** trained as all children do, lest they fall into rebellion, evil or laziness. Children need constructive things to teach them discipline and love. A willing child learns so much faster than a rebellious child.

The leaders in my kingdom do not have to be the brightest, but they are those with teachable hearts and willing spirits. I do not need the brightest because my ways are higher. I do not need the most able because I am more than enough. I need willing, obedient, and faithful servants I need sons and daughters who love me more than themselves, and thus, they can love others.

To be great in **my** kingdom, one must learn to yield his will to mine. I must be able to trust him with my kingdom; I paid so dearly for it.

Scriptures: Proverbs 3:11-12, Matthew 22:37-40, Hebrews 12:5-11.

Prayer: Father, I choose to yield my members to you,

totally. It is so hard, Lord, to yield without reservations. But with your help, I yield myself to you for correction and instruction. I want to be a faithful servant. I love you, Father, and want to love you more.

June 7

The kingdom of **God** must penetrate every area of human life. **I** came to redeem not only the spirit, but also the flesh and mind. A soul is a precious thing, but **I** also created the flesh. Once a man receives the new birth, his flesh should be brought under submission. As a man learns to control his mind and flesh, he really begins to see the evidence of kingdom living in his life. It is not easy to bring these areas into submission. However, when submission is done, the perfectness of **my Son** is shown in his life, and **I** am glorified.

A man must strive to bring the kingdom of **God** into his life. When the **King** truly reigns in every area of his life, then that man is truly free. The bondages of this earth are without power over one who has learned to let **Jesus** reign in each member. Rejoice in that you can be absolutely free.

Scriptures: John 8:36, II Corinthians 3:17, II Corinthians 5:17, II Corinthians 7:1.

Prayer: I rejoice in your freedom, Lord. Thank you for setting me free----free from death, sin, despair, hopelessness, pain, poverty and lack. I invite you, Father, into every area of my life. I want to be truly free indeed!

June 8

The **Lord** thy **God** knoweth your coming in and your going out. I do direct your paths. The church is my own creation, and I am putting it together. I am building stone upon stone with great workmanship. The work may seem slow to man, but I have eternity. The *enemy* would seek to dissuade **my** church from the work I have purposed, but *he* cannot! Each path, each stone and each life has been carefully laid out by the **Master** builder, the **creator** of the universe. There is no mistake in **my** workmanship.

The members of **my** body are being carefully hewed to come into the image of **Jesus**. **My** workmanship is of the highest quality. I put in only stones that have been carefully selected and perfectly formed. Those who conform most to the image of **my Son** will be in the prominent places; the obedient ones will be placed in the lovelier spots. The strong ones will be laid first, and the delicate ones placed later.

Scriptures: Psalm 16:11, Proverbs 4:18, I Peter 2:4-10.

Prayer: I thank you, Lord, for directing my paths. I also thank you for building your church "perfectly".

I want to be a strong stone, a perfect stone, like Jesus.

June 9

My mercy is to all who will call upon the name of **Jesus**. **My** mercy covers the whole man and provides him with an umbrella of protection. The mercies of **God** are as unfathomable as the depths of the sea, the expanses of space, the motivations of a human heart. Were it not for **my** mercy, man would (long ago) have vanished from the earth.

Through the ages, countless intercessors have reminded **me** of **my** mercy. Thus **my** hand was stayed, when **I** would have acted harshly. These intercessors will have a special place in **my** kingdom, because their love for their fellows was pure. This pure love has reminded **me** of man's frailty, of the deceit of his own heart against himself. Thus I am reminded again to forgive and find mercy. Come boldly to the throne to obtain mercy. **My Son** always reminds **me** to have mercy.

Scriptures: Genesis 18:23-33, Exodus 32:9-14, Psalm 98:3, Psalm 103:12-14, Hebrews 4:14-16.

Prayer: Father, thank you for your great mercy that endures forever. You are so good, patient and slow to anger; I delight in your mercy. Thank you for Jesus, our High Priest, who intercedes for your children, always. Father, I appreciate those you have called to be intercessors. Thank you for their faithfulness to intercede---and to remind you to have mercy on us.

June 10

The beauty of the earth is only one of the many blessings **I** have given man to cause him pleasure. No matter how hard the human heart, if a man will but look at the beauty **I** have made, he can find me. His salvation is not dependent upon a messenger, although **I** have commissioned my disciples to go into all the earth. **I** leave nothing to the chance that someone would be missed if the messenger did not go.

Thus, **I** have written my presence on every leaf, in every ray of sunlight, in every wisp of cloud. Man has no excuse for not seeing **me**. **I** am manifested in every chirp of a bird, the rustle of leaves, the crack of thunder. Man has no excuse. I can be found in every loving caress, every cool stone, every drop of water. Man has no excuse! A knowledge of **me** is given to every man. Pray that his heart will yield to the signs of **me**, that his will would not be resistant to my wooing.

Scriptures: Psalm 8:1-4, Psalm 19:1, Romans 1:19-20.

Prayer: Father, I pray that men will see you in the beauty of nature---in the sights, sounds, tastes, fragrances and feelings you have made to remind man of you. I also pray, Lord, that men will only worship the creator, and not the thing created.

June 11

The beauty of the earth is but a small part of **my** creation. **I** have created the inner beauty that comes from right thinking and abiding with **me.** The thoughts of love, joy and peace are all part of **my** creation. They were not present before **I** made and named them. The beauty of a kind word, a thoughtful gesture and a friendly smile are all evidence of **me**. Seldom does a soul question how the lovely, the pure, the good came into being. It was all part of **my** creative process.

I meant only the best for my children then evil appeared and brought forth the curse. Through the redemptive plan of **Jesus,** however, the regenerated man can live again with beauty. He can choose to have pure thoughts, good words, and a ready smile. He can have **my** peace and joy.

Scriptures: Psalm 15:1-3, Psalm 24:1-4, Philippians 4:8-9.

Prayer: Father, you are the only way to beauty and peace. Any other way is vanity. I will seek your face and fellowship always. It is the only avenue to joy. Thank you, Lord.

June 12

Be not afraid of the day's journey, for **I** lead. **I** choose only paths that are safe and secure. When you travel with me, the itinerary is preplanned and all items on the agenda are in order. This does not mean that you have no free will. **My** disciples choose **my** will, and thus are led through obstacles, over rough places, with victory in hand. The trials and the tests come, but victory is assured because my paths are taken.

To get a ticket to follow **my** route, you must follow **me.** The tickets are costly----the price is yielding your will to **mine.** The benefits are indescribable, however. The peace of journeying with **me** is a costly treasure that is worth yielding all. **I** meant for you to fellowship with **me**, to walk securely, to be at peace. **My** way is the only way and **Jesus** provides the gate. Follow **Him** closely and the pathways are secure.

Scriptures: Psalm 37:23, Proverbs 16:7, Proverbs 20:24, Proverbs 22:4, I Peter 2:21.

Prayer: I choose to follow Jesus and to submit myself to you, Father. It is with joyous expectation that I face each new day with you, Lord. I sincerely say, "Not my will, but yours."

June 13

The laws of the prophets and saints of old were

June 13

not abandoned with the coming of **my Son**; they were fulfilled in **Him**. **My** kingdom was never meant to bea set of rules, but a guideline for abundant life. As you seek **my** will for your life, you come into fulfillment of the law. I am the law and the law is love! As **my Son** declared, love **God** with all your heart, soul and mind, and your neighbor as yourself.

The action of living in **my** kingdom is a natural action. Just as a mother's loving her babe and breathing are natural functions, thus living in my kingdom is natural. So many have undeveloped spirits that they need support to function naturally. It was never meant to be so. Living in **my** kingdom and flowing in **my** will should be natural, not forced or difficult. As your spirit-man develops, the functions of the spirit will become natural. Attend to your spirit, so that the motions of the spirit are fluid and flow easily. Athletic skills must be learned; but once learned, they become natural. Thus it is in the spirit.

As the spirit develops, the actions and attitudes of the spirit are perfected----they flow easily and beautifully with little effort. All spiritual initiation comes from **me**. **My Spirit** is eager to lead you higher, deeper and wider in the spiritual realm.

Scriptures: Matthew 5:17-18, 22:37; Romans 10:4; Ephesians 3:14-19.

Prayer: Father, I desire to be led by your spirit higher, deeper and wider into the spiritual realm.

Thank you for having your Holy Spirit be my guide. I want to be always a willing follower.

June 14
The days of the wicked are full of worry and fear. They have no rest or peace. They cannot find satisfaction, and they seek vainly for something that will endure. I am the only rest, the only peace, the only thing that endures. Evil hardens the hearts of wicked men, and they cannot believe.

I have given **my word,** I have given **my** beauty, I have given **my** love----and they have rejected them all. I even gave **Jesus,** but they cannot see! Blessed are those who choose to see **me** in everything, who choose to believe the evidences of **my** presence. They shall receive the rewards of the kingdom.

Pray for softened hearts. Each man is so very different, but each has to decide----for **me**, or against **me**. Pray for the minds of men to yield to **my** wooing. It is critical! To lose a soul is an eternal loss. I would have my followers to pray.

Scriptures: Matthew 9:38, Luke 19:10, John 3:16-17, Galatians 6:1, II Timothy 2:24-26.

Prayer: Father, I believe your word that you want all men to be saved. I also want this, Lord, for all of my unsaved friends----that they would accept the good news of Jesus Christ. I pray that the eyes and ears of June 15, 16 their understanding would be opened. It is in Christ's name that I pray, Father.

June 15

The **words** that **I** speak are life to all who find them. So many do not yet realize that these **words** should be taken literally. **I** am life to the spirit, soul and flesh. Without **my** life, the spirit is dead and the heart full of evil. The spirit is dead to the things of my kingdom, and is unregenerated. It **works** for the god of this world.

My life gives new thoughts to the mind. As the mind is renewed on **my word, my** power replaces the negative thought of this world with positive thoughts: thoughts of good reports, pure thoughts, creative thoughts.

My life gives healing and health to the flesh. New life is literally available. **I** refresh the flesh and give it rest----true rest. The body is relieved of the anxiety that has tormented it, which causes it to decay and die. **I** do add length of days. Truly, a man gains life when he gains **me**.

Scriptures: Proverbs 6:23; Matthew 7:14; John 6:68, 8:12, 8:31, 12:46; Hebrews 4:12.

Prayer: Father, thank you for your word, for life, strength, guidance, peace and health. I praise you for the renewing power of your word. I always want to be close to you and to be ever in your word.

June 16

Trust in **my** ability to handle the needs of **my** body----the problems, difficulties and directions. **I** have not given that responsibility away. **I** am able to handle them easily. My disciples so often feel the burden of my kingdom in a measure they were not meant to bear. **I** give each one a load, but not more than he can bear.

I am able to coordinate **my** kingdom; have faith that **I** can. The ones who are following **me** will not be overburdened, unless they presume to take the jobs **I** meant for others. You ask, "But what if others do not do their part?" Is this the problem of the laborer or of the contractor? **I** alone take the responsibility for building **my** kingdom. Your only responsibility is to do your part! **I** will take care of the rest. Rest in the fact that **I** am in control. Trust me for directions and materials----and you will see the job completed. **I** am the **Master Builder!**

Scriptures: II Kings 19:15, Psalm 10:16, Proverbs 3:5, II Timothy 2:7-8.

Prayer: Father, help me to do my part. I want to know what your will is for my life. Give me wisdom in following you so that I may help (and not hinder) the building of the kingdom.

June 17

The ways of the spiritual life seem hard, but

there are no alternative to righteous living. The obedient, disciplined life is by far the best. It is so easy to be slothful and ignore right living. To be slovenly is to do nothing----but slothfulness will destroy life in the end. A vigorous, happy life must be one that is disciplined. Discipline lifts the spirit, it refreshes the mind, it heals the body. Do not shy away from discipline. Embrace it as a way to enjoy life to the fullest.

To change any kind of habit pattern, one must be motivated. When you realize that bad habits are inherently destructive---- and are causing not only harm, but grief----you will come to embrace and crave the discipline that renews and releases the whole man from this cycle. As the attitude changes, the fear, the reluctance and the hesitancy also change. Knowledge is the beginning of wisdom.

Scriptures: Proverbs 2:1-2, Proverbs 6:10-11, Proverbs 28:26, Isaiah 1:19.

Prayer: Father, I want to be wise. Because I want the best that life has to offer, I choose to end slothfulness in every area of my life. Help me to remember that my bad habits are destructive, so that I will be motivated to change them. Thank you, Holy Spirit, for leading me into this truth.

June 18

My peace is given to all who come into **my**

June 19

rest, but so often it seems difficult for man to find that rest. Man is involved in his affairs, what he assumes are **my** affairs, or he is simply rebellious. Entering into **my** rest requires no effort, as the world knows effort. It is a state of mind, a quietness of the spirit, a relaxation of the flesh. Entering into **my** rest is allowing the whole man to be ministered to by **my Spirit.**

You must put aside every encumbrance that hinders you from **my** rest----worry, fear, activity, inactivity. Put aside every weight that hinders your spirit from being at ease. Set apart a time to abide with **me**, a time to refresh your spirit. Let **me** instruct, build up and renew the inner man. Your spirit needs **my** rest.

Scriptures: Psalm 119:165, Matthew 11:28, John 14:27, Philippians 4:7, II Thessalonians 3:16.

Prayer: Father, thank you for granting me rest, peace and refreshing in this time of turmoil. I thank you, Lord, that I have nothing to fear because my security is in you.

June 19

The paths of life are strewn with boulders that cause you to stumble----boulders of frustration, evil, anxiety. *I am a lamp unto your feet, and a light unto your path.* You do not have to fear where **I** lead. Although the path is narrow, the way is secure. **I** am the guide to all spiritual riches and earthly blessings. **I** have given to all to partake of **my** goodness and mercy. **I** have given life to be enjoyed, yet so many are in lack and sorrow.

You must prepare yourself to meet the *enemy* on every front. *He* attacks, always. However, *he* is a defeated foe----always remember that! *He* can take no ground that is not relinquished. You have authority over him. Stand your ground and move forward only at **my** leading. **I** have given you mighty weapons of warfare. The path is shown to you. Put on your armor and defeat the *enemy*. *He* cannot stand against you!

Scriptures: Joshua 10:25, Psalm 32:8, Proverbs 3:6, Ephesians 6:11-18.

Prayer: Your word is truth, Father. It says that you will guide and keep me on the right path. If I did not know your leading and protection, Lord, I would be so very lost and afraid. The world is very threatening and dangerous. I praise you that I have your assurance of protection and safety. Thank you so much, Lord.

June 20

Fear comes in many disguises and in many forms. The purpose of fear is to have faith flee! If fear can rob you of faith, then **I** cannot work in your life. When fear begins to operate against you, you

June 21

must immediately retort with the **word** of faith. Do not give fear a toe-hold. Do not let the thoughts stay for a moment! The **word** of faith will drive fear out as surely as the sun rises. Faith causes the **Spirit of God** to work wonders in the earth. The saying that faith moves mountains is true. As faith builds in your life through the word in your heart, the **Spirit of God** will be manifested more and more in your life. As you recognize **God's** will for your life and obey **His** will, you will see more of the power of **God.**

You who can hear must obey. You to whom the **word** is revealed must receive the **word**----or you will be passed by and someone else will have the opportunity to act for **God.**

Scriptures: Matthew 17:20, Hebrews 10:22-23, Hebrews 11:6, Hebrews 12:25-29.

Prayer: Lord, help me to act on the word. I choose to use faith to answer every fearful thought. I choose to be a willing and obedient servant, who will not be passed over in favor of someone who is obedient. I choose life, I choose faith, I choose victory!

June 21

The real world is the spirit world. What man comprehends as the real world is the partial realization of **my** world. There is more life in the spirit world than there is in the natural world. As you develop all that you were intended to be, you will come into a whole man. I operate in the spiritual realm. **My Son** said he was spirit and truth. **He is!**

In order to function in my kingdom, the spirit must be sensitive to my ways. I direct by the **Spirit,** and by the **Spirit** are lasting objectives achieved. The natural man can only deal with natural cause and effect. He cannot touch the spiritual realm where real change occurs.

As you learn to heed **my** voice in ever greater measure, you will see results that are lasting---not the temporary ones of the flesh. Rest in the fact that I will guide you every step of the way into this awesome and wonderful realm. Is it not exciting?

Scriptures: II Kings 6:14-17, Zechariah 4:6, John 3:6, John 4:24, I Corinthians 15:44-46.

Prayer: Father, I am so grateful for spiritual eyes. I know, without a shadow of doubt, that your realm is real and what we call the world is only a part of your world. Thank you for the guidance and enlightenment from your Holy Spirit. I praise you that I do not have to live in fear---that I can live in trust.

June 22

The trials that come into your life are opportunities for victory. Do not look at them with alarm, but rejoice! I am able to take you through victoriously. I am powerful and have all things under

June 23

my feet. I have given you power over the enemy. You do not have to fear.

The kingdom of **God** must reign supreme in the hearts of all who love **me**. As the battles are fought and won individually, then will they be won collectively. I am able to bring the body into one accord, and I will! As obedient hearts are opened to my leading, the body will come forth victoriously. Is anything too hard for **God**?

Rejoice always that you have power over the enemy. Let **me** be your master, your guide, your leader. The paths that I have chosen are the best for you. You do not have to fear where I lead. You will see clearly as you seek **me**.

Scriptures: Psalm 34:19, Psalm 91:16-11, Proverbs 3:25-26, Isaiah 41:13, James 1:2-4.

Prayer: I praise you, Father, that I can live in victory. I choose to be confident, to put my trust in you and your Word. I will not fear, Lord, for great is your protection! Thank you, Father.

June 23

Just as each dawning brings forth a new day, so does the spiritual refreshment of **God** renew man. A man out of tune with me cannot know the freedom that my cleansing gives. He is burdened with all the sins of his past. **My** love must be shed abroad in the J hearts of believers so that others can see this freedom and desire it. Too often, even my followers, have not operated in the freedom that is theirs. They have not used the inheritance of love, joy and peace.

I have made it possible for all men to live an abundant life, but how few really live it! This is an exuberant life, full of pleasure and surprises. It is an overcoming and victorious life. Defeating the *enemy* should be exhilarating. When a battle is won, there is cause for celebration! Even the times of preparation should be done with victory in mind. Defeat and disobedience will bring pain to your life. Choose the higher life.

Scriptures: John 10:10, John 16:33, Galatians 5:22-23.

Prayer: Lord, I choose the higher life of obedience and the joyous rewards it brings. Thank you for your mercy and love. This life is possible only because of Jesus. Thank you, Lord, for Jesus and for the victory that he brings.

June 24

The time is short for those who do not know me. There is much to be accomplished in lives and hearts. The heart that does not heed me is in a fallen state----a state of loneliness, despair and despondency. Oh the joy of giving the burden of life to one who can take control! The pleasure of being able to let someone else take charge of the things you

June 25

cannot cope with. Relying on **me** is one of the greatest gifts.

The life that has come to rely on **me** has removed the stress and pain that worry brings. These will rob the body of energy and rejuvenation. The soul is robbed of creative thought when worry persists. The spirit is robbed of rest in me. I would that no man live a life of hurt, worry or fear. All must come to rely on **me**. **I** can handle all the hurts that cause a man to stumble. Give them to **me.**

Scriptures: Philippians 4:19, I Peter 4:13, I Peter 5:7-9.
Prayer: Father, I thank you that I can come to you, in the precious knowledge of Christ, relying on your help in time of trouble. I pray that all men, everywhere, would know this truth. Thank you, Father, for sending Jesus to be my savior. I rejoice in you!

June 25

Be patient with those you love. I am awakening them to spiritual truths in answer to your prayers. You must realize that every heart responds differently, for everyone is unique in creation.

Allow my love to flow through you to quicken spiritual hunger. Not only am **I** working in them, but **I** am perfecting you through them. **I** use one imperfect stone upon another to rub away the flaws in each. Do not chafe at the rubbing. Seek it as the means to perfectness as you seek to be like me. I am the Master Builder, the Master Creator, the Master of Perfection. You can trust me to finish what I have begun.

Scriptures: I Corinthians 13:4-7, I Peter 2:4-5, I Peter 3:15.

Prayer: Father, I will be patient with others for you have been so very patient with me. I know you are perfecting all of us. Thank you for working in our lives, tumbling us together so that we will rub off the rough places on each other. You do all things well, Lord.

June 26

My word is working in your life, even though you might not always see the visual evidence of it. The things of the spirit do not always follow the pattern of the natural. Only spiritual things endure. No one can hope to attain greatness in the kingdom, or true success in the natural, without spending time in **my word.** As the **word** becomes part and parcel of your mind and spirit, the flesh and circumstances change to fit the **word.** The **word** never changes. Flesh sometimes dominates man, but only because the **word** is lacking in him.

The trials that beset you have no influence on the **word.** If the spirit is fully developed, the trials

June 27

have no influence on you. The one who learns of my word is steadfast and sure. The word is a rock and it does not move. Endeavor to spend more time in the word. The scriptures are the revelation of me. They bless and keep you in times of abundance or lack. They change circumstances.

Scriptures: Isaiah 55:11, Malachi 3:6, John 17:17, II Corinthians 4:17-18.

Prayer: Father, I am determined to learn your word so that I will not be dominated by the flesh. I will no longer look upon the temporal things as being permanent. Only the Word is steadfast, sure and eternal. Thank you, Father, for your Word!

June 27

The reason that so much work done in **my** name fails, is the that preparation was faulty and the leading was awry. *Satan* knows a bluff, and *he* knows when a heart is full of faith. Also, much of the work is not ordained of *me*, nor did **I** bid it. Those who want success in spiritual areas must learn to heed **my** voice. **My Son** did only that which **I** told **him** to do. **He** did nothing on **his** own.

As **my** disciples learn to hear **my** voice, they will also have the success that **Jesus** had. **My** children have good intentions, but I have a larger plan. Those who are not prepared spiritually cannot lead in **my** kingdom. They would lead too many off

June 28

into areas of defeat. **I** need and will have only trained, disciplined, obedient leaders. Then will **my** body have the success that **I** intend it to have.

Scriptures: Matthew 22:29, John 8:28-29, John 15:5.

Prayer: Father, as Jesus did only those things that you bade him to do, so I want also to do only those things you tell me. I do not want my work to be done in vain. I desire so much to please you, Lord.

June 28

The lessons that **I** teach are always positive. Many things come into your life that are initiated by the *enemy*, but with me, the *negative* things become *positive*. This cannot happen in any other realm. **I** am the **creator** and **I** change things. The motives of *Satan* are to destroy **my** works, **my** people, **my** power. *He* cannot succeed!

I am Lord over all. If **my** principles and **my words** are acted upon, the positive reigns. There is no weapon that *Satan* has that you cannot defeat----if you are prepared in **my word** and rely on **me**. Learn more, more, more! Living in the spiritual realm is an ongoing process and cannot be neglected.

Great energy is derived from **my** kingdom, but energy must also flow into it. Discipline yourself, always. The rewards are so much greater than the input, not only in the spiritual realm, but in the natural.

June 29

Scriptures: Luke 10:19, John 10:10, II Timothy 2:15.

Prayer: Lord, I want to be a good, diligent, faithful student----not ever ashamed. I sincerely desire to be thoroughly taught the principles of your kingdom. Help me to be consistent in the study of your word, and faithful in prayer. I thank you, Lord, for your benefits.

June 29

The days of disciplining yourself will eventually pay off. It is not the big steps, although they are necessary, that cause great growth, but the small ones. A daily growing produces the most results. It is easy to get excited when you see spectacular results. It is difficult for this present generation to wait. The steady growth, the daily discipline and the consistent obedience are what produces abundant fruit.

It is necessary, occasionally, to recall where you were when you started. Do not look back frequently, only occasionally. Sometimes even maintenance of the status quo is a real victory. Desire discipline and seek obedience for your life. Learn to love bringing your mind and body into subjection. As with a well-trained athlete or animal, the results are beautiful to behold. Man needs freedom, but in this life, only obedience brings freedom. An unregulated, slothful life is not free. The **truth** will make you free.

June 30

Scriptures: I Chronicles 28:9, John 8:32, II Corinthians 4:16-17, I Timothy 4:15.

Prayer: Teach me faithfulness and discipline, Lord. I do not need spectacular results every day. I choose to be faithful, as you are faithful. Thank you for loving me.

June 30

I do not judge as the world judges. I look on the heart. The world's good works do not impress me unless the hearts are inclined towards **me.** Does man do good works out of love for **me** or to be seen of man?

An act of love is to serve your fellow, but to be well thought of by your fellowman should never be the motive. Do not let your right hand know what the left is doing. It is well to endeavor to do good, but always check your motives. You should always want to please **me**----not man.

I honor actions that stem from a pure heart, and **I** alone know the heart of man. If you seek to do good, ask **me** first. **I** will guide and direct every action. Trust in **my** guidance and hear **my** voice. I never withhold guidance. Only the hearer has the problem. Attempt always to please **me.**

Scriptures: I Samuel 16:7, Matthew 6:1, Matthew 6:4, Hebrews 6:10.

June 30

Prayer: Father, I repent of every action, every work which did not stem from love of you. I ask your guidance in every action I undertake. Help me to examine my motives. I want to please you more than I want to please people. I want to serve you with a pure heart.

JULY

July 1

Never fear the threats of the *enemy*. His power is limited----yours is not! **I** have given you authority to tread on the enemy and over all his works. Use it! *He* is a defeated foe, but *he* must be conquered. It is not any different today than it was in the days of old. **I** had given the children of Israel the land, but they had to take it. Faith is still faith. They had to believe in spite of overpowering physical evidence. Those who held fast and believed **me** inherited the promises.

Think of the promises you have been given. Is my **word** true? Am **I** faithful? Do **I** lie? Think on these things. Do not look at the circumstances, but believe **my word.** The **word I** give will always lead to victory. Cast down vain imaginations to the contrary. The *enemy* cannot stand against **my** anointed ones, and they are anointed with the oil of gladness----glad because **I** am conqueror over all. **I** am your **God.**

Scriptures: Luke 10:19, John 6:63, Hebrews 8:10, Hebrews 11:1.

Prayer: Father God, thank you for Jesus and that I am more than a conqueror through him. Help me to keep my eyes on you.

July 2

The fruit of the laborer is not quickly evident,

July 3

but with faithfulness, an abundance comes. Be willing to be patient in order to see the best fruit. In the natural world, vines are carefully pruned, fertilized and sometimes tied to train the limbs. I am the **Master Vinedresser**, and I know just what to do.

Never chafe at the disciplining you endure; **my** disciples must be trained. It all serves an ultimate purpose and works toward your good. As you choose discipline, the task is completed rapidly. A yielded heart is easy to train.

Do not get impatient with yourself or with others. Patience is part of the training, too. Just recognize my hand in all that is good, and reassurance will flood in to fill you with joy. I am still on the throne and in command. I love you. Trust **me** and see **my** power in greater measure.

Scriptures: Proverbs 3:13, John 15:15, James 1:17.

Prayer: Father, thank you so much for loving me and teaching me to trust you completely. Without you, I am nothing. I welcome your discipline; I want to please you in every way.

July 3

The thoughts that build one up in the kingdom of **God** are those to dwell upon. The enemy, *Satan*, comes to tear down lives and bring in confusion. **He** comes to let death and fear reign supreme.

However, the kingdom of **God** is outside *his* realm. *Satan* has no authority over the children of light, no means to bring them into terror or oppression. Because **I** give free will, my disciples can step out of **my** kingdom----into *Satan's.* You have free will and are able to control what you think, and whom you serve.

Choose **my** kingdom and live in its blessings. Choose light and love----over terror and darkness. Choose to abide in **me** and **my words.** Truly, the **wicked one** will not touch you. You need never step out of **my** kingdom. Choose rightly and wisely.

Scriptures: Deuteronomy 30:19, Philippians 4:8.

Prayer: Father, how I thank you for your Word. I make a quality decision to keep my eyes on you and your promises. I choose to see myself through your eyes, and you say I have authority over the enemy. I praise your name.

July 4

The call of Christianity is one of obedience and love. Because of your love for the **Father**, the love for his children comes. In obeying the voice of the **Father,** your life is spent in harmony and peace. Knowledge of the **Father** and **his word** brings *faith* to obey **his word.** The name of the Son gives authority to the **word.** As you walk the road of life in love, you will find many opportunities to serve **me**. A quickened heart, ready in obedience, makes the **Father** and the Heavenly Host rejoice. Prepare your heart so that you may be sensitive to the leading of the **Holy Spirit**. Then see the power of **Jesus** manifested in your life.

The Christian walk is not a mystery to those who are open to the message of the **Holy Spirit**. A heart that is eager to listen has no trouble in hearing. Obey your **heart**.

Scriptures: Jeremiah 7:23, John 14:26, I Corinthians 13.

Prayer: Father, I thank you for your love, and that you have made it possible for me to love those I would consider unlovely in my human thinking. Thank you for the Holy Spirit who guides me into all truth. Help me to walk the "love walk", so that others can see Jesus in me.

July 5

The road that leads to victory in a life is not easy, but victory is the promise to my disciples. As you progress along, remember that **I** have given you the authority to overcome all obstacles. Faith, however, must be steadily applied. Just because you do not see the end results, do not feel like you have failed. The battles must be fought with the spirit steady, and eyes fixed on **me**. Do not let doubt and discouragement change your mind. The victory is assured----if you faint not.

I know it would seem easier if the results could always be seen, but that requires no faith. See the challenge as an opportunity to grow and overcome, for indeed it is! There is no obstacle, promise or challenge that is outside my realm. **I will lead you on.** The determination to succeed and the authority of **my word** are infallible weapons. Realize what power has been invested in you, and act on it.

Scriptures: Colossians 3:17, Hebrews 10:23, I John 3:4.

Prayer: Father, thank you for the measure of faith you have given me. Thank you that faith grows as I spend time in your Word. It is not easy, Lord, for me to live by faith. However, it is such an exciting way of life----so simple, yet not easy. Help me not to faint, but to stand and fight the good fight of faith.

July 6

You are able to walk in victory, for **I** have given you mighty weapons of warfare. There is no weapon of *Satan* that cannot be stopped, no "tactic" that cannot be avoided or conquered. I have given you authority over all the power of the *enemy*. But as *he* is a relentless, persistent foe, so you must be a disciplined, well-trained adversary. Take the battle to *him!* Choose the advantage and stop the assaults before *he* gains momentum.

Be alert to *enemy* movements and do not fail to heed warning signals of impending attacks. You always have the advantage for *I* have given it to you. *Satan* cannot stop (or even hinder) the church, if the members are trained in spiritual warfare. Since the church is made up of individual members, you get trained and join others who are trained to fight and win! *One can put a thousand to flight, and two----ten thousand.* It does not take many, at those odds. *The weapons of your warfare are not carnal, but mighty through God to the pulling down of strongholds.* Seek strongholds, and pull them down! When the *enemy* is gathered in force, join with others to pull him down. I have given you the means and the victory.

Scriptures: Matthew 18:20, II Corinthians 10:4, Ephesians 6:10-18.

Prayer: Father, I praise and worship you. Thank you for giving me weapons of warfare that insure victory. Thank you for friends who will take time to pray and believe with me. Help me to be such a friend to others.

July 7

Self-pity is an indulgence no Christian can afford. Not only is it destructive, but it is evil and robs you of faith. *Satan* always tempts one with self-pity----fear and despondency follow closely. It is so important to be acquainted with the wiles of *Satan*. One has to be prepared for *him*, in order to ward off *his* attack. *He* is sneaky and cruel. *He* does not announce *his* coming to the unwary.

The follower who is grounded in **my word**, however, will recognize *Satan's* tactics and will rebuke him at once. There will always be a flicker of truth to quicken your *spirit*. It is at that moment that action must be taken. To indulge in self-pity following the alarm is to have to engage in heavy battles. If *Satan* is rebuked at the first hint of attack, the battle is won! Be spiritually sensitive always. I will always give you warning through the **Holy Spirit**. Heed **him**.

Scriptures: Psalms 119:105, John 16:13, James 4:7.

Prayer: Father God, I am so grateful to you for making me aware that pity parties are not pleasing to you. With your help I will <u>never</u> again give Satan this toe-hold in my life.

July 8

Because of **my** mercy, bought by **Jesus**, you do not see the wrath of **God** bestowed on men as in the days of old. My power and might have not changed, however. **My word** is being brought by my disciples so that men may know that **I am God**.

July 9

Men and women who are dedicated to **me** are coming forth in might and power. Miracles are abounding. Some will not believe, even though they see, but many will! To those with hearing ears and seeing eyes shall my miracles be seen. Then they will praise the **God** of Israel for **my** love and mercy on them.

The days of power are not ended, but just beginning. As the **word** of faith arises in the hearts of believers, so shall **my** power show forth. I am not only the **God** of the past. I am also the **God** of the future!

Scriptures: I Chronicles 16:34, Isaiah 32:3, Hebrews 13:8.

Prayer: I praise you, Father, for your love and mercy. Let me, also, show mercy to others. I want to be one of your children with seeing eyes and hearing ears. I give myself to you with no strings attached.

July 9

Do not worry about the state of affairs in the world. I am in control. The *enemy* causes much havoc and sorrow, but the end is coming for *him*. There is always a way to **God** for those who seek **me**. It is the responsibility of **my** disciples to be the *light* so that the world may see **me** more clearly and know **my** glory.

July 10

The mind of man is so limited (his thinking and reasoning). Trust **my** leading and your life will count. **I** only lead along the straight path. There is no crookedness or sorrow where **I** lead. The evil comes when the path is forsaken and when **fear** dominates.

I am developing saints who follow **my word** and can lead others out of bondage. Imagine a procession with many following the leader along the safe, sure passageway. Only the <u>very</u> trustworthy get to lead. Men are saved because of them.

Scriptures: Proverbs 3:5, Matthew 5:14, Matthew 7:14, John 16:33.

Prayer: Father, it is such a comfort to trust you. I see that worry is a sin, and I want no part of it. Worry is lack of faith, and you have said without faith, it is impossible to please you. Above all things, I want to please you. Help me to keep my mind centered on you.

July 10

As you live in **my** kingdom, the joy of the **Lord** will become more and more a way of life. No man can know that joy apart from **me.** The peace of having your burdens lifted bring health and wealth to spirit, soul, and body. **I** came to give joy and peace to you. Peace is a commodity of priceless value in the earth. Man tries so hard to earn it, buy it or steal it----when all he has to do is accept it.

July 11

This knowledge is to be shared throughout the earth. This is the good news. If **my** own do not exhibit what **I** give, how can the world receive it? You are given the lovely chore of living in harmony with me so that the world may see **me** through you. Is that not a blessing? As you live in the wonder and joy of **my** kingdom, others will see this joy and desire it.

What a job! To be a display item for life----a life full of joy, hope, faith, peace and love----is to be your portion. **My** disciples are all salesmen of my wares. My wares are the promises and the goodness of life. Rejoice in the position you have. **My** kingdom is one of joy, not drudgery. You get to model the most precious gifts in the world. Is it not wonderful? **My** gifts are precious, but free. As they are displayed before the world, they will be desired by all mankind. Remember, if **I** be lifted up, **I** will draw <u>all</u> men unto me.

Scriptures: John 12:32, John 14:27, Galatians 5:22-23.

Prayer: I come to you, Father, with my heart rejoicing. Thank you for your joy, your peace, and above all else, your love. I want to be a good salesman for you.

July 11

The rich heritage of the saints is not to be dismissed lightly. Prize the heritage which you have received. Talk of the miracles **my** power has wrought. Do not let the humdrum activities of daily life make the history of **God** seem out of place or past-tense. It is only as the miracles of the past are believed that faith rises for the future.

I have not stopped the power or the move of **God** in the lives of believers. I am the same, always. Expect the miraculous. Call on me for it! A faith that is strong will always move the heart of **God**. Am I not a faithful **God**? Can I not be trusted? The joy of knowing that I hear and move in response to a faith-filled request is without measure. Trust **me** more. Expect miracles. As you are lined-up with **my word** and will, the power flows.

Scriptures: Isaiah 54:17, Daniel 4:3, Malachi 3:6, I John 5:14-15.

Prayer: Oh Father, you are a mighty God indeed----the only true and living God. You are the Creator of heaven and earth, a miracle-working God! I will continually praise your name. Nothing is too difficult for you, and you even give attention to my little concerns. I love you so!

July 12

The life you enjoy in **me** is one of discipline, love and joy. The discipline must come before the others are manifested. Only a disciple (one who is willing to be trained) can enjoy the fruits of his labors. So many miss the fruits because they neglect to put in the time to cultivate their spirit. They have planted the seed (the **word** in their hearts), but have neglected to water, weed and harvest. It takes much endeavor to have a truly bountiful harvest to keep the spirit from becoming dry, cluttered with the cares of life or choked with weeds. The cultivation of the husbandman is a diligent, necessary job in order to gain a harvest that will sustain and supply.

Others are encouraged when they see that it is possible for anyone, through simple consistent acts, to have a good harvest. **I** can show anyone how to do it, if they will only seek **me.** Enjoy your fruits.

Scriptures: Matthew 6:33, John 15:5, II Timothy 2:15.

Prayer: Father, I know I need more discipline in my life. You tell me I can bear much fruit, and that is what I desire. Help me to be consistent.

July 13
Go forth always with the joy of thanksgiving, and as you go, the needs of the hour will be supplied. In the spirit world, as faith is applied, the power is loosed. The natural mind rejects this operation. It wants assurance of provision beforehand. That requires no faith.

In the spirit world, the power must be released

July 14

<u>as</u> faith has believed for it----<u>**NOT**</u> released and then believed for it. As the spirit develops, confidence in me grows so that fear does not hamper the operations of the spirit. Remember in **my word** that:

> The seas parted <u>as</u> the Egyptians approached
> The fire came down <u>after</u> the command of Elijah was given
> The dead arose <u>when</u> **Jesus** spoke.

Power has been given and is available.

In order for power to be used faith, built on my **word** and in the name of **my son**, must be there. Seek to develop your faith, and choose to develop your faith! It does come.

Scriptures: Romans 10:17, II Corinthians 4:13, Ephesians 4:17-19.

Prayer: Father, I thank you for always meeting my needs, and I praise your name. You are always right on time----seldom early, but never late! As my faith grows, so does my love for you. I desire great faith; I commit to spending more time in your word.

July 14

The cares of life can be so debilitating to the spiritual walk, if left unchecked and unheeded. Never allow your spirit to wane and become weak. You must guard it with all vigilance, because it is your life. The

July 15

spiritual life is *eternal* life. It is to be held more dear than natural life. As the spiritual life increases, the natural life and its problems grow less in importance.

As the spirit ascends, the mind and body begin to operate as they were created to do. You were not created to be dominated by your mind and body. You are a spirit creature and are meant to operate in the spiritual realm. When I breathed **my own** Spirit into you, your eternal life began. Because of this new birth, your spiritual life is established. Let the Spirit have **his** way in your life. Then the real pleasures of life begin to grow. Look forward to your spiritual life with **me**. It lasts forever!

Scriptures: Mark 4:19, I Peter 5:7, I John 2:24-25.

Prayer: Thank you, Father, that I do not have to go around with the cares of life weighing me down. I can give them all to you. I thank you, Father, for eternal life that began the day I accepted Jesus as my Savior and Lord.

July 15

I choose those who will follow, not those whose hearts are dead. I give <u>all</u> the opportunity to come, but not all will. The chosen ones of this earth are people who listen to the Spirit when **he** woos them. Good ground must be seeded! Seeding is the job of my disciples and **my Spirit.**

July 15

There is much fertile ground, and much seeding is to be done. Those who love **me** are the laborers. Seeds are planted by the lives, actions, and words of **my** laborers. Some will say, "Perhaps I was not chosen." That is an excuse. I would that all men might come unto **me.** I have breathed my Spirit into all men, but they must awaken to it and accept it! When they do, regeneration begins.

Be diligent to pray and heed **my word.** Thus, fruits and seeds are produced. Spread the seed of the gospel of **Jesus Christ** in your every action and word. You say, "How can this be done?" I will shine through you so that men can see me. Some will reject **me**, but many will not. Do not worry about the soil. Only be faithful to spread the seed. The fruits of your labors have been, and will be, your reward.

You will be surprised, sometimes, at who is fertile ground. The joy you see in seeded hearts will be the evidence of my love and approval. The sower reaps the same reward as the harvester, so sow with gladness and joy.

Scriptures: I Corinthians 3:6, James 5:16, II Peter 3:9.

Prayer: Father, I have always felt so inadequate in proclaiming you to the world. I will relax and let the spirit be in charge. As He makes opportunities, I will share what you have done in my life. Help me to be bold.

July 16

The beginning of eternal life is always in the spirit. Physical life is only a part of eternal life---a very small portion. The physical life will only serve to house the spiritual, to enable it to develop. Some will never come to the moment when the spirit becomes renewed with the life from above. Hence, their spiritual development remains an embryo.

The cause of a man is not measured naturally, but spiritually. The reason for a man's existence is to fellowship with **me**. He has the choice, of course. The end of the carnal life only marks the beginning of the eternal life that man can spend in harmony and fellowship with **me.**

Seek always the spiritual first. Do not neglect the most important part of life. **I** have made man to abide in **me,** and there is real joy there. The rewards are so much greater than the sacrifice.

Scriptures: Genesis 1:26-27, Genesis 2:7-8, John 3:7.

Prayer: Father, today I feel such a burden for those who refuse to choose you----whether it be through rebellion or just neglect. Life must be so dull without you. I shudder to think of the after-life that waits for those outside of you. Help me to think less about my carnal life and more about my spiritual one. I want to show Jesus to those around me. Help me to stay focused on you.

July 17

I have provided you with the weapons of warfare. It is your obligation (indeed, your duty) to use them effectively to defeat the enemy wherever he is found. **My** church has been wont to do what is necessary to help themselves, but now is the time for the body of **Christ** to move collectively on the enemy. As the church begins to love with an unselfish love that goes beyond its own immediate needs, then will the world realize and comprehend **my power.**

The world understands selfish love----it loves that way. When the world sees people who earnestly and sincerely desire the best for others, even as they desire the best for themselves, it will result in a love the world cannot understand. That kind of love will move the world. That kind of love will shake *Satan's* kingdom. Let that love start in the house of **God** and permeate every *iota* of this earth and all within it. That is **my** will!

Scriptures: Mark 12:30-31, Ephesians 6:13-18.

Prayer: What a great love you love us with, Father. I desire this same kind of unselfish love. With your love filling me and your armor clothing me, I can storm the strongholds of Satan. If we, who are called your church, would get on the offensive, we could indeed set the captives free. All praise and glory to you, Lord.

July 18

Never yield to the *enemy*. Guard yourself and your thoughts. Do not let the *evil one* manipulate you into doubt. Give him no place! You have learned to come into victory. Use this knowledge. As *Satan* is driven back inch by inch, *his* confidence weakens as your confidence grows! *He* is a defeated foe. Stand on that and declare it! Choose to believe it! *Satan* can only come at you with doubt, discouragement, fear, defeat; but *he* cannot stand against **my word**, applied in faith and held with patience. Stand firm and you will call *his* bluff.

Do not let other issues sidetrack you. Be single-minded and **I** will bring those things into line. Do not be diverted from the battle at hand with skirmishes on the homefront. Win the battle before you, and the guerilla warfare ceases. Trust me to help you endure, to bring you to victory. I cannot fail.

Scriptures: Philippians 4:13, James 4:7, 1 John 4:4.

Prayer: I do trust you, Father God, and I praise your name. I do not understand how people can live apart from you. Thank you for showing me that Satan is a defeated foe.

July 19

My word is comfort, power and joy. Those who dwell in it are made complete, for only as the Spirit becomes dominant in you, do you become complete. You were created to live in a spiritual world, to have dominion over the earth and subdue it. When Adam fell, the spirit was quenched, and until the resurrection of **my son**, the spirit of man was almost dormant. Now, however, you are re-instated to me. Your spirit can now have dominion over the earth once again. This dominion does not come automatically, but it is a growing process, just as the development of the mind and body are a growing process. As you feed your spirit, it grows strong.

Many of my children are spiritual cripples, because they have neglected their spiritual growth. Therefore, their spirits are left shriveled and immature. There are no limits, however, to the spirit's resurrection power, as nourishment stemming from **my word** and prayer are fed into it. I am the source of all life, especially of the spiritual life.

Scriptures: John 1:12, Romans 15:4, Ephesians 6:10, Colossians 1:13.

Prayer: Father, I desire to be strong in the power of your might. Help me to have victory in every aspect of my life. I pray that I will always be sensitive to the leading of your Holy Spirit. I believe that the same power that raised Christ from the dead dwells in me!

July 20

Never think that *Satan* will win this time. *He* will not, unless you refuse to act on **my word**! Have **I** not declared that he is a defeated foe? Confidence in **me** and **my word** always overcomes him. **I** have declared that *he* is a footstool. Is my word a lie? Do not let *Satan* stampede you into foolish action. *He* is all bluff. **I** do not cower at his barking. **I** tread on *him*!

You have been given the same authority. Just believe and act in **my** name. The name of **Jesus** is higher than any other name. The power that **I** bestow is greater than any force *old slewfoot* can throw your way. Do not allow yourself to fear his tactics. Be confident in me and what I have done for you. **I am** the **I am.** *I am the same yesterday, today and forever.* Keep this uppermost in your mind. **I** do not give you a spirit of fear! *He* does. You do not have to accept or act in fear. Be alert! You can always win.

Scriptures: Matthew 22:44, Luke 10:19, Philippians 2:10, II Timothy 1:7, Hebrews 13:8.

Prayer: Lord, I am amazed when I meditate on who I am in Christ. I can never be a failure when I act on your word. I am an overcomer. How I thank and praise you.

July 21

The price of your freedom was very dear----but it has been paid. In the package came love, peace, joy, and all the blessings that **I** have. **I** came, not to condemn the world, but to save it! Man's conscience will condemn him. Anytime a man is out of fellowship with **me**, he is back in the world where sin awaits. Man always has a choice as to whom he will follow and to whom he will yield his members.

Rejoice in the freedom **I** bought. The yoke **I** give is easy, so easy that it seems unbelievable. Believe **my word**. Trust in **my** power. *Lean not to your own understanding.*

Do not let the weapons of *Satan* (fear, doubt, despair) come in. Refuse them! Refuse them! Refuse them! *Satan* cannot gain entrance unless you allow it. Remember **my** sayings and rejoice that **I** have given you victory in all things. **I** am the victor, and you are a victor with me!

Scriptures: Proverbs 3:5, Matthew 11:30, John 3:17, I Corinthians 15:57.

Prayer: Lord God, I thank you for my freedom in Jesus. I'm just beginning to understand how precious that freedom is----so very precious that your Son would choose to die for me to have it. I will praise you forever.

July 22

The paths that **I** have laid for you are straight paths and are easy to follow. As **my Spirit** shows the way, you will be able to follow and lead others. The way is narrow, but safe. **I** am leading you with all the protection you need. None shall be able to move you, as you abide with **me**. Always make yourself come into **my** presence, when you feel threatened. Just as a baby runs to a parent for comfort and protection, you must run to **me**. There is no need to worry.

The trials **that** will come your way are already won, if you let me stay in control. If you choose to let **my Spirit** reign in your life, nothing can shake you. Do not fear the future. Look to it with anticipation and rejoicing. **I** have overcome the world, and **my** delight is in those who love **me**. Men need to know the joy of walking with me. Your life will help them see it.

Scriptures: Matthew 4:19-20, 8:19; John 6:44.

Prayer: Father, I love you. I know this is the key to everything and that even my faith cannot work without love. Help me to love you more.

July 23

The good *news* is being manifested in your life. The rewards are coming. A life of peace and joy is in store for those who believe and trust **me** without doubt. The warfare is difficult, but never impossible. Remember the battles of old. Were the odds not awesome? Did **my word** prevail? The giants, the armies, the enemies are no less real today, but they are defeated. Always remember that **I** have overcome them all, and **my word** prevails. The fear of the battle is the battleground. If you can overcome fear by faith, the battle is won before it starts.

Rest in my love. Make yourself get into a state of peace by meditating on **my word.** Do not neglect your spirit. **I** will always bring you victory, as you let me reign in your life. You choose daily to follow me. **I** am always available to give you aid and rest.

Scriptures: Joshua 11:6, Psalm 1:2, Isaiah 26:3, Ezekiel 12:25.

Prayer: Father, Thank you for your faithfulness. Thank you for keeping me in peace and safety. Thank you for victory, Lord. I praise your Holy name.

July 24

Do not be weary in well-doing, for **I** am using you in **my body.** You may not always want to go the way the **Spirit** directs, but trust me. It is the best way. Do not be fretful or anxious about the pathway; it is a safe and secure one. It will lead you to victory, rest, and refreshment.

Have an obedient attitude, always. Be willing

to serve me. *He who would be greatest must be least.* However, the blessings come to the giver in greater measure. Look at each opportunity to serve as a way to my heart, a way into my kingdom, a way to abide intimately with **me**. Be ready to be a doer of **my word**. The rewards of a doer are so much greater than just being a hearer of the **word**.

Let your heart rest. Lay down the anxiety and refuse to fear. I am leading you into a deeper relationship with me. There is no room for fear. There is only *the peace that passeth understanding.*

Scriptures: Numbers 6:6, Joshua 1:8, Matthew 11:11, Luke 12:32.

Prayer: Father, I refuse to let fear enter or stay in my mind. I will meditate on your love and mercy and the victory I have in Jesus. Thank you for your faithfulness.

July 25

I have made you to become like **my Son**. The Spirit that abides within you is in the image of **my Son**. Let the spirit-man in your heart develop to its full potential. Then you will look and act like **Jesus**. The decision to yield to the **Spirit** must be an act of your will. The growth comes proportionately to your yielding. I am developing spiritual giants in these last days. They will do great feats in *my name*.

Make ready the soil of your spirit. The soil

must be plowed with prayer, seeded and fertilized with **my word**, and sprinkled or watered with praise. A bountiful crop always results if these things are done. Trust me and see the harvest all about you. Yield continually to me; believe that **I** lead. As you believe, you shall see.

Scriptures: Psalm 4:5, Mark 16:17-18, Romans 8:14.

Prayer: Thank you, Father, that in your eyes my spirit man looks just like Jesus. I want to become more like Him with each passing day. As you lead, I will follow.

July 26

As the door of life swings open to you, you will enter in with a greater peace and understanding of my kingdom. The fruits of living with **me,** *abiding in me* work great wonders in your life. To live a life without fear, however costly it may be in terms of sacrifice, is worth it all. The peace that comes is more valuable than any riches imaginable.

Life is the highway that man travels in his union and communion with **me.** The man that seeks **me**---and comes to **me**----is blessed indeed. The soul that strays, seeking its own will is a soul in torment and despair. That one will never have the joy of living in peace with his creator, of finding solace in me. These needs will never cease to burn within him, so point the way towards me. Let others see your light and the glory that shines out. This is the glory that reflects a life dedicated to **me**, the glory that fills a man who communes with **me**-----*the Glory of the Lord.*

Let **my** will be your will. Delight yourself in **me**. I am faithful. I keep **my word.** Try **me!** Test me! I do not falter nor fail. You can be the same. Believe it! Rejoice in the **God** of Abraham, Isaac and Jacob. **My** seed and your seed are mighty upon the earth. In **my** joy and strength shall you go forward.

Scriptures: Numbers 14:21, Psalm 37:4, Malachi 3:10, Matthew 5:16.

Prayer: My Lord and my God, how I praise your name. I want to be in your perfect will, and I rejoice in you.

July 27

When the doubts of **my** indwelling come, remember that it is only faith that moves **me.** Never let doubt or fear remain. Cast them out. As the sun cannot be stopped in its progress across the sky, neither can fear linger in a **word**-ruled mind. You have infinite (yes, infinite!) power over your mind, when your mind is fixed on **me**. As your thoughts

July 27

come into line with **my words,** you have the **mind** of **Christ.** This means that infinite creativity, infinite ability and infinite depth are available, because **I** am infinite! Your will becomes **my will.** The thoughts you think will be godly thoughts---pure and clean. There are no limits in **me.** There will be no limits in you, as you are filled with **Christ.**

The mind that yields to me will never lack substance, peace or joy. I have all things under **my** feet. I freely bestow gifts. The gifts **I** give are priceless and are to be used for the edifying of **my** body.

Many are in bondage, lost and afraid. You must share your knowledge of **me**, the faith you have developed. Freely you have received, freely give. **My** unlimited love must be spread abroad. The task shall be easy, *for out of your belly shall flow rivers of living water,* easing the thirst of many.

Be faithful always. I have given you the will, the energy, the desire and the ability to be faithful. The joy you receive in so doing will increase and grow. There is no lack in **my** kingdom. Therefore, fear has no place. Look forward to life. It is abundant for **I** have provided for it. Enjoy it. **I** love you.

Scriptures: Matthew 10:8, Mark 16:15, John 7:38, I Corinthians 2:16.

Prayer: Father, thank you for the abundant life. As I keep my mind fixed on you, I have no fears or doubts.

July 28

I know that I can do all things through Christ who strengthens me.

July 28

Just as you want the best for your children, **I** want the best for **mine.** I have already provided the best, however----**my Son.** **He** has bought for all mankind the ability to overcome. Because of **him**, the battles are won. I told the children of Israel, "Go! Take the cities. They are yours!"

I am telling **my** children the same, today. All struggles, all obstacles, all hindrances are won. Believe it and you receive it. The battles are always found in the spiritual realm; there they are won or lost. Obey **my word** and no battle can be lost to you. It is impossible to lose where obedience is unconditional. Listen to and heed my instructions. The victory is yours. Do not fear. Do not waver. Just obey. Rejoice that victory has come, before you see it. It is surely done. It is finished!

Scriptures: Job 36:11, Mark 11:23, John 3:16.

Prayer: Father, I thank you for loving me so much. You have provided a way for me in every situation if I will only obey and trust you. Help me to quit fretting over the little things. I have learned to trust you with the big ones, and with your help, I will turn the seemingly unimportant ones over to you also.

July 29

Never give up! The **word** does work! Your prayers will be answered. **I** gave this promise, *if you abide in me and my words abide in you, you can ask whatsoever you will and it shall be given you.* Believe **my words.** Thus you meet the conditions. **I** have given you great power. **My Spirit** is working mighty things in your life. Do not relax your vigil. Do not weaken in well-doing. Resolve to press on, and you will see the reward of it. **I** am influencing others through you. The kingdom is founded on dicipleship; as you train others, they will pass it on.

Give **me** first place in your life, always. If you are determined to do so, the blessings are yours. **I** have promised them and **I** am faithful. The secret to abundance is **me,** and you have **me.** Rejoice!

Scriptures: Luke 14:26-27, John 15:7, Galatians 6:9.

Prayer: Father, I have been thinking about abiding in you. I think that if I could do this all of the time, I would have nothing to be concerned about. You would take care of everything! I give you first place in my life. Help me to leave you in this spot, and not for even a moment, replace you with someone, or something, else.

July 30

Be careful for nothing; but in everything by prayer and supplication with thanksgiving, let your requests be made known unto God. I meant that! You do not have to take the burdens upon yourself. That is why I said, *Come unto me, ye that are heavy laden, and I will give you rest.* You were never meant to carry burdens of fear, doubt or despair. I am able to carry them. You are not! I have already paid the price for them, and for you. So why let yourself be burdened? To do so is to doubt my ability to handle the situation. You can be thankful. I have taken the load of care, lifted it from you, and all is well.

You can go on your way with a merry heart, rejoicing in the knowledge of it. Your affairs and concerns are in the hands of the *Master*-Planner, the *Creator* of the Universe, the *All-Sufficient* One. What a revelation! *Let not yourself be troubled, neither be afraid.* I have overcome all situations! Believe it! Receive it!

Scriptures: Matthew 11:28, John 14:27, Philippians 4:6.

Prayer: Lord, I believe, and I believe I receive. What peace that passes understanding is mine. I praise you.

July 31

The good fight is one of faithfulness, consistency and determination. You fight until you win! You do not compromise. Even when things look hopeless, **I** have provided a way, not only of escape, but of victory! The race is given to the persistently determined. Run to win!

There can be no partial victory in **my** kingdom. The crowns are given to the overcomers. I am not creating a partial kingdom. **My Son** is going to reign with a spotless bride.

Do not yield your position in me to the *evil one*. *He* cannot move you when you stand steadfast. *He* has no weapons to do so, because *he* only operates on fear.

Be instant in season and out to declare **my word.** Sing praises unto **me.** Worship **me** with gladness and thanksgiving. It is a choice, and you have chosen **me.** Rejoice!

Scriptures: Psalm 108:3-6, I Timothy 6:12, II Timothy 4:2.

Prayer: Father, thank you for teaching me to stand, and having done all to stand. You are the "way" maker, and I know that I am an overcomer. I worship you and I praise you.

AUGUST

August 1

Courage is necessary in order to begin the assault on the *enemy's* strongholds, but it is faith that tears down the bulwarks. Faith is the substance that acts on, past courage. Many are courageous when they begin, but they are quickly put to flight when they see the size and power of the *enemy*. Faith recognizes, however, that the *enemy's* power is an illusion---a mirage---that will evaporate in the light of the truth of the **word.**

The world has many brave, courageous souls who have the inclination to fight *evil*. Without the shield of faith and the sword of the spirit, these stout hearted warriors are *overcome by fear*. Yes, the courageous are overcome by fear. Allow the seed of faith to grow in you, encourage it in others, and you will be amazed at the havoc it will inflict on the *enemy*. Faith consumes fear, and all of its by-products. *The kingdom of God suffers violence, and the violent take it by force*. Faith-filled warriors will consume the forces of Hell!

Scriptures: Matthew 11:12-15, Romans 10:17, II Corinthians 5:7.

Prayer: Father, thank you for giving each of us a measure of faith. I want to increase my faith, and I can feel it growing as I spend time in your word. Thank you that I can be a faith-filled warrior.

August 2

The fear that comes to you is a *wile of the enemy* to rob you of your faith. *Satan* is out to steal the word from your heart. You have the power to resist *him* and to nullify the thoughts that would destroy faith. Realize that *Satan* is a defeated foe. Give him no place in your mind, spirit, or body. *He* cannot stand against **my word**. He has to flee at **my word**

As this truth develops in your spirit, then you will begin to operate successfully in the spiritual realm. A deep belief in **my word** releases supernatural power in the earth. This is why **my word** must be ingrained in your heart and mind. You must be convinced of the truth of the **word**, which involves training, meditation and determination. As you begin to know the reality of **my word**, power and love, you, too, will operate in the fullness of **my** power. Make it your purpose to live in the fullness of *me*. It is a decision that can be fulfilled, with glory and honor of **me** resulting.

Scriptures: Psalms 119:105-106, John 10:10, James 4:7.

Prayer: Father, I make the quality decision to live in your fullness. I know your word is true, and I purpose today to spend more time in it and with you.

August 3

Nothing is wasted in the kingdom of **God**. It is not so in the world. *Satan* is a waster and a destroyer. *He* destroys bodies, energy, time and creativity. In **my** kingdom every action, every prayer counts. **I** answer every prayer offered in faith. Every minute spent with **me** is precious and adds to spiritual well-being. Each deed done in **my** name is observed and stored. There is no wastefulness in my kingdom!

The enemy would like you to think there is no time for **me**----no time to study, pray or praise. **I** say, make time. **I** am the creator of time and **I** make time! You must do so, too. As you do, you will see the other things done in an efficient and orderly manner. *Satan* is slothful and *he* wants you to be the same. Do <u>not</u> imitate *him*. Imitate me!

My Son set the example. Grow more like **Jesus.** Choose to take time with **me** and you will see that there is time for everything else.

Scriptures: Proverbs 8:17, Isaiah 55:6, Ephesians 5:15-16, I John 5:15.

Prayer: My Father, I have wasted so much time. Forgive me. I want an orderly life and I am trusting you to help me.

August 4

Put all things away that would hinder your walk with **me.** I let no other hindrances stand between me and **mine.** Neither can you. You must learn to hold yourself in perfect peace. You must learn self-control and discipline in all areas. Refuse to yield to your carnal nature. It is not of **me.** There is a time of action, but the **Holy Spirit** must be guiding you, not the lower nature. Stop, just a moment, and let the Spirit instruct you. That is his job! **He** is there to respond faithfully, if you will but listen.

Be diligent to keep yourself spotless before **me.** Then the power **I** send shall be seen. One who yields to anger and rage cannot be trusted to wield my power. Those who can overcome self and serve in complete objectivity will be able to use the power that **I** send. You can be one of these, if you set your mind and heart to its accomplishments.

Scriptures: John 16:13-15, Acts 1:8.

Prayer: Father, I thank you for giving me the Holy Spirit. I make such a mess of things when I act without His guidance. Help me to be more sensitive to His voice.

August 5

I am going to work my will in you, when you are committed to and united with my will. You will then be as unshakable and as unsinkable as **my** will. You can then face any situation, any threat, any opposition with perfect inner calm and tranquility. Nothing will defeat you! It cannot, because who can defeat **my will?** In any situation where your peace is threatened, where you feel fear or doubt beginning to grip you, look to see if you are in tune and committed to my will. If you are, you will face the situation **my** way.

Jesus saw the situation at Jacob's well quite differently from his disciples. **He** saw it differently because **he** was committed to my will. "**I** always do the will of **my Father**," **he** said.

Scriptures: John 5:19, John 5:30, Romans 12:2.

Prayer: Lord, today I give you my will, to unite it with your will. I want to see everything through Jesus' eyes, and to do the will of my Father, always. Thank you, Lord.

August 6

Be not afraid of the trials and tasks that you encounter. **I** have overcome the world, and thus, so have you. You may not feel victorious, but the results will be victory if you *abide in me* and act on **my word**. Listen to the **Holy** Spirit; **he** has all the answers. The prophets of old were led into battle and victory, through the leading of **my Spirit**. You cannot shy away from conflicts and battles, but you

August 7

must be led by **my Spirit.**

Rejoice in that **I** have given you victory in all things. Rest assured and be confident in **my** overcoming power. To win **my** way is to gain real victory, without the aftermath of retaliation and vengeance. Carnal weapons gain no lasting victories. Be obedient in all things. Do them willingly because I desire it, and because of your love for **me.** The rewards I give are great and endure forever.

Scriptures: John 16:33, II Corinthians 2:9, I John 5:4.

Prayer: Lord, I praise your name. I am so thankful that you are my Father, and that you have provided all that I need for a victorious life. I love you.

August 7

Believe and you receive. Throughout the scriptures, the message is given over and over. This is not by chance. **My** instruction to Thomas was to believe, even when you do not see. Faith is priceless and should be developed at all costs. Let nothing stand in the way of increasing your faith. As your faith grows, so does my power within you. The seed of faith that is given, the measure of faith, is to be nurtured and watered. This seed is essential to spiritual well-being because the kingdom does not operate without faith.

Faith is part of **my** character. I said that *faith,*

hope and love abideth. **I** am all of these. You must be, too. Do not let faith be quenched by circumstances, feeling and doubts. When the trying of your faith comes, rejoice! Faith always wins! Always! Cast down vain imaginations to the contrary and see the glory that follows.

Scriptures: Mark 11:24, Romans 12:3, I Corinthians 13:13, II Corinthians 10:5.

Prayer: Father, I thank you for your pastors and teachers who teach the word. You have made it so easy to walk in faith. Help me to discipline myself to spend more time with you and your word, so that my faith will continue to grow. You are wonderful, and I praise you!

August 8

When you **seek me**, you shall find **me.** I am so easy to find, for **my** eyes are constantly watching and looking for those whose hearts are pure toward **me.** When a man humbles himself, he becomes pure towards me. **I** will use those who have pliable hearts, whose desire is to please **me.**

Root out all rebellion and haughtiness in your life. Do not let pride, disdain or impudence keep you from coming near to **me.** *If you draw near to me, I will draw near to you.* The **Holy Spirit** is ever at work to woo your spirit. Listen to him and obey his instructions. The heart that is open will always hear

August 9

his voice. Seek the Lord and he will be found. The initiative is with you.

Scriptures: Psalm 24:3-4, Jeremiah 29:13, Matthew 5:8, James 4:8,10.

Prayer: Lord, with all my heart I seek a closer walk with you. Thank you for the Holy Spirit and His work in my life. I want to hear, and also, to obey.

August 9

I long to see **my** kingdom manifested in the lives of those who love **me**. The act of living in accord with me will bless and save others. I give grace to live in abundance and beauty, but the realization of this grace is often missed.

The world must see me through the lives of **my** disciples before it will accept me. **Jesus** said, *if I be lifted up from the earth, I will draw all men unto **me**.* **He** is lifted up in each individual life, and the world sees **me** through each of you. The abundance of peace, prosperity, happiness, joy, contentment and health will make the world take notice! They are wounded, scared, hungry and are looking for a way-out. **I** am *the way*; they must be given the opportunity to see **me** in **mine**. When you allow yourself to be blessed by **me**, you will in turn be a blessing. Open your heart and your life to all that **I** have. Choose the blessings, the good portion. All who see these things will want me, too.

Scriptures: Deuteronomy 28:2, Matthew 6:33, John 12:32.

Prayer: Father, help me <u>not</u> to compromise----to settle for nothing but your best. It is so easy to stray into the world's ways unless I keep focused on you. I always want to be in a position for you to bless me, and I want to be a blessing to others.

August 10

Be ready to do good, in and out of season, for this is **my** will concerning you. Those who follow **me** must be willing to lay down their lives for **my** cause, for my sheep. *No greater thing can a man do than to lay down his life for his brother.* The rewards come with such a sacrifice. Not only do you see your brother saved, but the kingdom of **God** is strengthened and so are you!

It is not in man's carnal nature to deal unselfishly. That is of **me**. The love that you show to your brother is of me, for **I** am love. To love your neighbor is the highest love you can give, for it is pure and unselfish. Attain to this love by dwelling more and more with **me**. As you give, it is given back, pressed down and running over. Love is a substance that will bless eternally and the rewards from it never end.

Scriptures: Luke 6:38, John 15:13, Romans 5:5, Galatians 5:14.

Prayer: Lord, thank you for your love that has changed my life. I cannot understand your kind of love, but I can live in it. With your help, I will love as you love. What a wonderful God you are!

August 11

The truth that you hear and receive will determine the amount of light that you walk in. Be diligent to hear the truth, to seek it and to make it your own. **My** disciples are to be a light to a dark and desperate world. There are many souls who are longing for a better way, and you can lead them into the light.

By getting your life in order, you affect the lives of so many others. You may sometimes feel that your life is stagnant, that nothing is being accomplished. Just persevere. **My** will is being done in your life, and growth is taking place. Be determined to go on with **me,** and you will see the "produce" of a fruitful life. The changes that take place in the life of a believer are not always obvious outwardly, but it is the changes in the heart that make the difference. Stay the course and only good things will result in your life. You have **my word.**

Scriptures: Psalm 25:3-5, Psalm 145:9-10; John 8:32, Galatians 6:9.

Prayer: Oh, Father, how I thank you for your word. I thank you for helping me to get my life in order, and for making it fruitful. I give you praise, and honor, and glory, forever!

August 12

I am the **God** that shall judge *the quick and the dead*. No one shall escape judgment, except those who belong to **my Son** and call him **Lord**. The ways of the world will surely lead to death, but **I** have given the world **my son** that all might be saved. If the world does not accept **him**, it must be judged. There will be many to whom you will be given the opportunity to share **Jesus**. Because you love me, and because you love them, you will share **Jesus** gladly and with honor. The glory that comes from winning a lost one will shine, not only on you, but on me. *My Glory will fill the whole earth,* and **my** children will share the glory.

Look forward to sharing me with all **I** send you. It will be a delightsome task, and the brothers (and sisters) you make in **Christ** will bless you eternally. **I** have special assignments for you. Look forward to them eagerly.

Scriptures: Numbers 14:21, John 3:16, Romans 10:15, II Timothy 4:1.

Prayer: Father, I want to share you with all those I come in contact with. I want to be bold. I realize that I have been too hesitant in sharing you. Help me.

August 13
Beware of the tendency to get lazy and slothful in meditation and prayer. Remember the enemy is ever ready to attack a believer in a moment of weakness. You must allow no point of weakness to come upon you. Weaknesses of the flesh are but symptoms of slothfulness in spiritual progress. Have **I** not provided full armor for every believer?

There is no time where you can say, "I've arrived!" and then rest on past victories. Just as you cannot say, "I've learned all there is to know", so you cannot be indifferent to spiritual growth. There does come a point of maintenance, where the development is not as hard. Work to enter into *my rest.* When spiritual maintenance is as natural as breathing, and fellowship with **me** is a routine part of your life, then the battles are easier to fight because your heart is full of **my word** and impenetrable.

Scriptures: Isaiah 40:8, Ephesians 6:11, Hebrews 4:11, I Peter 5:8.

Prayer: Father, I know it is easy for me to get lazy and be side-tracked by so many things. I do not want to be easy prey for the enemy. A war is on, and I thank you for giving me everything necessary to be a winner. I choose to stay close to you. Hence, I will never stop growing spiritually.

August 14

Before a soul is saved, he only knows the carnal life. As the **Holy Spirit** enters that soul, the life of the **Spirit** begins to reveal itself to his consciousness. Only those who yield their minds and bodies can ever really enter into my presence and peace here on earth. The carnal mind is at enmity with me and fights **my** influence.

Only as man's will is yielded, will that soul come into a deep relationship with **me**. *Satan* has tried to bias men into thinking that yielding to **me** means losing their identity and position in life. He wants a soul to think that life will be shallow and dull with me. But the opposite is the truth! *I came to give life, and that more abundantly.* The effects of living with me are: radiant health, internal peace, satisfaction, joy and hope. **I** give all the ingredients for everlasting joy.

Scriptures: Psalm 100:4, John 10:10, Romans 6:16.

Prayer: Father God, how I praise and bless your name. I yield myself anew to you this day. Life with you is more meaningful and more exciting than I could have imagined. I do not understand how anyone can even survive in the world as it is today, without you. Thank you for Jesus.

August 15

The love you give freely will be returned unto you abundantly, as will all the gifts you give in **my** name. I am a generous giver, and you must also be. Never feel that you must hold back anything that I have given you. I will furnish it again, as you believe me for it. I give so freely to the world. However, the world has failed to receive most of my gifts. Because you know the truth, you are able to receive gifts.

If you will put **me** first, and trust in **my** ability to provide all your needs, you will never see lack or have want. I am faithful to provide abundantly. Rejoice in this, and feel the freedom of abundance in all things. I have provided it to you. You can freely give----physically, emotionally, spiritually. There will be no lack. *Trust me.*

Scriptures: Psalm 34:10, Psalm 37:5, John 4:11, Matthew 10:8.

Prayer: Lord, I am so thankful for your love. Help me to love as you do. You have told us that love covers a multitude of sins, and that faith works by love. I think if I could really love like you, everything else would fall in line. About the time I think I am doing great, I catch myself with an unloving thought or action. I need your help!

August 16

Because you are learning to come into my presence, you will see the power bought by **Jesus** manifested, more and more. In times of old, and even in the present, men have feared when my power came forth. After all, man was created to walk in authority and power. Only the regenerated can be trusted to use this power---one who is found faithful and obedient.

Choose always the paths of trusting and obeying. The more you do, the more you will see **my** presence in your life. Many have come a little way, but would go no farther. They were not willing to pay the price in obedience and faithfulness. The price, however, is not too high, considering the rewards. I reward abundantly for work done in **my** kingdom. The joy, alone, is worth it all, but there are many additional benefits----besides power.

Scriptures: Psalm 18:2, Isaiah 1:19, Luke 10:19, II Corinthians 9:8.

Prayer: Father, I praise you. You are God of the universe and worthy to be praised. Forgive me for not being quick to be obedient. Thank you for loving me enough to correct me. I choose you, Lord.

August 17

You must always yield to **my** will, for this will bring deliverance and peace. In the carnal life, men

August 18

are subject to the ways, thoughts and actions of the world. Not so with believers, those who call Jesus, Lord. To receive deliverance and peace, you must relinquish your thoughts, ways and actions to my word and will. In so doing, you defeat the enemy at every turn. He can establish no stronghold if you give him no place in your life.

Your mind and flesh will not want to bow to me. You must train, even command, them to obey. You have the power to do this, because of Jesus. Do not fall into the traps set by Satan. He can only try to deceive you, but he has no authority over you. Dwell, think and meditate on my word! Learn it! The word will bring you out of bondage every time, and into peace, joy and contentment. These are attributes that the whole world seeks. They are yours for the willing. You will to do my will. I will never fail you.

Scriptures: Joshua 1:8, II Chronicles 30:8, Psalm 1:2, Colossians 2:8.

Prayer: Father, Jesus is lord of my life. Help me always to be a yielded vessel unto you. As I spend more time with you and meditate on your word, I can see my faith growing. Thank you for never failing me.

August 18
This is the day the Lord has made; I shall rejoice Aug and be glad in it. The psalmist knew that as you go

rejoicing, the blessings will come. Believing and expecting the blessings are necessary parts to receiving them. The cares, the worries, the things that would hinder you are temporal. They will surely pass. The blessings, however, endure. Overlook the things that are temporal and gaze towards the eternal. My blessing will come to those who are prepared to receive them. I have commanded them, and they cannot be reversed.

Just think! The God of the whole universe, creator of all that is and ever will be, has commanded the blessings on you. Let that thought dwell with you and permeate your being. As it does, new horizons will open before you. You will truly go on your way, rejoicing.

Scriptures: Deuteronomy 28:1-14, Psalm 118:24, Mark 11:23.

Prayer: Oh, Lord, when I think of all the blessings you have for me, I am overcome with joy and thanksgiving. I know I can never be good enough to deserve them, so I praise you and thank you for Jesus, whose blood has made me worthy!

August 19
   The way to a successful life in Jesus is to make it the highest priority in your life. There is nothing so valuable as a bounteous life in Christ. The daily
August 20

August 20

discipline of spending time in prayer and in **my word** will produce much fruit. As faith grows and develops, many miracles will also be brought forth. The **Christ**-filled life is not dull or uninteresting. It is rich, full and alive.

A life in me could not be dull! The *enemy* tries to deceive all men into thinking that yielding means giving up something. Yielding, however, means gaining the best, living life to the fullest, as it was meant to be lived, in joy and peace.

Scriptures: Matthew 13:44-45, Matthew 13:52, John 10:14-15.

Prayer: Father, nothing is more important to me than Jesus. Sometimes I do not act as though this is true, and I ask your forgiveness. As I spend more time with you, I find it easier to give you first place in everything. Life without you would be pretty boring! Help me to stay focused.

August 20

A song will I put in your heart. A song to gladden your ways, and give you delight. You just have to rejoice in the melody of love that I alone provide. I meant always that my children should go rejoicing. You have much about which to rejoice. You are an overcomer----victorious in all of life. The cares of this world will not defeat you, for you know the source of power. Choose to act on it!

Do not let thoughts of defeat stay for an instant. Rebuke them! Then watch the joy return. Let the melody of love permeate your being. See the music of joy fill the air around you. Be as a happy child, delighting in **my** world. Enjoy my presence, **my Son, my word.** Life is to be lived, and you know the source of it. It is **Christ Jesus,** the **Hope** of the World, the **Redeemer** of Mankind. *Rejoice!*

Scriptures: Psalm 40:3, John 15:11, Philippians 4:4, James 5:8.

Prayer: Father, just to think that I am your child, the child of a King fills me with wonder. I go forth this day rejoicing. I do not accept defeat because I am more then a conqueror. I delight in you, and I know that I have the desires of my heart. Thank you for Jesus, my Savior.

August 21

*In the world you will have tribulation, but be of good cheer, for **I** have overcome the world.* What a glad message that is! To think that the world with its trials no longer dominates your life is such a blessing. You must keep this thought in your mind. You are a victor. Nothing can take that away. The victory is not for you alone, however. It is for **my** kingdom. You must train yourself to do battle on every front you see. There are many who are unprepared for battle. You must not only help them, but trainthem! Then they in turn will do the same.

Resistance to evil will grow until evil is conquered by **Jesus,** and conquered by love of man for mankind. **I** alone can inspire this love, for **I** am *love.* Stay ready for battle. It has been won. Be prepared at all times and see the *enemy* flee at your command. *He* has to do so!

Scriptures: Psalm 19:14, John 16:33, Romans 8:37, I John 4:7-8.

Prayer: Father, it is such a comfort to me to know that you have overcome the world. Thank you for the victory I have in Jesus. I want my life to show this Jesus to others. Help me to help others.

August 22

I have blessed and who can reverse it? As this concept is accepted and sublimated into the hearts of believers, the evidence will be manifested. The only hindrance to blessing man is the receiving of it, for the blessing has been given.

The world sits in pain, poverty and lack of blessings only because it has not accepted this gift. There is no lack of any blessing with **me.** The heart that receives this message is blessed in that it can accept what **Jesus** has paid for. I have blessed **my** children and they must learn of **me,** of **my** gifts and how to receive **my** gifts. Thus, the whole earth will benefit, for nothing shall stop the blessings from flowing. Let nothing hinder your reception of them.

Scriptures: Proverbs 10:22; Ephesians 1:3, Ephesians 4:8.

Prayer: Father, thank you for your blessings. I choose to receive each and every one of them, and I want to show others what wonderful gifts you have for your children. Help me to be bolder.

August 23

Never let fear dominate your thinking. Be concerned about circumstances enough to pray, then trust the results to **me.** **I** will not fail you. When you hear or see something that needs to come before the throne of grace, bring it there, immediately. Then rest in the fact that it is taken care of.

My children were not meant to be burdened with the cares of this world. **I** am faithful and trustworthy to handle any difficulty. Learn to trust **my word** more than you would trust the word of any man you know. Trust that **I** will handle the situation in the most effective and efficient manner. Then thank **me**, as you would thank a trusted friend, for taking care of it.

The blessing of knowing that the petitions you have asked have been granted are given to those who trust, and are not afraid. Fear is not of **me** and will not move **me.** Faith will! When you believe that I will, **I will!**

August 24

Scriptures: II Samuel 22:3-4, Psalm 56:3-4, Mark 4:19, II Timothy 1:7, I Peter 5:7.

Prayer: Lord God Almighty, Creator of heaven and earth, and my father! It is hard to believe that I can call on one as great as you! It amazes me to realize how much you must love me----small, insignificant me! I come before you as a little child. You are my daddy and I know you have a plan about everything I bring to you. I give you all my cares. I trust you with my life. Now I thank you, Father, for taking care of me.

August 24

Come unto me, all ye who are heavy laden, and I will give you rest. Have you ever thought that this statement is already an accomplished fact? All you have to be concerned with is "the coming". **I** have done the rest. The *rest* that **I** give refreshes the heart, mind and body. My rest brings under control all anguish, anxieties and worry. Come unto **me.** You have to purpose in order to come, but once you do, my rest is assured. **I** will give you rest! There should be no doubt that the rest will be yours.

I see **my** children anxious about many things, and I am grieved. *Be anxious for nothing. . . . let your request be made known . . . with prayer and thanksgiving.* Follow **my** instructions and you will see the results you desire. Make yourself rest in **me.** Labor to enter into **my** rest. **My** rest is worth whatever effort it may cost you. **I** am always waiting for you, to comfort you in **my** rest.

Scriptures: Matthew 11:28, Philippians 4:6, Hebrews 4:11.

Prayer: Father, I thank you for the rest you have prepared for me, and I thank you that I know to run to you whenever I stumble. I have discovered that I tend to faint when I get weary. This is when I need to revive myself in your rest. Help me to remember this and to make time to relax in your love. I love you, Father.

August 25

The victory belongs to those who persevere and press on. There is no room for quitters in the kingdom. The quitters have had the **word** choked by cares and persecution. The victors press on at all costs. It is easy to get sidetracked from the kingdom principles. This is *Satan's* greatest ploy to get your mind on the unimportant, the immaterial, and the mundane. The victor will not be moved from **my word** and purposes in the earth. If your heart is fixed on **me**, you will not fail.

To make sure you are established on **my** word, consider your priorities. Are they in pleasing **me** or yourself? **My** purposes are not at odds with your gain, but they are opposed to the carnal life. The blessings that come from me will enhance life and **my** kingdom. These are parallel goals, and the heart that lines up with me will see success and peace in this life. Do not be deceived by the goals of *Satan*. They always fail.

Scriptures: Psalm 112:7, Mark 4:19, Romans 8:7, I John 5:5.

Prayer: Father, I choose not to be a quitter. I will play until I win! I make this confession to you today, and I ask you to help me not be sidetracked. I want to please you.

August 26

Just as a man sees many things that will benefit him, so must he be aware of evils that lurk in his paths. Each (the beneficial or evil) is awaiting you; therefore, discernment is imperative. You must always be aware of spiritual opportunities (blessings or pitfalls), just as you are aware of physical opportunities. To be able to discern spiritual truth requires knowledge, training and sensitivity. Discernment needs to be taught and learned. As a disciple, you must be open to discernment. Then many things heretofore hidden will become evident.

Although you live and operate in the physical and mental realms, the spiritual is also there. It is more important to health, wealth and peace than the natural realm. *I would not have you ignorant,* brethren. My best is that you are not ignorant of spiritual truths. When you walk in the spirit, you walk in reality!

Scriptures: Ecclesiastes 2:13-14, Isaiah 2:5, I Corinthians 12:1, I Corinthians 12:10, Galatians 5:16-18.

Prayer: Lord, I ask you to give me a discerning spirit. Sometimes I feel so gullible, and I know that this does not please you. Help me to be sensitive to the leading of the Holy Spirit.

August 27

The way to life is through me. Although this way is narrow, it leads to abundant living. How many have tried to take shortcuts to abundant living? *Man has a way that seemeth right, but the end thereof is death.* There is no shortcut----only heartbreak, pain and death! If **my** words are followed consistently, **I** have guaranteed the results. No guarantee has greater force or power than the one **I** give. **My** ways are not hard----**my** yoke is easy! But it is a yoke and you must place it yourself.

To those who have chosen the **way,** there is peace, joy and abundant life. The way seems so simple that many miss it. They cannot believe that this is all there is to it. I said it so often----in many forms----but it amounts to the same thing. *If you abide in me and let my words abide in you,* you will find the **way.** Walk ye in it.

August 28

Scriptures: Proverbs 16:25, Matthew 7:14, Matthew 11:30, John 14:6, John 15:7.

Prayer: Oh Father, I thank you for Jesus. And Jesus, I thank you for dying for me. I am so troubled over the people I know who do not know "the way". I ask you, Father, to prepare their hearts for the truth. If I am the one to share Jesus with them, open the door and fill my mouth with the right words. How I praise and bless your name----Father, Son, and Holy Spirit.

August 28

Because the yearnings of your heart are toward **me**, and because you are choosing to obey and please **me,** you will see **me** manifested more in your life. **I** reveal myself to those who seek **me**. **I** abide with them. Your act of coming voluntarily into **my** presence opens the door for blessings. When you choose to worship and praise me, you enter into **my** divine holiness. **My** glory is shown through the lives and acts of those who love **me**. **I** rise up and overflow in them as rivers of living water issuing forth.

The life in whom **I** manifest **myself** must be holy, for **I** am holy. You are made holy through **my Son,** and by coming into **my** presence. **I** have washed you clean. You choose to stay clean by continually abiding in **me**. *Whom the Son sets free is free indeed.* You are free from sin and, therefore, clean.

Scriptures: Leviticus 11:45, Psalm 100:4-5, John

7:38, John 8:36.

Prayer: Father, I thank you that you have given me the freedom to choose who I serve, and I choose Jesus! I come into your presence with thanksgiving and praise, and want my life to show your glory.

August 29
    The joy that comes from living in me is worth all the effort that you might put forth. Yours is an exuberant life that affects everyone around you, everything you do. *I came that your joy might be made full.* Joy makes your days brighter, the air fresher, the day better in every way. There is none who will not recognize this fruit in your life.

    Joy comes in the morning, but it should last throughout the day, if your mind is fixed on me. When you have the confidence that all is right with the world, because your **Father** is in control, you are free to enjoy life. There are no nagging worries to hold you down.

    Refuse to let worry, doubt, despondency or fear enter your mind. These are enemies of your soul and spirit. They will defeat you if you give them entrance. They cannot come without permission---and you do not have to give it! Be free in **me.** Let joy dominate! Enjoy yourself.

Scriptures: Psalm 30:4-5; John 17:13; Philippians 4:8.

Prayer: Lord, I wish everyone could know the joy that comes from living in you. I have found that it is contagious. If my life shows your joy, it rubs off on others I come in contact with. Help me to be diligent about keeping this joy.

August 30

A "glad" heart takes practice----practice in letting my peace overflow you until the joy and gladness come. You must learn to reject all thoughts of worries, chores or anxieties that nag at your mind. These will rob you of the delight of truly living in **my** kingdom.

I said, Take no thought for the morrow. . . . and . . . Your burdens will be light. This does not mean that you should not plan. It means that once the plans have been formulated, leave the rest to **me.** I am **Lord** over all. I will bring the best to pass when the best is expected. What joy fills the soul when one anticipates life with joyful expectation. I said to come as a little child. A child, when expecting a special treat does not worry about the things that could go wrong to hinder that treat. He just looks forward to it. Be ye likewise. Enjoy the peace **I** give.

Scriptures: Proverbs 17:22, Matthew 6:34, Luke 18:17.

Prayer: Father, I'm so glad you said to come to you

as a little child. You have made it so simple. As a child trusts his parents, I trust you, knowing that you will do what you have said. How I praise and love you!

August 31
Always delight to do **my will** and **my will** will be shown to you. A life cannot achieve success and happiness apart from **my will**. A man may possess material things, but real success and happiness come only from **me.**

When you yield yourself, your mind, emotions and flesh to **me, I** will direct your path---easily and clearly. Yield as a matter of obedience at first. Then, it will be a matter of habit, as natural to you as breathing.

As my will begins to be done in your life, you will see power manifested there. Power to change lives, and heal broken hearts. **My** kingdom will come on earth as **I** intended from the beginning. Live in **my Spirit.** Let **him** take precedence in your life, and you will see **my** love come forth. It is an exciting day! Choose to be part of it, and you will enjoy the fruits of your labors.

Scriptures: I Chronicles 29:11, Psalm 40:8, Proverbs 3:7-8, Matthew 6:9-13.

Prayer: Father, as I yield myself to you, material things seem so unimportant. Since I know you must

August 31

meet all my needs, I don't even have to be concerned. My concern is to be so closely connected to you that I will be able to show others your kingdom. Thank you for the Holy Spirit who guides me into all truth.

SEPTEMBER

September 1

Because you have accepted **me** and **my** covenant, you will see **my** glory, the glory that I promised in my word. This glory will cover the whole earth. *All the earth shall be filled with the glory of the Lord.* The world cannot and does not comprehend **me.** They have no idea of **my** character, my love or **my** blessings. The glory that comes out of my children is all the world can see. As Christ's representative of **me**, you have the privilege of presenting the glory of **me** to the world. Through your life, the glory will be manifested to all who accept and receive the covenant.

As **I** open **my** kingdom to you through the **Holy Spirit,** the glory will fill the earth. There is no greater blessing than this. Rejoice, rejoice! The blessings of **my** glory have been given and who can turn them back? Go forward rejoicing, knowing that **I** have already provided the way. **I** am the way.

Scriptures: Numbers 14:21, Isaiah 58:8, John 14:6.

Prayer: Father, I get so excited when I think about your glory filling all the earth. To think that I can play a part in your glory thrills me! I rejoice and praise your name as I expectantly wait.

September 2

The dissatisfaction that the world feels is due to

September 3

a lack of harmony with **me**. **I** put a knowledge of me in every man's heart, and he hungers for his creator——though he might not recognize the hunger. The gnawing in his soul is very uncomfortable. Man's will is involved, and sin can cloud his direction.

As **my** word is heard, light enters the soul, and a release of the soul's spiritual bondage begins. Man has the option of yielding to that release or of letting his reasoning dominate. Man can refuse to yield himself to my wooing. I do not appeal to the mind of man, because the mind is unregenerated. It does not know **me**. The spirit of man, however, recognizes me. I give every man an opportunity to accept **me**. I use **my** children to reinforce that opportunity, to give man's senses an opportunity to respond. **My** children are a **light** to this world.

Scriptures: II Chronicles 30:8, Psalm 119:105, Matthew 5:14, Romans 1:17-22.

Prayer: Father, you said I am the light of the world, and that is what I want to be. I have friends who need you. Help me to light the way. Thank you, Lord.

September 3

My banner over you is love, the love of the Father for his children. **My** love is so great that I even extend it to those who do not love me, *raining on the just and the unjust.* Those who are under my umbrella of love *abide in the secret place of the most high.* Their lives are truly blessed as they partake of **my** mercy and grace, which is poured out on them in abundance.

The evil in this world would long ago have destroyed the world, were it not for **my** grace and **my** promise to Abraham. Because there are righteous ones who love **me** and are pleasing to **me**, I have spared the world. The day is approaching, however, when **my** righteous ones will reign supreme, and *every knee will bow to the name of Jesus.* The blessings have already begun to those who have made **Jesus** their Lord.

Scriptures: Psalm 91:1, Song of Solomon 2:4, Matthew 5:45, Romans 14:11, I John 4:19.

Prayer: My Father, how I thank you for your mercy and grace. I thank you that I can run to you and be refreshed by your life. I praise your holy name.

September 4

The trust that you give to **my word** is the portion of faith that you have. Seek always to build up your faith and choose to trust **me. I** will always answer faith. Trust comes from knowing **my** character, and from knowing **my** faithfulness. Trust is not developed apart from knowing **my word.**

The **Holy Spirit** will lead you into all truth.

September 5

You must then choose to allow **Him** to lead you and to believe that **he** is leading. There is so much to learn and so many to teach. The job is not more than **my Spirit** can handle, however. **He** is adequate for the task. The **Holy Spirit** only needs your cooperation. Choose to cooperate with **him**. Choose to trust in me, your **Holy God.** Choose to call upon the name of **Jesus,** your deliverer and **Savior.** You will then see my works manifested in your life.

Scriptures: Proverbs 3:5, Psalm 119:11, John 16:13, Acts 5:32.

Prayer: Father, I trust you with all my heart, and I feel faith rising up in me stronger and stronger as I learn more of your word. Thank you for this hunger I have for your word. I do not ever want to lose it. Thank you, Father.

September 5

For the body of **Christ** to be victorious, the preparation must be intense. This is why so many teachers are being prepared and sent out. Exhortation is coming forth as never before. A great battle is being planned which has been ordained since the beginning of time. *Satan* and his **evil ones** have had their time of victory and harassment. Now my army will come forth to defeat *him.*

You ask, "When will this occur?" Only **I** know,

but **my** army will be prepared. **My** army is the *body*, with **my son** as *the head*. **He** is leading with victory and a sword in **his** teeth. *Satan* quakes at the thought of **him**. *Satan's* desire is to thwart the formation and preparation of this army of believers. Because **my** people love **me**, they are busy preparing. They are yielding themselves to be taught and are disciplining their lives. *Satan* is doomed!

Scriptures: Joel 2:11, Matthew 28:19-20, 1 Corinthians 12:27, Colossians 1:18, Revelation 1:16, Revelation 20:10.

Prayer: Father, thank you for your teachers who are boldly teaching your word. They have been such a help to me. Help me to be quick to learn. I want to be a part of your army. I do not want to stand on the sidelines watching.

September 6

The times of tribulation seem long, but not nearly as long as another cure would take. Even in Job's tribulations, there was just a brief expanse of time. As you are built-up in **my word,** the time that the enemy can test you will grow shorter and shorter, until you come into the perfection of **my son.** Then you will only need a word to send *Satan* fleeing.

The goal you must seek is perfection, like **my** son. As **my word** abides in you in greater measure, truly written upon the *table* of your heart, you will see more immediate results of **my word** in your life. It is the **word** that turns *Satan* back. *He* cannot stand against it. Desire the **word** in your life. Endeavor to put it there in greater measure. *Meditate in the word day and night.* I have given my promise as to the results it will bring. I am truth.

Scriptures: Deuteronomy 4:30, Proverbs 3:3, Joshua 1:8, Hebrews 4:12.

Prayer: Father, I thank you that even in times of tribulation, I know I win! If you are for us, who can be against us? I just praise you for giving me your word----my sword. With it, I can make Satan flee!

September 7

If you will seek **my** glory and **my** honor, I will give glory to you. A pure heart and faith are all that you need for you to come before me, knowing that I am ready to answer you. When your desires line up with my desires, the answers to your petitions are on the way.

I long to commune with my children. I long to hear their voices raised in praise and worship. Worship must be real----not feigned. Worship is a heart attitude that can and must be developed. I will teach you how to worship, if you choose to learn. Choose wisely and see the rewards come. I will share my honor with no other, so search your heart to make sure your motives are pure. I give glory, but I do not share honor. Glory can only be given; it cannot be taken. There is a difference.

Scriptures: Psalm 37:4-5, I Chronicles 16:28-29, Matthew 5:8, John 17:22.

Prayer: Father, I can see my desires beginning to line up with yours. Many things that used to be so important to me, no longer are. I praise you for your word. It is helping me to get my life in order. When I remember how much I enjoy visiting with my own children (and how sad I would be if they didn't call, or if I felt they didn't care), then I think how many times I must have grieved your heart. Forgive me for not taking more time to talk to you, Father. I love you.

September 8

Remember always who the *enemy* is----*he* is the destroyer, killer and thief. When *he* would come upon you or those who you love, rebuke *him!* Do not let *him* have *his* way. I have given you power over serpents and scorpions. You go, therefore, and defeat *him* at every turn. He *will* try all sorts of diversionary tactics to keep you off target. You must remember to be wise as a serpent, though gentle as a lamb.

Do not be afraid! You must never let fear of failure dominate your thinking. Know in whom you believe and in whom you trust. *Satan* cannot stand

September 9

against you. If you falter or fail, repent. Then go forward, again! You get up----and go on, and on, and on! You are an overcomer, and you will win. I have decreed it, and **I** am **Lord** over all!

Scriptures: Matthew 10:16, Luke 10:19, II Timothy 1:12, Revelation 12:11.

Prayer: Father, you are so wonderful! How I praise you and thank you for your word which provides everything. I need to succeed! You have taught me who the enemy is, and you have made me an overcomer!

September 9

If your motives are pure, **I** will direct the rest. **I** can work with those whose hearts are ready and prepared. Those who choose to obey **me** have no difficulty in hearing my voice. **I** can guide them! Just make sure you choose correctly. Examine your heart daily to see if your desire is to please **me**----or to please yourself. **I** am able to guide you easily if your heart is fixed on me. **I** speak guidance through **my word** and through other servants. **I** speak to a receptive heart. The preparation of the heart takes a decision----a decision to please **me.** As you decide to do this, **my Spirit** will gently show you the way. No father is harsh with a child who wants to please him. Would **I** be harsh----your **father** who knows the frail frame of man and his weaknesses? **I** look on the heart.

Scriptures: Psalm 51:10, John 10:27, Hebrews 10:23.

Prayer: Thank you, Lord, for always being with me and loving me. I want to have pure motives and a clean heart. Thank you for correcting me when I stray. Help me always to be quick to obey.

September 10

Doubt and discouragement are not of **me.** Do not be deceived by these tactics or let them stay. Refuse the influence of doubt and discouragement. Recall my words of faith. Choose to allow faith to rise within you. This will cause your expectations and hope to soar again in joy. The *enemy* wants you defeated. *He* will try to arrange circumstances or cause symptoms that would suggest that the things you desire will not occur. If you will let your spirit reign and just pause a moment or two, to allow the **Holy Spirit** to assert **himself,** you will find your joy and peace returning.

Faith is a substance that must be acted upon to have it operational in your life. Your *Christian* walk ----indeed, your whole life----centers on your will and the choices you make. Choose to believe **me** and accept **my word.**

Scriptures: Deuteronomy 1:21, Matthew 21:21, John

September 11

14:27.

Prayer: Lord, thank you for teaching me that nothing bad ever comes from you, and that our fight is the good fight of faith. I choose to believe you and to act on your word. I praise you, Father.

September 11
　　Believe and receive. These are very important concepts in the spiritual realm, for good or ill. Most people do not realize that when they refuse or neglect to receive from **me,** they are receiving and believing *Satan's* lies. **I** have given **my word.** If it is accepted and believed, the **word** will come to pass in your life. To know **my word,** to know **my** character and to have **my Spirit** abiding in you is absolutely necessary! Believing is not just an act of your will, although that is important. Believing is the action of faith in your life---faith bringing forth fruit, with an explosion of the seed of **my word** resulting.
　　The spiritual realm is difficult to explain in natural terms. It is supernatural! There must first be the *will* (good ground). Next comes the **word** (seed). Then *faith* (water) must be applied. Finally, the manifestation (fruit) will come. This process will never fail. I have decreed it.

Scriptures: Mark 11:24, John 15:4, Hebrews 11:1.

Prayer: Father, I always want to choose your way.

Help me to be wise in all things. Help me to remember that I have the *mind of Christ*. I love you, Lord.

September 12

Guard your thoughts at all time. Do not let the *enemy* deceive you with his lies and guile. You have the **Holy Spirit** to lead you into all truth, so you do not have to be deceived. You can only be trapped if you choose to listen to *Satan's* lies. It is easy to be lured away---but always possible to resist. Did **I** not say **I** would always make a way of escape? I have given you the keys of the kingdom. Use them! I have given you mighty weapons of warfare. Use them! I have given you the **Holy Spirit** to lead and guide you. Hear **Him**! You have power and authority over all the works of the *devil*. Use them!

You must keep yourself! You have the *power* to do so. I have not given **my** kingdom to a bunch of babies, but to those who are mature in **Christ**. Keep yourself in readiness to defeat the *enemy* at every turn! You have the *power!*

Scriptures: Matthew 16:19, John 14:26, I Corinthians 10:13, II Corinthians 10:4.

Prayer: Lord, I do not want to be a weak, baby Christian. I thank you for the growth I'm experiencing. It is not quite so easy, as it once was, for Satan to deceive me. I know that I will continue to grow if I am diligent to spend time with you and in your word. I commit to do this, Father.

September 13
The joy of the Lord is your strength. A heart full of joy is a testimony of its trust in **my word, my** ability and **my** faithfulness. It is impossible to have joy without first being steadfast and established in **my** word. Only then can you know that the power of the universe is behind you.

Joy is not happiness, although happiness is a manifestation of joy. Joy is a confidence, a *knowing* that **I** am in control, and that there is nothing to fear. A joyful heart is not anxious or worried. You may see troubles----even have them lap at your doorstep----but you have the assurance they will not harm you. It is so blessed to be in the shadow of the Almighty, to rest in **my** love. I do keep you, and your joy can be complete. Believe and receive.

Scriptures: Nehemiah 8:10; Psalm 16:11, 91:1-2; John 17:13; Romans 14:17.

Prayer: Thank you, Father, for your joy. You are so wonderful. Help me always remember to praise you and to tell you how much I love you.

September 14
Praise will lift the soul to new heights of joy. Praise is a sweet incense unto me. A heart full of

praise is a joyful heart; it is strength to a believer.
Joy permeates everyone who hears praise----just the opposite the effect of depression. **My** gifts lift the spirit! *Satan's* gifts drag it down.

When a believer truly lives with me, he has a joy that is like a mantle of fruit on his body. Joy is a fruit that is visible to the whole world. Joy testifies that hope and faith are secure, enriching the flavor of the other fruits. All men are seeking these fruits, and joy is the most evident of them. A happy face is a mirror of the joy of the soul.

Cultivate this precious fruit by trusting in **me**. When you trust **me**, the soul is at peace. A joyful heart results. Joy comes, because the heart must have expression, and there is no room for depression. **I** give a happy, joyful heart. So praise, praise, praise!

Scriptures: Psalm 30:4-5, Proverbs 17:22, Galatians 5:22, Hebrews 13:15.

Prayer: Oh Father God, I have thought I spent a lot of time praising you, but I realize that I probably spend only minutes a day. Forgive me, and help me to live a life of praise.

September 15

The commission that I gave to **my** followers, *Go ye into all the world and preach the gospel to every creature*, is still in effect. Since you are in the world already, just live your life before men and they

September 16

will crave **me.** Each individual in **my** body has a special task that none other has. Man is always looking for a pattern to follow, a plan he can use to become like me. The only pattern that can be used is that of **my son. He** obeyed **me.** The **Holy Spirit** will direct your paths to function appropriately as your heart seeks and yearns for **my** will for your life.

Allow the **Holy Spirit** to direct your coming in and your going out. I have already given **my** blessing to you. Let the **Holy Spirit** teach and lead you into all truth. I have given him authority to do so. Your function is unique for you. With the mind of **Christ** being the same in all believers, you are all one, but function differently.

Scriptures: Proverbs 3:6, Mark 16:15, John 16:7-12, I Corinthians 2:16, I Corinthians 12:28.

Prayer: Father, I do not know of any big task you have for me, but help me to be faithful in the little things. I want to be quick to hear and quick to act on your direction, Lord.

September 16

To come into your full inheritance, you must only accept my gifts. This inheritance was provided in a moment of time. When **I** gave **my** only begotten **son, I** gave it <u>all:</u> all salvation, all health, all deliverance, all wealth, all peace, all, all, all. Acceptance of these gifts, however, has not taken place among all who qualify for this inheritance.

To be qualified, one must be wearing the robe of righteousness provided by **Jesus.** This inheritance was clearly given as stated in **my** will, which is **my word.** All lies and deception must be stripped away before regeneration begins. This regeneration is only possible because **Jesus** has redeemed man from the curse. Man is reinstated to the position he had when he was created. As faith grows, knowledge of the inheritance comes. Faith comes from the **word** and the word is **Jesus.**

Scriptures: John 3:16, Acts 16:30-31, Romans 10:17, Galatians 3:13-14.

Prayer: Father, I thank you for Jesus who has made me righteous. I am a child of the King! Praise the Lord! I have inherited everything I need. I have an abundance of health, wealth and happiness! I cannot thank you or praise you enough!

September 17

Never be afraid of anything! You must always fight the temptation to doubt or fear. **I** have taken care of your redemption----physically, mentally, emotionally and spiritually. **I** can be trusted for **I** am faithful. When you have thoughts of doubt, recognize the author of them. Do not entertain these thoughts, but answer them with **my word.** Learning the **word** is essential, if you are to have a ready answer on your lips. *Satan* can only tempt you; he cannot make you act. **I** have always made a way out of the temptation, a way of escape. *Satan* cannot win against the power of **my word**, said in faith.

Renew your mind with the *washing of the water by the word.* This is a command! There is no compromise with a **word**-filled mind. It is impregnable to the darts of doubt and fear. When you can release your will to mine, then the fear goes. Trust me always to bring you glory as **my word** is active in your life. **My** glory will **I** bring you.

Scriptures: Deuteronomy 7:9, Psalm 118:6, I Corinthians 10:13, Ephesians 5:26.

Prayer: Father, you are so wonderful, and your word in full of so much wisdom. I praise you, Lord. As I fill my mind with your word, doubts and fears leave, just as you have said. Help me to stay full of your word so that I give no place to the devil.

September 18

I have given **my** disciples the opportunity to come before the throne of grace to receive mercy and to have their petitions granted. They have the opportunity to receive joy, strength and peace from **me**. However, they often worship **me** with their lips, but not with their hearts. Many are so self-centered that they refuse (yes, refuse!) to come before the throne to let **me** be the center of their attention, instead of themselves. **I** made man to yield his will to **mine,** to yield his love and adoration, so that he would be complete. The old rebellious nature hinders him, although **I** paid the price to kill it.

Worship is an act of the will. "Whosoever will" may enter into **my** presence, clothed with the garment of righteousness. Thus clothed, he may be filled with **my** glory. Choose to enter in. **I** command it!

Scriptures: Psalm 29:2, Matthew 22:37, Mark 7:6, Hebrews 4:16.

Prayer: Oh Lord, I do not ever want to be guilty of saying things to you, or about you, that I do not mean with my whole heart! I want your love above everything else, and I think you feel the same about me. I choose to be completely filled with you.

September 19

Sin shall not have dominion over you. This is **my word**, and its veracity is undisputed among believers. How, then, do **my** children still yield themselves to **Satan's** lusts and deceptions? Ignorance! Ignorance of my word. Ignorance does not indicate that a believer has never heard the truth. Ignorance occurs when you do not know how to accept and act on the truth. *Be ye doers of the word, and not hearers only.* You have the power to train your mind to receive and act on **my word**. If you *will* to do **my** will, your spirit can be developed to take control over *evil*.

Scriptures: Romans 5:20, Romans 6:14, I Corinthians 10:1-6, James 1:22.

Prayer: Father, it is easy to get so excited about your word that I fail to do it. I do not want to be a "fat cat" who sits around feeding on your truths, but never acting. Help me, Lord, to act!

September 20

My grace is sufficient for thee. **I** have given you the means of overcoming. You must learn to use it. Many are living lives of despair and pain. **My** disciples must teach and love those in pain. Before you teach, however, you must do your homework. You must learn how to use authority and power. Unless the heart of the teacher is prepared, no lasting results will occur in the spiritual realm. Heart knowledge will always sustain you when harassments, afflictions, trials and temptations come.

These harassments can be removed with the *sword of the Spirit,* **my word.** The preparation in **my** word must be thorough. Use your time wisely, *redeeming the time, for the days are evil.* A prepared warrior and a prepared army will always win the fight of faith. Be prepared and pray that others will likewise be.

Scriptures: Proverbs 18:15, II Corinthians 12:9, Ephesians 5:16, Ephesians 6:16, II Timothy 2;15.

Prayer: Father, I want to be a help to others. Help me to prepare myself and to listen to the Holy Spirit for my marching orders. I realize that by myself, I can do nothing. Thank you for the Holy Spirit, who is my Counselor and Guide.

September 21

Ye have not because ye ask not. . . . , or because ye ask amiss. **My** people need to know **my word** to have an effective prayer life. Often **my** mercy has overcome a request made in ignorance, but **I** desire a knowledgeable people. It is necessary that **my** people prepare themselves for warfare. They have battles to do in the heavenlies in order to establish the conditions for **my** return.

I am directing, through **my Spirit**, the necessary groundwork, and **I** am leading disciples into specific areas of combat. **My** body will prevail over the enemy and will come into the mature person **I** said it would be. As committed people take up the standard and desire **my** will in their lives, the universe will be shaken with the heavenly battles being won in **my** name.

September 22

Scriptures: Lamentations 3:22-23, Matthew 16:18, James 4:3, I John 4:4.

Prayer: Father, I thank you for teaching me to pray your word. I do not have to worry about praying amiss, if I stay in the word and pray what it says. I do not have to wonder what your will is, either. You have told me in the Bible. Thank you, Lord, for the church, your body. I have come to see how much we need one another.

September 22

The greatest growth in your spiritual life often comes when there is no evidence of progress. The quiet times of meditation and prayer are the really productive times, although no fruit is evident. Preparation spiritually is always necessary for future use. No lasting progress will be made without this preparation. The world recognizes activity and visual clues to indicate progress. The spiritual realm, however, operates differently. Feverish activity usually means a draining of energy spiritually and must cease before spiritual progress can proceed.

Rejoice in these quiet times. Open up and allow **my Spirit** to minister to your every need. Count your blessings; thank and praise **me** for them. See your joy rise to new levels.

I do not place unnecessary or heavy burdens on my children. The burdens come from the *enemy*---- and you do not have to accept them. Trust in me and see that all is well. Know that **I** hear your petitions, and believe that **I** answer your prayers. As you do this, you will see your spirit being freed to rejoice and joy in **me**. I have provided a way of escape.

Scriptures: I Chronicles 29:11-13, Psalm 46:10, Matthew 11:30, John 8:36, I John 5:15.

Prayer: Father, I am at that time where no progress is evident in my spiritual life. I know I need to be patient and rest in you. I choose to relax and just enjoy you. Thank you for my blessings.

September 23

When the testing of your faith comes and you are tempted, you must have a knowledge of **my word** to sustain you. Furthermore, you must be determined to use it! The **Holy Spirit** must be given free reign in your life to hold you in readiness.

Many people learn scriptures, but neglect the other conditions. Many others seem determined, but have no weapons with which to fight. And again, those without the **Holy Spirit** are unready and without power to do effective combat. The weapons are not carnal, but spiritual. Only on a spiritual plane can the battles be fought.

Many attempt to fight on the carnal level, but ultimate defeat is inevitable. *Satan* is the god of this world, the carnal world; *he* rules the old man! The new man----the man freed by me----does not have to

September 24

submit to him, nor does he have to use carnal weapons. There is much to learn about spiritual warfare. Be a ready hearer, an eager doer of **my word**. You will then see the **Holy Spirit** lead you in the victories you desire.

Scriptures: John 8:31, John 18:36, Acts 1:8, James 1:2, James 4:7.

Prayer: Father, I thank you so much for your word. There are so many temptation in the world. Without your word, I would be completely helpless. And thank you for the weapons of warfare you have given. Because of Jesus, I can be more than a conqueror. I praise your name, Lord.

September 24

Always take time to renew your spirit, to *wash your mind,* to build yourself up in faith. You would not neglect your hair, your teeth, your family! Do not neglect **me** and the **Holy Spirit,** who dwell so richly within you. **I** have given you a heritage, a covenant, of priceless value. It, too, cannot be neglected----if you want the full benefits of its power. Do not neglect the meditation of **my word**; allow its revelation to become life to you. **I** paid so dearly to provide the word for you. Do not take it lightly nor neglect it.

Do not neglect your prayer life. Commit yourself to intercession and prayer. Pray for yourself, your family, the *body of Christ* and your country. In all these things, remember **my** promises and pray accordingly. Bombard the heavenlies with the power of prayer, and see the angels busy to carry out the commands brought by prayer. Use your authority over *Satanic* forces, wherever you find them. Learn of your authority as a believer and grow adept at warfare. Use the weapons **I** have given, with skill and cunning. Go forth boldly, and unafraid. The *God of Glory* goes, too!

Scriptures: Joshua 1:9, Luke 18:1, I Timothy 2:1, Hebrews 1:13-14, Hebrews 10:16.

Prayer: Father, I know you are grieved when I neglect you. I never want to cause you grief, so help me keep my priorities straight. Thank you for your angels who minister for us, and for your provision for our victory. I love and bless your name.

September 25

Above all, take the shield of faith to quench all the fiery darts of the wicked. This shield is impenetrable when used according to **my word** and will. The shield will protect you absolutely as you use it in power and might. **I** have given this shield to overcome the darts of doubt, despair and darkness that come against the mind which are manifested in the body. When the darts are extinguished as planned, there is no entry with which to concern yourself. The faith of others may not be strong. Cover them, also, with your faith, until their faith is matured. There is nothing to limit the size of your shield of faith. It will grow and expand as much as you allow the **word** to enter and remain in your heart.

Purpose always to expand your faith. Put your ears in places to listen. Open the windows of your heart to receive and retain **my word**. Be determined to have **my word** indelibly imprinted on the tables of your heart. Faith will never fail you even as love never fails you. And **I** never fail you; **I** am love.

Scriptures: Psalm 11:1, Romans 10:17, Galatians 6:2, Ephesians 6:16, I John 4:16.

Prayer: Lord, attacks on my mind cause me more trouble than anything else. I thank you that my shield of faith protects me from all these fiery darts. I want to keep my faith growing so that my shield will grow larger and larger. I am so grateful for your love.

September 26

Trust me to bring order out of chaos, to bring peace out of fear, to bring love out of strife. **I** am the only one who can do it anyway, and without faith being applied, there is no peace. When you see situations arising that might produce division, bring them before the throne. When you see personalities bent on being obstinate and unyielding, bring them before the throne. When you see hate filling the air and impossible situations developing, bring them to the throne of grace.

You must come, however, believing that **I** can and will change things. Do not just come with distress in your heart and unbelief filling your mind. Come as a child who knows that his **father** will fix it! Else why bother to tell **me** at all? So often, **I** only hear unbelief. **I** operate on faith and faith always moves **me**. The joy of an intercessor is to bring cares, situations, problems to **me** in faith, knowing that to do so is to find an answer. Pray always in faith----believing that **I** not only have the power to change situations, but that **I** will! It is declared in **my word** that it is **my** will.

Scriptures: Mark 9:23, Mark 10:15, Romans 4:17, Hebrews 4:16, James 5:16.

Prayer: Father, I trust you for all things. I used to believe you could change things. Now I believe that you can and you <u>will</u> change things. I give you praise and glory forevermore.

September 27

If the salt loses its saltiness...? **My** people are the salt and they are responsible for sharing the gospel. Too often, the gospel has been corrupted by the traditions of men. The gospel has been a yoke of oppression and bondage instead of the way to freedom. Guard yourself from the traditions and bondages of religion.

September 27

Act in accordance with the truth and leading of the **Holy Spirit.** There is no reason to fear being lead astray as your heart desires **me**, as you feed upon **my word,** and as you continually humble yourself before **me.** A heart cannot be deceived, unless it is drawn away of its own lusts and enticed. Guard your heart and trust **me** to lead you in the straight paths.

The gospel is the key to freedom for a dying and suffering world. It should be a joy to share **me**, and not a burden. If it becomes a burden, check out the yoke. Is it my yoke or one of bondage? I am a creative **God.**

Trust **me** to lead you in creative, spontaneous, joyful ways. I love you, and I would <u>not</u> put a yoke of bondage upon you. I came to set you free. I did not come to condemn you.

Scriptures: Matthew 5:13, Matthew 11:29, John 3:17, John 8:32, Colossians 2:8, James 1:14.

Prayer: Father, there are so many "traditions of men" in the world. Until I began to spend time in your word, I did not realize this. These traditions turn your simple ways into complicated ones.

I ask that you open the eyes of your children, everywhere, and to help us all to be receptive to your truth. Thank you for loving us.

September 28

Be bold when you come before the throne of grace. Boldly ask for mercy and boldly expect your prayers to be answered. This boldness is not one of haughtiness or pride, but one of sonship, of belonging. Because **I** have given you the place of being a joint-heir with **my son, Jesus,** you need no longer be timid and afraid. Boldly declare **my word** in the land. Boldly rebuke *Satan* and nullify his works in my people. This is the boldness of one who knows his authority and power in the kingdom.

Can you perceive of a timid general amassing armies against his enemies? Was David timid before the giant? Did Moses go timidly and cowardly before Pharaoh? How about Joshua and Caleb? Think on these mighty men of valor, when you act in a situation for the kingdom. These men had boldness, but with the reverence and fear of **me** that comes from loving their **Creator.** A haughty and prideful attitude they did not have, but one of obedience and bravery as they met the *enemy* head on. Come boldly as you realize what a mighty kingdom you represent. This is an injunction to you! Follow it!

Scriptures: Proverbs 16:18, 28:1; Romans 8:16-17; Hebrews 4:16.

Prayer: Father, I thank you that I belong to you---that I am a part of the family of God. I need help to be bolder. I am beginning really to know who I am in Christ, and I can feel boldness rising up within me. I desire your help to declare your word whenever or wherever. I believe I receive it, and I thank you for it.

September 29

I have blessed you with the abundance of Heaven and earth. Receive it! This abundance of health, prosperity, and salvation was redeemed and bought back for you through the *Son of man.* The realization of this abundance must come through spiritual revelation; otherwise it would be misused and abused. I provided it for the children who called on the name of **Jesus** to be *Lord.* I gave it to all who would believe.

The abuse and misuse have come through *Satanic* action, but he cannot act in a heart that is full of **Jesus.** *Satan* has no ingress into a life that has the love of **Christ** emanating from it. *Satan* would like to steal this abundance to corrupt and enslave men. He has used the counterfeits of deceitful riches, corrupting power, and covetness to deceive men into thinking they are being blessed. The true abundance of life, however, *he* cannot give.

I give good things, with no sorrow added. Believe in **my word.** Receive the real abundance of life. *I am come that they might have life, and that . . . . more abundantly.* It is yours.

Scriptures: Matthew 28:18, Mark 4:19, Luke 2:32, Luke 19:17-19, John 10:10, James 1:17.

Prayer: My lord and My God, I receive the abundant life you offer. Help me to show it to others. Praise your name, Lord.

September 30

Your faith must be built-up at all times so that you are ready to receive, give, or act in faith. If you are to operate effectively in **my** kingdom, you must not allow neglect of **my word,** prayer or meditation in **my word** to hinder your faith. I have given the seed of faith. You must see that it is watered, cultivated and allowed to bear fruit.

Faith is the believing of **me, my word, my** character, **my** promises. Faith moves circumstances in ways the natural mind cannot comprehend. Faith pleases me, because it is the normal operation of the spiritual realm, just as speech is the natural operation of the physical realm. The difference is:

> We declare in the natural realm what we see or think is already a fact. In the spiritual realm, we declare what we want to be, before it is a fact.

In **my** word, I have declared many things to be facts that have not come to pass. They will come to pass! I have purposed them. Who shall disannul them? You

September 30

must learn to operate more and more in the faith realm. You must speak words of faith in confidence, words that line up with **my** will and purpose. Then expect your words to come to pass. This is walking in faith. Walk ye in it!

Scriptures: Isaiah 55:11, Luke 17:6, Romans 12:3, II Corinthians 4:13, Hebrews 11:6.

Prayer: Father, as I spend more time with you, the natural world grows dimmer, and the spiritual become more real. I praise you for your promises, and for the fact that they are mine! Glory to God!

OCTOBER

October 1

Fear not, only believe. I have granted the petitions you have asked, but do not weaken in faith. You must not let fear or doubt rob you of what you believed you received. Many ask in faith, but when a circumstance proves contrary, they lose confidence in me. Confidence comes from being steadfast in the **word.** It comes by digging into your innermost being and believing, even though you have no natural evidence to confirm your desires.

Confidence comes from an assurance of **my** love and character. If you remain steadfast and established on **my word,** you will always see the results you have asked. Refuse to doubt. You have the ability through the **Holy Spirit** to do so. It is not will-power, but trust, that can muster up this confidence in me.

You must also endeavor to keep your faith-level high. That comes from spending time with **me** and in **my word.** I do not fail. I cannot fail! I always react to immovable, steadfast, faith. Seek **me** with all your heart, and you will see this faith produced in your life. It costs to do so, but the rewards are so great! Trust **me.** I am faithful.

Scriptures: Mark 11:23, Luke 8:50, I Corinthians 15:58, I Peter 5:9.

Prayer: Father, when I spend time meditating on

your word, strong faith rises up within me. I feel that I can overcome anything Satan throws at me. I know what to do to keep my faith level high. Help me to remember this if I tend to "faint". Help not only me, but your other children, to realize what a great God you are.

October 2

Waiting is often the most difficult part of victory, but it is necessary. Patience is a fruit of the spirit. Let *patience have her perfect work, that you may be perfect and entire, wanting nothing.* Think of **my** patience. I am waiting on you, the body, to come into the fullness of maturity. Many are approaching maturity, but many still need to come.

When circumstances seem slow, continue to pray and praise. Many heavenly battles are being fought. The prayers of the saints are necessary to bring down powers, rulers and principalities that would stand against the kingdom of **God.** Be not weary in prayer. Be not weary in patience. The rewards will come to the faithful, persistent warrior. . . . . *Doing all to stand, stand therefore.* Do not stand idle! Stand in faith. Pray **my word;** pray in the Spirit. Intercede fervently. Your prayers "availeth" much! Pray on the behalf of all saints, everywhere. **I** will lead you in prayer. **I** will show you for whom you should pray. Patience is a virtue. Do not be weary in patience. It will serve you well.

October 3

Scriptures: Psalm 33:20, Isaiah 40:31, Galatians 6:9, Ephesians 6:13, Ephesians 6:18, James 1:4, Jude 1:20.

Prayer: Father, I know that patience is not one of my strong points. I also know that with your help I can become one of the most patient of your children. Thank you for the lessons you are giving me. I will continue to praise you.

October 3

The faithfulness of **my** people will always be in direct proportion to their determination to follow me and their knowledge of **my word.** Faithfulness cannot be developed by will-power, nor can it be developed just by knowledge alone. Faithfulness is developed by the combination of dedication and word-power. These enable a man to be faithful to me. Without the **word**, you do not know your place or power. Without a decision to grow, you are tossed to and fro and nothing gets accomplished.

Be ready to be faithful. Be prepared and disciplined. These are reachable goals for you. These are attainments that are in **my** will and are blessings to all who come after them. Desire faithfulness because the action brings blessings. The closer you come to **me**, the closer will **I** come to you. **My Glory** will become more evident in your life. Choose the good life. **I** have given it already in abundance. Receive it, thou good and faithful servant.

October 4

Scriptures: Deuteronomy 30:19, Psalm 119:11, Psalm 119:89, Matthew 24:45-47, Matthew 25:21, I Peter 2:9-10.

Prayer: Father, I want to be your faithful child, and I choose to grow. I thank you that you direct my paths. To you be glory forevermore.

October 4

You do have faith in abundance, so apply it. Let your mind relax and your spirit take control. If you will but loose those natural thoughts to **me**, then I will fill your mind with **my** thoughts. **I** give thoughts of victory, of success in **my** kingdom, of domination over the harassments of *Satan*. He would have you think, "There is no way out!" But that is contrary to **my word**.

My word renews and refreshes the mind and spirit. **It** gives the mind positive thoughts, thoughts of victory, thoughts of overcoming power. **I** have said that my thoughts are higher than your thoughts; so start thinking my thoughts. You have them clearly stated in **my word**.

Choose to learn **my word**, think **my word**, say **my word**. Then see your life changed. There is no limit with **me**. As you think, say and act on **my word**, there will be no limit with you, either. You are bound by your will. Come into conformity with **my** will, and see sickness flee, poverty dissolve and despair cast away. **I** am *the way* to earthly success, emotional stability and spiritual maturity. These are yours for the taking. Choose to act wisely.

Scriptures: Joshua 1:8, Isaiah 26:3-4, Isaiah 55:9, II Corinthians 4:13, II Timothy 1:7.

Prayer: Lord, I thank you for your word. It gives me the confidence I need to live a victorious life. Help me to think your thoughts always. I love you.

October 5

Rest in **my** presence. This rest renews the spirit and refreshes the soul. It gives new vigor to the body; it fills a void that cannot be touched by any other source. As you come into my rest, remember my blessings and give praise to **me.** I have blessed you and it is good that you remember. **I** long to have fellowship with **my** creation---that is the purpose for which you were formed---and you need **me** to have the fullness of life.

Sacrifice to **me,** and see the rewards come in abundance. This time of refreshing is a blessing to us both. You have many things that would call your attention away from this time of refreshing, but if you will purpose to let nothing hinder your coming into rest, you will see all things come into order. Believe they will, and they will.

I hold this time to be needful. How could you not think the same? Look forward to it, as you would a good night's sleep or a cleansing bath. **My rest is even more essential than these.** Be warmed by **my** presence, filled with joy and blessed with **my** comfort. **I** have given these things freely so that you may be complete. Receive them.

Scriptures: Deuteronomy 28:2, Matthew 11:28, Romans 8:32, Hebrews 13:15.

Prayer: Father, I need rest in your presence. Sometimes my life gets so complicated. Without your rest, I would not have the strength to continue. Thank you for this refreshing rest.

October 6

The goodness and mercy of **God** cannot be measured. But through the mind of **Christ** the human spirit begins to comprehend what is unfathomable to the carnal mind. As your spirit comprehends this, you begin to love your neighbor as yourself. Carnal man cannot love his neighbor in this way. You begin to have compassionate thoughts for your neighbor. Carnal man may feel empathy for his neighbor; but to love your neighbor truly requires the agape love that comes from walking with **me**. **I** require you to walk in love.

Walking in love may be the most difficult walk there is, because it involves relationships outside of selfishness. This walk may involve others, who may not know what you know, and who may not respond

October 6

as a Christian. Other temptations, other trials are more clearly defined. The *enemy* is recognizable as *Satan* as *he* deals in sickness, lack, fear, and depression. To walk in love means to be forgiving when you are rejected----not to "lash back". You know you are walking in strength, but the world thinks you are weak.

The world looks on; these trials are not a personal, intimate fight. You are open to public view and, therefore, must use more spiritual insight. To walk in love is to expose yourself to ridicule, rejections, humiliation, and perhaps even violence; it will not be understood by the world.

My spiritual ones know the cost and sacrifice to you, however. You will have those spiritual ones cheering for you, even though you may not see them. They will be encouraged; **I**, too, will give you strength to be victorious in it all.

The rewards will be worth whatever pain it may cost. Do not fear the love walk. Do not fear the world's disdain or scoffing. Know that to please me is the only important task you have. Love **me** that much! *To whom much is given, much is required.*

Scriptures: Psalm 86:15, Luke 6:37, Luke 10:27, I Co-rinthians 2:16, Ephesians 5:2.

Prayer: Father, I thank you for teaching me to walk in love. When I keep my mind on you, it is easy. When I am not spending enough time with you, it is difficult. Thank you for helping me to love.

October 7

The **words** that **I** have spoken are as sure as the sun that rises, as the air you breathe, as the water you drink----and just as essential to life. I refer to the spirit life, your life with me. Unregenerate man only has life because of these **words**, for it is only my mercy that allows him to exist at all. Do not judge him too harshly, because you were once as blind as he.

Endeavor with all your strength to walk more in accord with my **word**. **Make** receiving life and my **word** your priority, your life's goal and desire. I paid <u>all</u> to give spiritual life unto you. You must receive it at all cost----it is the *pearl* of great price. If your heart's desire is to receive life, you will have victory in your flesh and over your flesh.

Scriptures: Proverbs 4:10-11, Matthew 13:45-46, John 6:63.

Prayer: Lord, I know that walking according to your word is the only thing that brings true happiness. Give me strength and more determination to follow you, no matter what the cost may seem to be. You are my heart's desire, and I praise you.

October 8

Watch **my word** comes to pass, just as **I** declared it long ago. Observe **my words** bearing fruit as **my words** are heeded and believed. See the glory of the **Lord** manifested in the lives of those who truly love **me**. I am the **Lord God** and I change not. Just as **I** was in the days of Abraham, so **I** am now. *I am the same yesterday, today and forever.* Therefore, trust **me!** Believe always in **my** might and power. See the results of unswerving faith.

As you dare to believe, be prepared to receive. **I** am ready to deliver that which has been promised. The faith that must be used to bring **my** glory to the earth must be steadfast and unshakable. This is the faith that comes from abiding in **me.** I said that *if you abide in **me**, and **my words** abide in you, you can ask whatever you will and it shall be given you.* Watch **me** fulfill those **words.** Watch **me!**

Scriptures: Jeremiah 22:29, Malachi 3:6, Mark 5:36, Hebrews 13:8, I Peter 1:25.

Prayer: Father, when I believe on your word and see it come to pass, my faith grows by leaps and bounds. How could I ever fail to trust you? You are truly a wonder, and I love you.

October 9

Watch **me** work! See **my** miracle-working power come into operation and see **my word** fulfilled on the earth. Rejoice in the acts of your **God.** Know you are a part of this kingdom, connected to the

October 10

mightiest force in the universe. The requests you have made have been heard. Your prayers are being answered. If you ask according to **my** will, **I** always answer those petitions.

Faith changes things. Is anything too mighty for **me**? Have faith that **I** will, and **I** will! The world cannot see or understand this power, but that does not matter. **I** *have purposed, and who shall turn it back?* Be exceedingly glad and continue to trust **me**. You choose to do so, and you will!

Scriptures: Isaiah 14:24, Luke 10:23, Luke 17:21, Hebrews 11:1, I John 5:14-15.

Prayer: Lord, I choose always to trust you and to do it with a heart filled with joy and praise. I want the world to see what a miracle working God you are! Walking in faith is the most exciting way to live, and I thank you for leading me into faith.

October 10

Never doubt **my** love, **my** leading, **my** power, **my** authority. This is a choice you make. Get yourself always into the position to receive. This is done by abiding in me. To abide with **me** is to spend time with **me**. Then you know when you hear **my** voice, because you know me! You cannot live with someone without knowing him, unless you do not communicate or unless you ignore one another.

Abiding means to live with **me**, taking time tobe

with **me**. I will reveal **myself** more and more to you, as much as you will allow. Choose to trust **me** and believe that all is well. I would not deceive you, and I cannot fail. The times of testing will prove this, so rejoice when they come. Victory comes with them. This is the opportunity to win the contest, and victory is so sweet! I have given the land, my kingdom, so take it! As you do, you will lead many into new areas of victory that were heretofore closed to them. Go forward unafraid, knowing that all is well.

Scriptures: Joshua 1:9, Joshua 14:9, John 10:27, John 15:4.

Prayer: Father God, thank you for loving me and leading me. Because I can trust you, I know that all is well. Fear is the opposite of faith, and I choose not to fear. Thank you for the victory I have in Jesus.

October 11
    Come singing into my gates because the **Lord Jesus** reigns. There is cause to rejoice, because **His** kingdom is being established on the earth by the children of men! For too long, the god of this world, Satan, has dominated politics, societies and nations. It is time for the redeemed to take hold and to take responsibility.
    Your weapons are not carnal, however. If you live by the sword, you shall die by the sword. If you live in the **Spirit**, you will overcome all things. You

will reign in this world by overpowering *Satan's* world.

My son is coming for a bride that is without spot or wrinkle. This is a people who are holy, and who love **me**. Rejoice as you see the kingdom of **God** manifesting itself in your midst. Look for signs of it---they are bountiful! Use your weapons to bring my will into the earth.

This is an exciting time and you are part of the victorious army. Let this thought mature in your mind and you will see mighty fruits manifested. Sing songs of gladness and praise. Let your lips tell of the greatness of **God**, the **Holy One of Israel**, and of **my son** who is now **King of Kings**.

Scriptures: II Samuel 7:16, Psalm 97:1, 100:2, 115:16, Isaiah 35:10, Ephesians 5:27.

Prayer: I rejoice in you, Father. My God reigns! Praise your name. I am so excited because the New Jerusalem is surely coming. I ask you to open doors for me to share Jesus with those who do not know him.

October 12

Be quick to grasp spiritual truths, and you will see the fruitful results, shortly. The **Holy Spirit** is eager to show you insight into **the word**, to reveal **his** plans to you. **He** has a purpose in the earth----to comfort, guide and convict. Be ready to yield to **his** leading and you will be amazed at how rapidly you will learn. Choose not to grieve **him**, and he will teach you the truths of the kingdom. Listen closely for **his** promptings. Decide to open your will to **his** direction. Then you will quickly perceive spiritual insight directing your life. The **Holy Spirit** always confirms the **word**, magnifies me and exalts **Jesus** as the **Messiah.** If ever you have doubts, ask **him** to identify **himself. He** will!

Learn to trust the leading of the **Holy Spirit**. Learn to rely on **his** information and promptings. **He** will show you paths that you would never have noticed. **He** will lead you quickly into the *Holy of Holies.* **He** will bring you before the *Throne of Grace.* **He** is your personal escort, teacher, counselor, and friend. He is provided to all who accept **Jesus**, and he is a priceless treasure.

Scriptures: John 16:7-15, Ephesians 4:30.

Prayer: Father, thank you for your Holy Spirit who leads and guides me. I want him to have free reign in my life. I thank you that I am now aware of how important he is to me. For many years, I didn't really know who he was or what he did, so I did not give him credit for working daily in my life. He truly is a priceless treasure.

October 13

When you go, the **Holy Spirit** goes with you to

October 13

prepare the way. Trust him to prepare hearts ahead of time. Be diligent to pray for those to whom **I** would have you speak. A man cannot receive me unless his heart is open. Prayer can soften the hardest of hearts. Be sensitive to **my** leading and let your heart be open to suggestions for prayer.

There are so many in bondage who need to be set free. **I** am sending out faithful ones to set them free. **I** have an army, fully equipped to defeat the enemy. It is marshalling forces against *him* and taking ground daily. As you daily yield yourself to me and daily take up your cross, you are doing your part. Determine to go only where **I** lead----not where guilt, tradition or man leads. As you walk more with me, you will learn to easily hear the promptings of the **Holy Spirit** to receive my guidance and directions.

Stay instant in season. Be prepared to do battle at all times. Pray for others and be open to my leading. You will see great miracles wrought by a caring, loving *body*. **My** *body* is led by the **King of Kings** who cared so much that he gave himself for all men. **He** cared enough to obey. Do ye likewise.

Scriptures: Mark 10:21, Galatians 4:3, II Timothy 4:2, Titus 2:13-15.

Prayer: Father you have laid on my heart friends and acquaintances who do not know you. Holy Spirit, I ask you to prepare their hearts, and I wait for your guidance. If I tried to witness on my own, I would only mess things up. How I praise you, and thank you, for Jesus.

October 14

The words you speak in faith are full of power and might. Always determine that they line up with **my words**, before you speak. Many bring themselves harm because they speak wrong words in faith, causing untold havoc in their lives and in the lives of others. *Out of the abundance of the heart, the mouth speaketh.* Choose wisely what you want in your heart in abundance. Then see to it that it gets there! If you choose wisely, then you will live wisely and in blessings. Every choice you make affects your life----and the lives of those around you. Be at peace in your heart as you trust me to bring forth **my word** in your life. Trust means overlooking circumstances that do not confirm **my word. My word** is reality.

You have chosen the narrow pathway that leads to life and peace. Choose always to stay on it, and you will! **I** decree it for you as your faith in **me** is steadfast. Life with me is worth it all!

Scriptures: Isaiah 26:4, Matthew 7:14, Luke 6:45.

Prayer: Father, thank you for making me aware of how important it is to watch what I say. As I spend more time with you, I find your word rising up within me. I know it is necessary to speak it out. I praise you for bringing your word to pass in my life.

October 15

It is never too late, where **I** am concerned, for **I** am the maker of time. **I** can turn circumstances around in a flash of light, and circumstances that were, no longer are. When you pray, pray for impossible situations. All things are possible with me. Pray for men who are lost, corrupt, and damned----for **I** redeem mankind. Pray for the unknowing, unseeing, and unhearing---for **I** open hearts, eyes and ears. Pray, pray, pray! Through prayer, things are brought into being. Anyone can pray. It takes no special preparation, paraphanelia or place. To pray in **my** will, one must either know **my word** or **pray** under the anointing of the **Holy Spirit**, so as to pray not in vain. **Spirit**-led prayer is always in **my** will, because the **Holy Spirit** always does the will of the Father. To pray effectively in the understanding, much time must be spent in **my word**. I cannot go against **my word**.

A humble heart moves the mercy of **my** love. Pray in faith, in the fear of the **Lord**, and with a heart ready to receive **my** mercy and grace. **I** will not refuse such a prayer. Come into **my** gates with praise and thanksgiving. Enter boldly into the Holy of Holies, ready to receive mercy, love and grace. **I** am your **God** and **I** love you. You must leave **my** presence, ready to love others. That is **my** will for you. The blessings you receive will be without measure.

October 16

Scriptures: Psalm 10:17, Psalm 100:4, John 15:12, I Timothy 6:19, Hebrews 4:16.

Prayer: Father, how I praise and bless your name! You are worthy to be praised. Thank you for loving me. Thank you for your word that tells me all things are possible, if I only believe. I believe, Lord. You are my God, and I love you!

October 16

Trust **me** to lead you in straight paths. The *enemy* is forever lurking to pick off one of the elect, but as long as the armor is intact, nothing can touch you. **My Spirit** is there to lead and guide you, as long as you choose to listen and yield. Yielding requires practice. Your flesh must be trained to yield. Your flesh is not the will in your life; it will do whatever you train it to do. When you *walk in the spirit, you will not fulfill the lusts of the flesh.*

Build up your spirit man, renew your mind and train your flesh. As you do this, you will see the glory of **God** operating in and upon you. The freedom that accompanies the glory is too wonderful to comprehend. This blessing makes you a steadfast, victorious *Christian* who overcomes in every area. Is not my grace too wonderful to behold? **I** have given you the kingdom; the joy that is there for those who receive it is indescribable. Rejoice in and share what you have received. This is the joy of the **Lord.**

October 17

Scriptures: Psalm 23:4, Habbakuk 3:18, Galatians 5:16, Romans 12:2, I Peter 3:13.

Prayer: Father, I thank you that I can rest in peace, knowing that my steps are ordered by you. You are such a good God!

October 17

To love with **my** kind of love is to risk pain, betrayal and rebuke. However, the one who holds you in **his** hand will never let you fall. When you give your will to **me,** you have given **me** the opportunity to let love have her perfect will in your life which is to yield to **my** will. I was rebuked, I was in pain and I was betrayed. I loved anyway! In so doing, I broke the curse of it and gave love back.

Never fear doing it **my** way, for I will never fail and am incapable of failing. When you feel you have to protect yourself from being hurt, you are saying, "I do not trust **you, Lord,** to take care of me." But I have said over and over in **my word** to fear not. You must heed those **words** and let love and trust of **me** take control of the fear. Do you love **me** enough to do this? Do you trust me enough?

I loved **my** disciples enough and believed in their **faith** in **me** to trust them with **my** kingdom, **my** body, **my** church. Are you one of these? If you truly love **me,** obey my commandments. *Love your neighbor as yourself.* Be willing to risk your heart, your safety, and your life to **my** keeping. I never fail, for **I** am love.

Scriptures: Psalm 118:6, Mark 12:30-31, John 3:16, John 14:23, I Corinthians 13:13.

Prayer: Lord, I thank you for all you have done for me----just because you love me! I am overwhelmed. Help me to love as you do.

October 18

There is no pain in any area that you could feel that **I** have not already borne. Give your every need to **me**. It is the only way to overcome. To fail to give **me** your needs, to try to take action on your own, is to invite disaster. **I** am the overcomer! **I** prevail! **I** will lead you always into victory. Your love and forgiveness must not be conditional. If you do otherwise, you will never reach that realm of steadfast love that protects, shields, gives and receives.

There is nothing that can prevent this plateau in your life----unless you refuse to accept **my word**, **my will**, **my** shield and compensation. Always let **my word** reign. Do not listen to your carnal mind. Do not let your fears take control. **I** am **Lord** over all and **master** of all. Trust in **me** and win! Have victory in every area. Refuse to let *Satan* have his way in your life. You choose!

You can choose rightly, for **I** will strengthen you. **I** will give you peace and will work all things to your good. **I** promise not to fail you, because **I** do not fail!

Scriptures: Genesis 15:1, Mark 11:25, I Peter 3:18, I Peter 5:7.

Prayer: Father, I give you all my cares; I promise I will not take them back. You have made the way so simple that even I can understand it. I do not have to live in confusion any longer; I just have to come to you. I choose to trust you and to be obedient to you.

October 19

Let the oil of gladness flow over and through your being. Rejoice always, for this is my will for you. If you truly trust **me,** you will rejoice, for **I** have overcome all things. Joy and gladness are attitudes of the mind, brought about by a spiritual solidity, a trust in me. When you choose to trust in **my** power, **my** ability to act and move, in **my word**, then your spirit becomes established and strong. You must first decide if **I** am worthy to be trusted. You may protest, "Of course you are worthy, Lord." If **I** am, and if you really think so, then you must trust **me.**

The joy and peace, the abundance of life are only possible to a confident believer. There are many factors besides the decision to trust that must be incorporated before the established heart becomes a reality. A knowledge of **my** character and of **my**

word is essential to the established heart. A reverent fear of **me** and a confident hope for the future are essential to the established heart. A willingness to lay aside your desires and fears, to lay aside your aspirations, perhaps your very life for **my** kingdom are inclusive in an established heart. But the established heart will not be moved and will not be afraid!

Scriptures: Psalm 112:8, Isaiah 51:11, Hebrews 1:9, Hebrews 13:9.

Prayer: Father, my heart is established in you. Even when I feel troubled or afraid, I choose to believe your word. Thank you, Lord, for the opportunity to be established on your word.

October 20

I have told you of a truth: that **I** am making you one, that the petitions you have asked for are done, that **my Spirit** is working on your behalf, that you must trust me and not yield to vain imaginations. **My** love is unconditional to a trusting child. Your love must be the same towards **me.** Fear is a powerful force and it tends to allow much *evil* to invade, once it has its way. You can refuse evil. You must allow patience to work. You must love with the **God**-kind of love. You must refuse fear and choose to trust. As you do, you will see **my** perfect work manifested.

October 21

The trials and tests are never over, but neither are the victories. Not until that perfect day of my return. Learn to count it all joy, knowing that experience does indeed bring hope of future conquests over the *enemy*. Battles prepare you for greater use. Every battle that is fought and won, gives greater force to your testimony, which overcomes the *enemy*.

Refuse to fear the battle! Refuse to give in to *Satan's* vile tactics. *He* cannot stay if you steadfastly resist *him*. Meditate on the good news. Build-up your spirit and you will see victory upon victory in your life.

Scriptures: Deuteronomy 31:8, John 16:33, Romans 5:3, Hebrews 10:36.

Prayer: I thank you, Father, for loving me. I thank you for the trials and the tests that have made me "stretch". Now I can go through these tests and trials, knowing that I can win! You are my strength, Lord.

October 21

I have provided you with the opportunity to pray into being the miraculous----in areas of salvation, healing, revelation, love. There are such needs, but **my** body is capable of the task. Remem-ber that old saying, "Many hands make lightwork." As you assist the rest of the body in your calling, it all flows so easily. **My** ultimate will does not rest on you alone, but if you love **me**, you will do **my** will. Others who love **me** are flowing in the stream of **my** will, with you. As a result, many are going to be saved, healed, delivered.

Nations will line up with **my** will. The earth will come into the fullness of my kingdom, with **Jesus** on the throne. The task of each individual believer is training for the eternal kingdom. Not only will you have the joy of serving, you will also have the rewards of serving! Look for opportunities to pray, to serve, to do **my** will on the earth. I have carefully prepared you for your task. You will not fail, as long as you stand on **my word**, believe **my word** and act on **my word.**

Scriptures: Luke 11:2, Romans 8:28, Romans 12:4-9, I Timothy 5:17.

Prayer: Lord God, I thank you for teaching us how to pray. I thank you for your other children. We need one another so very much. Help us all to be diligent to pray and to follow the leading of the Holy Spirit.

October 22

As you are led from victory to victory, you will learn many things of kingdom principals. Trials and temptations are not easy things to endure, but the taste of victory is so sweet. Many extraneous blessings are

October 23

shared as you overcome.

At first, no one enjoys discipline or fiery encounters. As conquests and victory become more a part of your life, however, you will look forward to overcoming the *enemy.* You will look forward to seeing others freed, to seeing your flesh under submission and to having your heart steadfast and sure. Your confidence in these areas will grow and grow, until you are looking for opportunities to share the love and power of **Jesus Christ.**

An unsure heart is hesitant to venture into the unknown. Make your heart sure by meditating on my word, spending time with **me** and purposing in your heart to believe **my word.** The kingdom life is sweet and rewarding. You will not have the empty success of the carnal life. You will have a rich, satisfying life- ---with the **Father**, through the Son, and with the leading of the **Holy Spirit.**

Scriptures: Psalm 77:12, I Corinthians 15:57, I John 4:4-6.

Prayer: Father, my heart overflows with praise for your wisdom. I welcome your discipline so that I may grow more in the warmth of your love.

October 23

Put on the garment of praise for the spirit of heaviness. Then watch your spirit soar. You cannotbe

October 23

in my presence without feeling the lift of **my** love and power. The spirit of heaviness should never be allowed to remain, once you realize that it has come upon you. **I** have given you authority in the earth. Speak to the oppression, speak to the lack, speak to the pain, speak to the jealousy, speak to the evil thing---and watch it go! Then turn and praise me for the results.

Believe, then, that all is well. Heaviness comes as a result of fear, a lack of trust in **me**. Recall **my words,** *Fear not, only believe.* Bring words of comfort, words of power, words of wisdom from your heart----**My words.** Then watch the *enemy* flee. *He* is no match for a **word**-filled *heart*, for a believer who is determined to stand and withstand him. He only pursues those who run from *him*, like a predator after his prey. But those who withstand *him* on the power and authority of **my word**, they will not be touched! **I** said to rejoice that the demons would flee from you. Rejoice more, however, that *your name is written in the Lamb's Book of Life.* Rejoice!

Scriptures: Isaiah 61:3, Matthew 21:21, Luke 8:50, Luke 10:20, James 4:7.

Prayer: Father, I am rejoicing that my name is written in heaven. I only have to think or talk about what wonderful things you have done for me to begin to rejoice. I count my blessings, daily. Thank you for teaching me to speak to the mountains in my life. You are so great!

October 24

Trust **me** to provide you with guidance, wisdom, materials, strength and health. **I** am the great provider, and **I** keep **my** covenant. **I** have never failed to uphold **my** bargains with those who were faithful, who trusted **me** and acted on **my word.** You are in a wonderful position. All you have to do is believe!

Satan will try to steal the **word** from your heart, but *he* cannot if you do not let *him.* Always remember this: *Satan* is unable to overcome **my word**, and *he* has no defense against the sword of the **Spirit. Jesus** has defeated *him* and it is an accomplished fact! *Satan's* acts of terrorism are ineffective on a covenant man. If your armor is in place, there is nothing he can do to you. Choose to allow the **Holy Spirit** to develop your battle plan. **He** will lead you into areas where success is already given, when you listen and obey **his** strategies.

Remember Jericho! Those men had to do nothing but obey the **word** of the **Lord.** Listening ears and an obedient heart will enable you to win every time. Choose to listen to and obey the **Holy Spirit;** that is what **I** sent him for.

Scriptures: Deuteronomy 28:1-13, Joshua 6:2-5, John 16:13, Ephesians 6:17, Philippians 4:19.

Prayer: I could not live without trusting you, Father. You are Jehovah Jireh, my provider. Your word is forever true; it never fails! I want to be obedient; help me always to hear your voice.

October 25

The *enemy* would have you to believe that a failure means all is lost. However, my servants, though they might stumble, get up and fight again---- resolved to keep on until victory is assured. **My** servant David (a man of great faith), had moments of doubt, despair, anxiety and failure. Abraham, too, doubted at times. So did they all! Look at Elijah! he ran from Jezebel in fright. He weakened, but he arose again to do the miraculous! Elijah was strengthened by **my** ministering.

Each victor, when he looked into his heart for strength, relied on his **God** to bring to pass those things that he had believed for. Many times, a stumbling heart makes you realize how really dependent you are on **me, my power** and **my word**. Be always ready to repent, for you are but frail man.

When you are convinced of my might, power and authority, however, you are also a mighty warrior. Forget the failures, and choose to believe. Be strengthened in **my word.** Be strengthened in your heart. Let **my** love and surety of forgiving mercy permeate your being. As **I** have had mercy on you, you also have mercy and forgiveness for those who fail you.

Scriptures: I Kings 19:1-9, Psalm 51:1-2, Proverbs 24:16, I John 1:9.

Prayer: Father, I am so glad you let me see that the men in the Bible were human, too. You have given directions in your word. When I sin, I must repent. Then I am eligible to receive your wonderful mercy and grace. Thank you, Father, for your mercy and forgiveness.

October 26

My glory is shed abroad in your heart by the **Holy Ghost.** This is a spiritual mystery, but it is evident in the physical life. The world sees **my** glory in you. The world is in pain, in lack, desperate for hope and full of doubt. Those who wear **my** glory are confident, full of joy and abundantly supplied. The world can see the difference.

When **my** people who are called by **my** name fail to have **my** glory, it is because they have failed to believe **my word.** The glory is automatic to those who truly walk in the light. Some have more glory than others, and some just manifest the glory at times.

The difference comes from the amount of time that is spent in **my** presence. No one can be in **my** presence and leave without the glory. Remember how Moses looked when he left my presence? Remember when **my** glory filled the temple as Solomon and **my** people worshipped in **Spirit** and truth? When you come into my presence (and the choice is yours), I fill you with **my** glory. *All the earth shall be filled with the glory of the Lord* as **my** children walk closely with the **Creator** of the Universe, in the name of **Jesus**, and in the power of the **Holy Ghost**.

Scriptures: Numbers 14:21, I Kings 8:10-11, Psalm 62:7, John 4:24, John 8:12.

Prayer: Father, I thank you for the glory that is shed abroad by the Holy Spirit. You are worthy of our praise. Thank you for Jesus. Thank you for allowing me to spend time in your presence. I love you!

October 27

If you will put **me** first in your life, you will not have to worry about order in your life. As **my words** fill your heart and mind, the **Holy Spirit** can quicken you to act accordingly and thus bring the best results in the shortest amount of time. **I** created order and look at my universe. The seasons are controlled by order----the migrations of millions of animals and the oceans of the world yield to it. So **my word** in you will bring perfect order to you physically, emotionally and most importantly, spiritually.

Often it is easy to neglect the spiritual life because of the demands of your physical life----work, family, friends. But **I** say that there is no more important time than that spent in prayer, in meditation on **my word**, in reading of **my word**. I am a jealous **God** and **I** must have "first place" in your life. This is not for **my** sake alone, for **I** do desire fellowship with you, but so that you may fulfill these other obligations in power and with joy.

No man is able to walk successfully without **me**. He will stumble and fall. The curse will eventually kill such a man. In accepting **Jesus**, you begin your life of order in me. It changes your life and the lives of all you meet. Seek **me** first!

Scriptures: Deuteronomy 4:23-24, Psalm 19:7-14, Zechariah 4:6, Matthew 6:33, Galatians 3:13-14.

Prayer: Father, thank you that you have put order in my life. I choose to give you first place, Lord, for I have found that unless you are first, nothing else is in order. Help me to keep this foremost in my mind.

October 28

The weapons of your warfare are not carnal, but are mighty through God to the pulling down of strongholds. Make sure your armor is on and ready for battle at all times. The *enemy* is forever waiting to catch you off guard, so that *he* can penetrate and wound you. *His* main weapon is fear, so your shield of faith must always be in place. *He* cannot even get near, with your shield ready to quench all the fiery darts. If your faith should weaken, should a dart or two penetrate, there is no major damage done to a warrior who has his vital areas covered. The helmet of salvation and the breastplate of righteousness are sure safeguards for the heart and brain.

But do not give *Satan* a place! Give *him* no place! *He* should not be allowed to hit you ever. Fear is painful, It hurts. Do not let *Satan* confuse you. Renew your mind so that you think on the **word,** not on *his* lies. Make yourself meditate on the **word**. Drop everything, if you have to, and think on **my word** until it crushes the *lying serpent!* Then the peace that passes understanding comes and envelopes you, giving you rest.

Scriptures: John 14:27, II Corinthians 10:4, Ephesians 6:11-17.

Prayer: Father, thank you for showing me the way to victory in my life. When I have on the full armor of the word, I can resist Satan and he does flee! I want to spend more time in your word, so that I will never be caught off-guard. I praise your Holy name.

October 29

Yes, there is no fear in my perfect love. Coming into this knowledge will free you as nothing else has done. Seek this truth with all your heart. Let it invade every fiber of your being. Meditate on this nugget of truth until every doubt has vanished. Then you will truly see the glory of the **Lord** in great manifestations. Remember, **I am God**. There is nothing impossible to those who believe, and faith cometh! Make sure it comes in your life by choosing to receive it. It, the receiving of faith, is worth every price you might pay. It is the pearl of great price. There is nothing greater than believing **my word**, and in turn, acting on **my word**.

Rejoice in this truth. Let it lay hold on your heart. Do not allow the dark thoughts to rob you of faith. You can recognize dark thoughts, because they torment and give pain. This truth will set you free. Words are inadequate to describe the freedom that comes from believing on **my words**. *If you abide in me, and my words abide in you, you shall ask whatsoever you will, and it shall be given you!*

Scriptures: Hosea 13:4, Mark 11:22, Luke 1:37, John 15:7, I John 4:18.

Prayer: Father, I am so thankful that I do not have to be afraid. Before I knew the truth, I operated in fear. It is a most miserable way to live. I will never go back to that kind of life. Thank you for your word, Lord.

October 30

When the *enemy* comes, rest in **my word**. *He* has no authority to rob, steal from, or destroy a believer who is declaring and believing **my word**. Not only can you rest and rely on **my word**, but you can send him fleeing at **my word**. *Resist the devil and he will flee!* He will not stick around. He will flee!

If you give *him* any ground, if you entertain *his* lying thoughts, *he* will remain to hinder, destroy and torment you.

There are so many who are in torment, pain and distress. They are meant to be free. You are given the weapons to help them to be free. I will send them to you as you are ready. These are precious ones who will in turn learn to make the enemy cower and cringe when *he* sees **my** glory in them.

Scriptures: Joshua 10:8, Joshua 10:25, Luke 10:19, John 8:36, John 10:10, Hebrews 10:23.

Prayer: Father, thank you for teaching me how to recognize my enemy (Satan). For such a long time, I blamed you for his works. Forgive me. Some of your other children need to make this discovery, too. Prepare their hearts, Lord.

October 31

Great is the Lord and greatly to be praised. I am teaching you about worship and praise. Have listening ears and an open heart. The joy that comes from entering into **my** presence is an experience to be desired and coveted. There is a rest in **me** that refreshes, empowers and satisfies. This is the rest that all men seek.

I made my priests of old go through many physical preparations before they could enter into the

October 31

Holy of Holies. So must you also learn to prepare spiritually---- otherwise you will not be able to enter. Spiritual preparation requires desire, submission, gratefulness and an attitude of worship of **me.** As these requirements are met, the entering into **my** presence is fluid and smooth. **Jesus** has made it possible for you to be a priest. Do not neglect the priestly functions. It is essential for spiritual growth and refreshing.

Scriptures: Deuteronomy 4:30, Psalm 48:1, Psalm 100:4, Hebrews 4:11, Revelation 1:6.

Prayer: I desire to be a priest, Lord, so that I may honor you more. Help me to learn better how to praise you and to worship you. I am not sure I know the difference! But this I do know----I love you with all my heart!

NOVEMBER

November 1

Do not limit **my** power, **my** ability, my creativity or my abundance. **I** will do what **I** say. **My** people have a tendency not to expect too much of **me**, for they wish to protect my reputation. They do not want to see **me** fail them. Do you not realize that this hinders **my** performance on the earth? Nothing is impossible with me!

I raise up; I cast down. I am able to do <u>all</u> things. Do not limit **me**! Expect great things. Build up your faith to receive them, and you shall have those things! As your faith rises to meet the challenges of life, so will your maturity. Faith does not come without the **word**. It is the **word** that renews your mind. Look forward-----and be not afraid!

Scriptures: Jeremiah 32:27, Matthew 4:4, Mark 10:27, I Corinthians 4:20, Jude 1:20.

Prayer: Father, I have been guilty of trying to protect your reputation. I am so sorry. Forgive me. I know nothing is impossible with you, and I will not limit you again. I will expect great things and praise your name.

November 2

I have magnified **my word** above **my** name, and there is no higher power! When you choose to

November 2

believe **my word** and act on it, you are invincible to *Satanic* influences, actions and deceits. Be determined to have unquenchable faith----faith that flows like a river from your innermost being. This river will touch others and give them refreshment.

How lovely are the feet of those who bring the good news. Their whole countenance is lovely. You can be a blessing to so many others. Choose to be! As you go, the **word** of faith will shield you. The **word** of truth will defeat the *enemy* before you. The robe of righteousness will clothe and warm you. Look forward to the journeys that I will take you on. My word is the key to spiritual success. It looses---- and binds. It looses my children and binds Satan. Use is as it was meant to be used. I have given it to you, and you can go forth in power and love. Trust me. Enjoy my kingdom. Enjoy my service. Enjoy my sonship. I have given you the land.

Scriptures: Joshua 1:13, Psalm 138:2, Matthew 16:19, Luke 17:5-6, Romans 10:15-17.

Prayer: Lord, I love your word, and I believe it. I want to be a blessing to others by sharing it. Prepare hearts and open doors for me. Help me to speak and act like you.

November 3

Walk in the spirit and you won't fulfill the lust of the flesh. This is true for every facet of your life. The flesh will try to over power the spirit. It does what it has been trained to do, i.e., be ruled by the emotions, its cravings and desires. It wills to gratify itself at all costs.

But remember, flesh is just flesh. It cannot have dominion over you when you yield yourself to the **Holy Spirit's** promptings and direction. Your flesh can be retrained to glorify **God** and to be a blessing to you. You must make your will submit to the **Holy Spirit** within you; then your flesh will submit, too.

This act of determining to follow after the **Spirit** is the first step. The next step is to build your spirit up in the most holy faith, so that you will be strong and courageous. The flesh has no will; thus it will follow after your will and spirit.

Rejoice that you have learned the secret to being victorious. Walking in the spirit means walking in love. And love never fails! Love is absolute trust in the **Father,** the originator and completor of your faith. Oh, rejoice! rejoice! for victory over the flesh, and victory in the world.

Scriptures: I Corinthians 13:8, Galatians 5:16, Galatians 5:25, I John 5:4, Hebrews 12:2.

Prayer: Lord, I rejoice! I rejoice because you have

made a way for me to be victorious. I praise your name.

November 4

Take time to come into **my** presence. You need the refreshing and the rest. You need to abide in me, so that **my** power and glory can flow through you. I want **my Spirit** to influence your life. However, without your willingness to allow **me** in, there is no "flow".

I do not impose **myself** on others and neither should you. My Spirit can work only where there is a desire for **him** to work. This does not mean that you cannot attack *Satan's* strongholds! But you attack in power (and in the **Spirit**), not in the flesh. Where there is a desire to be free (and the **Spirit** knows the heart), the **Holy Spirit** will lead the way. You must let him instruct you----and work through you---to unbind fetters, loose chains of bondage, and release the downtrodden from inequity. It is glorious to live in **my** kingdom. Others will see **my** glory in you and desire it. Be ready to help. This is done by abiding in **me.**

Scriptures: Psalm 91, John 15:4, Romans 8:1-4.

Prayer: Father, I desire always to be led by the Holy Spirit. I choose to abide in you and to let your love flow through me to others. I thank you that I don't have to do things on my own. Without you, I am nothing. I love you, Father.

November 5

I told Joshua to be very courageous, not to tremble or be dismayed. Do you think the desire to "tremble and be dismayed" was in his heart ere I told him? Of course it was! He was a man and used to living by the signs around him. However, he also had faith in the might and power of his **God.** He chose to believe **me** and went on to have victory. He defeated the giants. He had learned to hear **my** voice and to trust **me.** This trusting is a learning process that is initiated by an act of the will.

When the seed of faith is planted in your heart, it must be fed! You feed it on the **word**, and water it with my presence. This takes time spent with **me**, meditation on **my word**, and abiding in me. As you become assured of **my** veracity, then your faith grows. Trust is established. Divine faith must be nurtured. It must be protected from conflicting thoughts.

This is where "choice" begins. Do you choose to believe me, or to believe the signs the **enemy** would bring? Choose to be courageous. Choose to trust in me. Choose to think **my** thoughts, believe **my word** and say **my word**. You will see your faith blossom and grow. Mighty works will I do also through you.

Scriptures: Joshua 1:5-6, Psalm 37:5, John 10:28-29, John 14:12-14.

November 6

Prayer: Father, I thank you that I can be courageous. I choose to listen to you instead of the world----to think your thoughts and to speak them out. You are so wonderful!

November 6

Remember in times of old when **I** delivered **my** children out of the land of the heathen with great and miraculous acts? **I** am still doing that today---in individual lives. **I** did collective miracles for the Jews, but **I** have done individual miracles for the Gentiles.

The times of miraculous works are not over, either for the Jew or Gentile. Faith in **my word** and power is bringing even greater miracles to the forefront. Watch and see what **I** do wherever believers gather in faith to honor **me!** Be aware and enlightened at my mighty works. **I** am the **Lord** and **I** change not. **I** am the same. The miraculous is still happening. More and more you will see visible miracles----even while the less obvious is still being worked.

Expect great things. Let the power of **my word** work in your life, too. It is not just for others! I am the **Lord God**. The power and might of **my** kingdom has been given unto you by my son, Jesus. The body will function and will be the entity that it was created to be!

Scriptures: Leviticus 18:4-5, Malachi 3:6, Matthew

18:19-20, Hebrews 13:8.

Prayer: Father, I thank you that you are a miracle-working God, and that you never change. Thank you for loving me and working miracles in my life. Thank you for your word.

November 7

As you come into **my** presence, let your soul be refreshed. This is a decision you make. As you do, you will feel the cares of this world vanishing. I have given you this time to renew yourself, to be built-up, to be empowered with **my** might and by **my** Spirit. Neglect not so great a salvation!

As you find time to eat, to refresh your body, and to stimulate your mind, thus determine to refresh your spirit. It is imperative that you do so---for victory in your life. I will lead you victoriously in all areas. Give no foothold to Satan; then he will not influence your life. I have given you protection. I have given you weapons, I have given you rest. When all of these gifts are operative, you are victorious! Your protection is the robe of righteousness. Your weapons are the sword of the spirit and the shield of faith. Your rest comes from abiding in me.

Satan is powerless against these. *He* can have no part of your life as long as these are intact. Make sure that all three are used (and done) consistently. I

November 8

have spent a great deal of time in training you, but it will be worth it. You are a mighty warrior for **me**!

Scriptures: Isaiah 61:10, Acts 3:19, I Corinthians 15:57, Ephesians 6:13-17, Hebrews 2:3, James 4:7.

Prayer: Father, I thank you that as I spend time with you, I am refreshed. The cares of the world slip away. You have provided everything I need for an abundant life, and I receive it all! I give no place to Satan, and he has no power over me. How I praise and honor your name.

November 8

My keeping power is real. You are becoming aware of the abundance of my love, grace and peace. Because of **my** mercy, you are able to dwell in love, safety and security. I am creating in you a hunger to share this peace with the world as you see people in frustration, pain and agony. You have had to learn some of the principles the hard way, but the learning must come so that teaching may begin.

All learning does not have to come through experience, although it seems to be the most effective way of learning. Choose to learn by **my Spirit** so that the learning can be anointed----and as painless as possible. Then see who **I** will put before you to share my *good news* of peace and joy.

The inner contentment of abiding in **me** is priceless, and you have found it. Refuse to let anything disrupt it. Then you can stay in **my** presence. **My** glory will then rest on you. The world will see it, and through you, see **me.** This is **my** will for all **my** children. You must lead the way, so that others may follow.

Scriptures: Psalm 3:3, Isaiah 54:10, Lamentations 3:22, II Timothy 2:15.

Prayer: Lord God, I praise your name. To relax in your love is wonderful----the peace that passeth understanding. Prepare me, Lord, so that I can share this with friends who are hurting.

November 9
Be steadfast on **my word** and there will not be an entrance for *demonic* activity. Allow the **Holy Spirit** to rule and reign in your life. You can trust him to lead you aright. Your senses are deceptive, and so are your emotions. **My word** is always true, however, and **I** can be trusted.

Rejoice when temptations come. They are opportunities for victory. The struggles you endure need not be defeats. Determine to win the victories through the love and lordship of **Jesus Christ**. You have all the weapons you need. Just remember that *Satan* is a defeated foe.

Scriptures: Psalm 112:6-10, James 1:2, I Peter 1:22.

November 10

Prayer: Father, I am asking you to help me to be steadfast in all situations. Help me to remember to rejoice when I am tempted and struggling. I know there is victory in Jesus. Thank you for being so patient with me. I love you.

November 10

Come into **my** presence with gladness of heart. The joy of being in **my** presence supersedes all pleasure, when you come in with praise and singing. **I** have made this for you and all men. The joys of being with me are eternal joys; they will never fade! All the earth will someday cease, but joy in **me** will never cease.

Begin preparation for eternity now. Release your joy here and now! Let your heart ring out with joy! The rewards are unmeasurable as you rejoice in life. A merry heart fills many. Choose to be merry. Choose to allow my blessings to flow; allow gladness to permeate others around you. They cannot help but be moved by the joy of the Lord. Be exceedingly glad. **I** have given you the land and all the inhabitants must yield.

Scriptures: Joshua 1:3, Psalm 9:2, Psalm 32:11, Proverbs 15:15, Ephesians 1:3.

Prayer: Father, help me always to be joyful. Your joy is contagious, and I want to spread it around. I believe that I receive your blessings, so how could I have anything but gladness of heart! I sing praises to your name.

November 11

Always remember the grace and mercy I have had toward you. You, in turn, must be merciful. It is so easy to be critical and unyielding. Choose to love, to have compassion and to be truly Christian in word and deed. I didn't look with haughtiness or disdain at the woman at the well. I did not approve of her lifestyle, but neither did I condemn her. I showed her a better way, and so must you.

I have given you peace, joy and a loving family. As you have freely received, freely give. The more you give, the more you will be given. You may give unreservedly and without fear because **my** love and spirit enfold you. Do not fear giving liberally. You cannot outgive me; I will return more than you can imagine. Give with the thought of unlimited supply. I will bless it!

Scriptures: Zechariah 7:9, Matthew 10:8, John 4:7-29, I John 3:18, II John 1:3.

Prayer: Father, I praise your name and thank you for your grace and mercy. I want to have the kind of mercy and compassion you have, Lord. You have given me so much, and in return, I want to give to others. Help me to be more like Jesus. I love you,

Father.

November 12
The joy of the Lord is your strength. Joy only comes to a heart that is carefree; it comes to a heart that trusts in my love. **My** joy is unquenchable and full of glory. It will shine out with radiance. As you exercise your body, also exercise your heart. Have it grow in joy and magnitude. Let nothing hinder your joy in **me.**

You must develop an attitude of trust. Trust is an act of your will, and will produce joy. This strength will lift many out of the mire of despondency and depression. Your strength is needed in the world. Then, in turn, the world will be filled with **my** joy.

Scriptures: Nehemiah 8:10, Psalm 9:10, Isaiah 62:10, Nahum 1:7.

Prayer: Father, thank you for making your directions so easy, that even a child can follow them. I know that rejoicing and trusting in you has turned my life around---no more "pity parties"! You are my strength.

November 13
My ways are higher, and life is more abundant when it is lived in **me.** There is life without **me**----life filled with pain, frustrations and defeat. In life with **me**, there is hope----and an assurance of victory. **I** have given you the land, but it must be taken! It takes

a courageous heart to battle in the spirit, because natural man lives only by his senses. Once the power is tapped in the spiritual realm, however, victory results.

In order to live a victorious life, you must decide to trust **me** for guidance. Man is reluctant to let go of his independence out of fear. He is afraid his desires will be thwarted and that **I** will fail him. This is why the learning of **my** character and limitless love is so essential. When you understand that my love for you is sure, then you will not let fear rob you of victory. You will trust **me** more than you fear!

Perfect love cast out fear. When you love me enough to trust me in all areas, then you will truly walk, act and live in **my** kingdom, as **I** intended from the beginning. You will be in tune with **me**.

Scriptures: Isaiah 55:9, Romans 5:17, I John 4:18.

Prayer: Father, I love you, and I thank you that I do not have to live my life in fear. It is such a blessing to trust you----to know my steps are ordered by you.

November 14

My ways may seem confusing to those who do not know **me**, but **I** will always reveal myself to those whose hearts are open. Having an open heart is an act of your will. It is a decision to seek **me,** to do **my** will, to see my power manifested and to come into **my** presence.

November 15

If you seek **me,** you shall find **me**. Many times in **my** mercy and wisdom **I** have revealed myself to those who were not actively seeking **me**. However, when you seek **me,** I will be found by you. You have my promise, **I** will be found.

Scriptures: Psalm 37:4, Jeremiah 29:13, Matthew 7:7.

Prayer: Father, I seek you. I want to know you more. I love you, and I want to love you more. Help me, Father.

November 15
My purposes in the earth will come to pass. As **I** have decreed it, so will it be! Rest assured in this fact. I am moved by the prayers of saints to do those things which conform to **my word.** I even put the desire in your heart to do my will. There is such mighty power in **my word**----power than has never ceased and will never cease. You must decide to learn **my word**, so that its power will be evident in your life. Words that are spoken in faith bring results. You must always remember where faith originates. *Faith cometh by hearing and hearing by the word of **God**.*

Make it your goal to learn **my word**, speak **my word**, think **my word**. As you do, you will see the results of miraculous power being loosed. *In the beginning was the **word**, and the **word** was **God**.*

November 16

Scriptures: Ezekiel 12:25, John 1:1, Colossians 1:28-29, Romans 10:17.

Prayer: My Father, I praise you and I thank you. You are such a mighty God. I am so thankful that you want only good for me. Help me to learn more of your word.

November 16

Say often to yourself,
"I am full of faith."
"I am victorious."
"I am child of the king,
courageous and unafraid!"
for indeed, you are.

I see you through the eye of faith, and you must do likewise. Learn to see all things through the eye of faith. Then your heart will swell with confidence and love. This love will be shed abroad by the **Holy Ghost,** and will thus touch so many other lives.

Do not allow any doubt or fear to rob you of your faith and victory. *Be strong and courageous. Do not tremble or be afraid.* This is a commandment to you. Obey it!

Scriptures: Joshua 1:7, Romans 5:5, Romans 8:16-17, II Corinthians 5:7, I John 5:4.

Prayer: Lord, help me to see myself though your eyes. You are so merciful and loving. I want to be like you. I will not doubt or fear, because I am a child of the King! Hallelujah!

November 17

Be ready to put off the old man, with all of his hang-ups, his failures, and his curses. That old man is dead, and you must reckon him so. I have given you a new nature and a new spirit. That old nature shall not have dominion over you, if you walk in the **Spirit.**

Your old nature is dead, but the *enemy* would have you believe otherwise. Think of that old nature as a carousel whose power has been eliminated. It will coast round and round for a while, with the appearance of having power, but unless the electricity is turned back on, it will eventually cease turning.

All your old habits, the abominable things in your personality that you detest, you will see less and less of as your spirit waxes stronger and stronger. The new nature, created by **me** and freed by **Jesus**, will begin to govern your mind and body. You will indeed be delivered. You will begin to walk in newness of life that invigorates and brings joy.

Rejoice in your deliverance. As far as is possible, assist the **Holy Spirit** in letting that old nature die gracefully. **Jesus** has done the hard work. You just agree with him, and yield yourself.

Scriptures: Romans 6:4, II Corinthians 5:17, Galatians

5:16, Ephesians 4:22-24.

Prayer: Father, I thank you that I do not have to be controlled by my carnal nature. I can see the Holy Spirit changing my life, my thoughts and desires. I praise you, and I yield myself to you.

November 18

The times of sowing and reaping are times of hope and rejoicing. You sow in hope and reap with joy. The times in-between are the difficult times, however. This is the time of patience. Patience cannot be rushed or pressured. Patience stands until the fruit is ready for harvesting. If patience is lax or lacking, the sowing was done in vain.

I have given the power to you to hold yourself strong until the time of reaping. Do not allow discouragement or trouble to hinder your patience. You shall surely reap! The confident heart does not faint or grow weary. You know the rewards are sure because you are confident in the rewarder. I am *the rewarder of them that diligently seek* **me**. You may begin now to rejoice. I have given you the land, and no man is able to stand against you.

Scriptures: Joshua 1:11, Isaiah 40:31, Romans 8:25, Galatians 6:7, Hebrews 11:6.

Prayer: My Lord and my God, I rejoice in you. Thank you for teaching me patience. As I spend the waiting period praising and thanking you, it seems much shorter. I love you so much, Father.

November 19

I have made you different, and **my Holy Spirit** abides in you. You will not be understood by the world----not until it accepts me. If they rejected **me**, how will they accept you? But, love them anyway. Be forgiving and not offended. **I** want you to influence them----not for them to influence you. If you will stand steadfast, **my** glory and light will shine out. The world needs light. Do not fail to shine!

Scriptures: Jeremiah 1:17:19, Matthew 5:44, John 15:18, I Peter 2:9.

Prayer: Father, I want to please you, and not the world. It is not hard to be loving and forgiving when I stay close to you. Help me always to be sure I am abiding in you.

November 20

Be compassionate and considerate of others----their lives may depend upon what they see in you. When you live before men in spirit and in truth, they will be drawn to **me**. I am faithful to turn you to those who need **me**. You be faithful to turn them toward **me**.

I have much planned for those who desire to please **me**. A life with **me** is filled with excitement, joy and adventure. Do not hesitate to seek it out. You will not be disappointed.

Scriptures: Jeremiah 29:11, Colossians 3:17, I Peter 3:8.

Prayer: Father, a desire of my heart is for others to see Jesus in me. I want to fit into the plans you have for me. I want to be used to your glory. I praise and honor your name.

November 21

Do not feel like life is in vain----that rewards are illusive and unreachable. Do not be discouraged at failure, especially in yourself. I am doing a work in you and growth is sometimes painful, sometimes hidden. The persevering heart will reap great rewards, however. Just remember who it is you trust, remember **my** awesome power, and remember **my** ability to save, heal, prosper, and deliver. Then you will not grow weary of "growing".

There is so much to learn. It takes a dedicated effort to absorb **my** teachings. You can receive some teachings by being around others who receive. You can receive some teachings from just desiring to please **me**. The real meat of learning, however, comes from a determined heart----like that of Elisha! (Elisha would not be deterred from going with Elijah.) And then there was Jacob; he would not turn loose until he had been blessed.

Those who hold on and are determined reap the greatest rewards. It is true that **I** am impartial to man, that I am no respecter of persons, but the man who determines to receive more of **me**, will! I treat all such men the same----**I** give them a double portion!

Scriptures: Genesis 32:24-26, II Kings 2:1-15, Acts 10:34, Galatians 6:9.

Prayer: Father, help me to be determined to stay the course. Sometime I feel so strung-out. With your help, I will persevere. I want to receive all that I am capable of receiving.

November 22

The comforting power of **my word** is immeasurable. The peace that **my word** can bring to a troubled heart is beyond price. **My** heart yearns to comfort the broken-hearted----those in physical, emotional or spiritual pain. But they will not let **me**! Think how your heart yearns to comfort those you love when you know they are suffering. You would like to take their suffering and bear it yourself, if it would give them even a little comfort.

Well, **I** did bear it! **I** gave it to **Jesus**, and **he** broke the curse of it. *Evil* now has no hold on **my** children----yet **my** children have not accepted this gift. They have not received **my** comfort, peace, healing or delivering power! It grieves a father's heart to see his children in stress. Share the *good news* that

it is done! ----all grief, pain and suffering have been borne. Let **my** children know so they may receive it! Tell them how----they need to know.

Scriptures: Psalm 22:1-5, Isaiah 53:4-5, II Corinthians 1:3-4, Galatians 3:13.

Prayer: Father, your word is true, so powerful and so wonderful. There is nothing that comforts me so much when I am troubled. I want everyone to know what marvelous things your word can do. Help me to share this with others.

November 23

When you begin to realize how truly blessed you are, what power you possess, and how filled with knowledge you have become, you will have *the joy of the Lord. Joy unspeakable and full of glory* is the manifestation of **me** in a believer's life. What a thrill it is to have the manifestation of gifts, of prayers, of healing, deliverance, prosperity and love. These are my blessings that **I** have given unreservedly and they are free to whosoever will receive them. This realization of **my** blessings will come as your spirit grows, and it grows from knowledge of **my word** and abiding in **me.**

There are no substitutes; there are no shortcuts! Choose more than ever to make these (knowledge and abiding) a priority. Then the manifestations will come more quickly----and in greater power. Look forward to the future. Revel in the loveliness of life. **I** have made it fruitful and full of abundant grace----*every favor and earthly blessing.*

Scriptures: John 15:5, I Corinthians 12:4-5, II Corinthians 4:15, I Peter 1:8.

Prayer: Father, it is hard for me to understand how much you love me! Life with you is so exciting. Thank you for all the blessings that are mine.

November 24

Give thanks unto me this day, and receive the blessings of a loving **Father**. No area of your life is too small or too large to be neglected in your *thanksgiving*. As you give thanks, you will open your heart to receive more and more of **my** blessings.

Scriptures: I Chronicles 16:34, Psalm 105:1, Daniel 2:23, Romans 1:8.

Prayer: Father, how I thank you. My heart overflows with thanksgiving. Every good thing I have, or am, comes through you. Blessed be your name.

November 25

Every thought you think must be disciplined by my word in order to have victory in your life. Learn to sift your mind for impurities of thought.

November 26

Concentrate on the good, the pure and those things that edify. The *enemy* would have you dwell on negative, destructive, confusing thoughts----so that *he* could brings those things to pass in your life. Since you are no longer under *his* domination, you do not have to yield to *his* promptings. You are learning to be aware when *he* sends *his* doubt and unbelief into your mind. You are becoming cognizant of *his* deceptions. Therefore, *his* power is broken----for whom *he* cannot deceive, *he* cannot abuse!

Train your mind to dwell on **my word**. You will then experience the fruit of peace. You will not falter nor fall. Release **my** power to work and the results are forthcoming! Hallelujah!

Scriptures: Joshua 1:8, Psalm 19:14, II Corinthians 10:5, Galatians 5:22, Philippinans 4:8.

Prayer: Father, how good life is, when I think on your word. There is no place for doubt and unbelief. I choose to think on lovely things today, and every day. Thank you for prompting me to do so.

November 26

The door to life must come through **Jesus. He** is the only way, but so many try other doors. I need for you to be an arrow, to point the way to **him**. So many of **my** children point the way to other sources before they consider **Jesus. He** is the only answer to

November 27

every need; **he** is the only one who can solve the problems of man.

I can understand how someone in pain would seek symptomatic relief. However, the root problem is still there. Until the root is dealt with, the problem reoccurs again, and again. Endeavor to show the way, through **Jesus**, to the core of the problem. Pray that spiritual eyes would be open to receive the answer. Until the root is cut, the symptoms will never leave.

Do not yield to the temptation to solve only extraneous needs, while leaving the core untouched. Do not be satisfied until the root is completely cleaned----and detached----so no more growth is possible. You have the tools to cut cleanly. Use them!

Scriptures: Matthew 3:10; John 10:9, John 14:6, Acts 26:18, Romans 11:16.

Prayer: Father, I want to point the way to Jesus. I know he is the answer to every problem. Help me to be a good witness.

November 27

Allow **my Spirit** to permeate every fiber of your being, to quicken every cell to renewal, and to open every pore to **my** cleansing. As you do, you will begin to walk with **me** in new power and might. Your permission has to be given, however, before the **Holy Spirit** can operate effectively in your life. You must have no reservations about my entrance into your life. No fear must be left to hinder the flow of **my** power, no doubt must be allowed to hinder faith. Your decision must be founded on trust and fidelity. It must be grounded in truth, and cultivated daily. The determination to open your life to my leading must come far in advance of actual habitation, so that you will be ready for the forces that would hinder you.

Preparation always precedes growth. Prepare your heart, your mind and your body. This preparation is **Spirit**-inspired and **Spirit**-led. Remember, I give not only the power to do my good pleasure, but also the *will* to do it. However, you must be ready to receive it.

Scriptures: Proverbs 3:5, Matthew 14:31, Romans 6:4, Romans 8:14, Philippians 2:13.

Prayer: Father, I thank you for giving me the Holy Spirit to be my Comforter, my Teacher, and my Guide. I yield myself to him. Help me to hear him clearly, I praise you, Father.

November 28

The *enemy* seeks entrance into your life, to stop the power of the **Holy Spirit** from operating through you. *He* seeks to dominate your thinking, to destroy your faith, and to defeat you in every area of your life. Rejoice, however, because *he* is a defeated foe. *Satan* has no power to possess, harass or hinder you.

November 29

I have made a show of him openly, and *he* is powerless in *his* efforts----as long as you act according to **my word.**

Do not allow *Satan* to bluff you! Do not allow him to bring fear into your heart! Refuse to give *him* ground in your *life*. *He* no longer has any authority or right to act against you. As you rebuke *him*, and stand against *him, he* has to flee. Take offense at *him* and give *him* no place! You have the power and authority to do so! *He* cannot harm you.

Scriptures: Psalm 68:18, Mark 16:17-18, Romans 8:37-39, Hebrews 2:14-15.

Prayer: I praise and thank you, Father, for Jesus, who has defeated Satan. I thank you that Satan is powerless as long I stand on your word. I will not fear him, because you say I am more than a conqueror. Hallelujah!

November 29

Be instant, in season and out! This is preparation raised to its highest level of performance. A prepared heart, mind and body cannot be defeated, hindered, or bothered; it is immune to all *the wiles of the devil*. What a tremendous position for a believer! You are steadfast and strong in the faith of your **God**, trusting and trustworthy!

November 30

I am raising an army of such men and women. **My** kingdom will be governed by the *pure in heart*, by those whose lives reflect **me**. This army is taking ground daily. Victory is assured because of **Jesus.** The victory here is a foretaste of the eternal victory that is the ultimate end for believers. Those who are trained and prepared will see it all----and share in the conquest.

Make inheriting the kingdom your highest aim. *Seek ye first the kingdom of God, and his righteousness; and all these things shall be added unto you.* When your aim is perfect, the path is straight. I have given you the land. Receive it!

Scriptures: Joshua 1:13, Matthew 5:8, Matthew 25:34, Matthew 6:33, I Corinthians 16:13, II Timothy 4:2.

Prayer: Father, I seek your kingdom above all else. Help me to prepare myself. I want to be a part of your army. I will praise you and love you forever.

November 30

The door to my heart is through acceptance of **my son,** and through faith in his power to deliver. *Without faith, it is impossible to please me. . . . no man commeth unto the Father, but by me.* The implications of this profession of faith are beyond imitation. I have opened possibilities to you that will take a lifetime to explore. However, the joy of

November 30

coming to **me** will be more compensation than you can imagine. Because you have dared to believe and act on **my word**, you shall see the fruit of your faith. Your prayers are answered and your position is strong.

In order to maintain faith and to grow, you must not be hindered in your spiritual life. Make it the priority above all priorities. This is not for **my** sake, but for yours. **I** long to fellowship with you, but even more, **I** long to have you in the position to receive from **me**. **My** love for you is without measure. Man can hardly comprehend this---and except in the spirit---he cannot at all!

Scriptures: John 14:6, I Corinthians 2:9, Hebrews 11:6, I John 5:14-15.

Prayer: Father, I thank you that because of Jesus, I can come to you at any time. And when I base my prayer on your word, I know I receive what I ask for. How I praise your name! How I thank you for your love! How I love you!

DECEMBER

December 1
 Be above reproach in your dealings with all men. Be honest and let me guide your every move; be sensitive to **my Holy Spirit**. *Judge not, that ye may not be judged.* Let me deal with the hearts of men. Your job is only to obey me, and to be submissive to those **I** have put in authority over you. As you do this, you place yourself in position to receive. I have given you the land. I will bless you in it.

 Give no foothold to the enemy. Do not let the accuser rob you of the victory that **I** have given you, by hearing his lies. Lay your burdens on **me**. I am able to carry them---you are not! I will work all things to your good. Just trust **me**. You will not be disappointed.

Scriptures: Jeremiah 7:23, Romans 12:17, Ephesians 4:27, Hebrews 13:17, I Peter 5:7.

Prayer: Father, I want mercy, not judgment, from you. Help me to likewise be merciful and not judgmental. I rest in you, and I give you my love.

December 2
 As you grow in your spirit, the things of this world will influence you less and less. You will rise above the earthly problems. Living on a higher plane enhances the pleasures of earth---and diminishes the trials. I meant for man to be always above the

December 3

troubles of life. **I** meant for him to enjoy the fullness of life, and to be productive in life. But because of his disobedience and slothfulness in spiritual growth, he has not received the rewards of my creation.

As you learn to walk in **my** paths---paths of light and love---the darkness will roll back before you. You will have new visions of conquest, new hope springing forth to excite and enhance your life. **I** meant for life to be a thrill and reward. It was not meant to be, nor is it, a drudgery to be endured. Victory in life brings rewards. Victory renews, regenerates and reinvigorates the spirit, soul and body. Learn to win in spiritual warfare. Prepare yourself to win, and refuse to faint. Set your mind on **my word**; refuse to let anything, anyone or any condition move you. *I have given you the land.* **I** repeat, ***I HAVE GIVEN YOU THE LAND!*** Enjoy it.

Scriptures: Numbers 33:53, Ecclesiastes 3:13, John 16:33, I Timothy 6:17.

Prayer: Father, I choose to believe your word, no matter what the world says. Thank you for the victories I see in my life. Thank you for making me a winner! How I praise you!

December 3

The overflowing abundance of **my grace** is being comprehended by you in greater measure. his realization is the foundation for security and peace.

Comprehending **my** grace will enable you to rest assured of my faithfulness and to dare to believe for great miracles. You are beginning to know **my** character and manifest presence. Therefore, you can act with a greater sense of direction.

I am teaching you to walk in the **Spirit**; as you do, you will see the *fruits of the spirit* springing forth. The time you have spent with **me** has been foundation-building time---time used to hear **my** voice, to feel **my** presence, to listen to instructions and obey.

More time is needed. You will have to make time by yielding your spirit to **me** at every spare moment. It is a natural act for a spiritual man, but is very hard for the carnal man. Abide in **me** and see the glory of **me**. You will not be disappointed!

Scriptures: Psalm 1:2, Jeremiah 24:7, Hebrews 3:12-14, III John 1:3-4.

Prayer: Father, I give thanks to you for your grace. It still amazes me when I think of how much you love me. I want to walk always in the Spirit. Help me to make more time for you.

December 4

Never be discouraged with the trials before you, for victory is always yours. As you learn to rest in **me,** you have the energy, enthusiasm and courage to tackle any task that is presented to you. The desire to

December 5

retreat and hide from trouble is not a spiritual desire, but a carnal one. There is no hiding place outside of **my** love and protection. *I am your hiding place.*

When you walk with **me, I** give you rest. I hide you under **my** wings in the secret places, and you are protected. You can be in the midst of a crowd----but carefully hidden away in me. I am come that they might have life, and that they might have it more abundantly. I give enthusiastic, energetic, overflowing life that produces wealth, happiness and peace.

The thief cometh to kill, steal and destroy life. His wiles and deceptions have no power over those who are not ignorant of his tactics. Be strong in the word; be strong in your faith; be strong in determination! Then you will see the forces of evil flee from you----and at your command. **My word** works! Use it!

Scriptures: Psalm 61:4, Psalm 119:114, Matthew 11:29, John 10:10, Ephesians 6:10, James 4:7.

Prayer: Father, I praise you. There is no way I can be discouraged when I keep my mind on you. You have provided all I need for success in every area of my life. I receive your word, and with your help, I will be an overcomer. I love you.

December 5

As you wait upon me with expectancy and

December 6

anticipation of good to come, **I** am already preparing the blessings to flow. **I** react to faith and hope, based on my faithfulness. If you trust in my power to perform, **I** will!

Just as you would never disappoint someone you love----who is trustfully believing you according to your promise----neither will **I**! As you stand, stand in faith. **I** act on faith!

Scriptures: Psalm 37:34, Psalm 119:90, I Corinthians 2:9, I Corinthians 16:13.

Prayer: Father God, I am filled with excitement and expectancy over the good things you have planned for me. Help me to stay so close to you that I will not miss out on any of your blessings. You are wonderful, and I adore you.

December 6

A wayward heart is unstable and cannot know the peace of **God.** A heart that is not true in love, in purpose, in desire towards **me** is a heart without meaning. It is doomed to frustration and failure. To have a heart that knows **me**, its **Master** and **Lord**, is to have a heart that is full of joy. I have come that your joy may be full. This overflowing, abundant joy will lift you up in the darkest hour, and will bring you into the light of love that every man seeks.

I am the creator of the heart. **I** know its every function, the rhythm of its beat, the need it has to be complete. When you walk with **me**, the **God** of the Universe, you have a complete heart. **Jesus** points the way to **me**. Follow **him** into *fullness of life*. Then your heart will be stable, and abundant life will be yours.

Scriptures: Isaiah 40:28-29, John 14:9, John 16:24, James 1:6-8.

Prayer: Father, I thank you for sending Jesus. Because of him, I know you, my Lord and my God. I want my heart to be true to you always. I love you and give you praise and glory.

December 7
    Be diligent to follow my leading. The **Holy Spirit** will always lead you in safe paths. He will shorten the time and the distance necessary to obtain success in life. **He** will quicken your spirit so that you may indeed walk in victory. **I** have plans for your life. If you heed my directions, you will live in **my** kingdom.
    Choose to allow the **Holy Spirit** free reign in your life. This will keep your heart in peace, and your mind at rest. It is a glorious thing to *walk in the Spirit*. As you set your mind and heart to do so, you will see the product of a fruitful life.

Scriptures: Psalm 23, Isaiah 26:3-4, Jeremiah 29:11, Galatians 5:25.

December 8, 9

Prayer: Father, I am so grateful that I have the Holy Spirit to lead me. On my own, I couldn't choose the right paths. I give him free reign in my life. Thank you, Father.

December 8
The act of giving mercy is more than compassion or empathy. It is a desire to see **my** will performed in the earth. It is a wish to see **my** love manifested in a glorious way.

Do not confuse mercy with compassion. Make sure you are desiring the higher blessing. Mercy is everlasting, while compassion is temporary. Learn to desire the mercy of **God** for all mankind----that man's end would not be futile. **I** have blessed, and who can reverse it?

Scriptures: Numbers 23:20, Psalm 103:17-18, Micah 6:8, Matthew 9:13.

Prayer: Father, I want to be merciful like you. I have much compassion, but I desire to have much mercy. Help me to really understand the difference.

December 9
Be sure your heart is set on things of the **Spirit**, before you venture into compromising situations. **My** disciples were meant to be victorious in every area, but they must be prepared. **I** have given the desire and ability to do **my** good pleasure,

but do not treat **my** gift lightly. I put in you the urge to please **me**. Your love----not only for **me**, but for your neighbor----is growing mightily within you.

The *things* of this earth may cloud holy initiatives, if not checked and halted in the embryo stage. *Satan* has always known this premise, in an *evil* sense. If you can but check *evil* impulses with the **Holy Spirit**, then good will proceed instead of *evil*. *Walk in the Spirit* at all times. It is the only safe haven.

Scriptures: Ezekiel 36:27, Mark 12:28-31, Romans 8:1, Galatians 5:16.

Prayer: Father, I desire to please you. I love you so much, and I thank you that I can see others through your eyes and love them, also. Thank you that I have a safe place as long as I walk in the Spirit. Help me to be alert.

December 10

I have given you abilities and gifts to do **my** will. As with natural talent, your abilities must be developed according to kingdom principles----in order to be a blessing to others instead of a curse. The gifts that are received by faith can certainly be abused or misused. However, they can abundantly bless and deliver, as well. **I** have made it possible for you to discern evil, the wolf in sheep's clothing. **I** have given you authority and power over the evil one. **I** have made it possible for you to succeed----and not fail.

The ways that **I** have given are through **my word** and through time spent with **me**. These develop **my** gifts and abilities. This is how you learn to have listening ears and eyes that see. You can then make right decisions, and your talents will not be cursed or wasted. You are blessed!

Scriptures: Psalm 119:105, Isaiah 32:3, Luke 10:19, I Corinthians 12:28, Ephesians 4:8.

Prayer: Lord, I do not want to waste any talents you have given me. Help me to recognize my strong points and to be a blessing to others.

December 11

I will send you into paths traveled by those who need **my word, my** way, **my** life. Some will accept your words eagerly, but many will not. Your job is to be a living testimony of **my** wares, being not brash nor hard. You are to be a vital, enthusiastic representative of **my** kingdom. You are to be a good salesman of **my** wares-----the wares of peace, love, joy, prosperity, health, hope and faith. The ones to whom I send you are needful of **my** wares. They are sick, desperate and despondent.

The joy and life you bring will be in stark contrast to their lives. Some will think you weird; others will be afraid of change. Many, however, will

December 12

be open-minded to the wares you bring, and will respond enthusiastically. These are the ones who will enter freely and will receive the benefits. All, however, will know that the kingdom of **God** has been in their midst.

Scriptures: Psalm 46:10, Isaiah 6:8, Matthew 5:14-16, Luke 9:2.

Prayer: Father, I'm filled with wonder thinking of myself as a living testimony of you. So many need you, Lord, and I am willing to be used. Prepare me and help me to bring you glory. I praise your holy name.

December 12

The thoughts that **I** give you are life-breathing and build you up. They restore your soul and renew your mind. They enable you to walk in the paths of light and love. If you ever allow yourself to atrophy in spiritual matters, you will feel the crushing weight of despondency and desperation. **I** am the shield that keeps you protected. You can abide in **me** and in the *secret place of the most high*. Always remember your source. Keep yourself and the wicked one cannot touch you.

Scriptures: Psalm 23:3, Psalm 51:10, Psalm 91:1, Proverbs 12:5, I John 5:18.

Prayer: Father, thank you for renewing my mind and restoring my soul. It is so good to know that I do not have to feel despondent or depressed as long as I abide in you. I choose to have the joy of the Lord. You are worthy to be praised, and I will praise you all the days of my life.

December 13

As **my** love develops in you in greater measure, you will find yourself reaching out more to those in need. You will find it much easier to allow others to come into your affections and thoughts. Yea, you will invite them into your heart. You will feel the pains and yearnings of others, even as **I** feel your pain. You will begin to love as **I** love (without the need of returned love). You will know that this kind of love will heal, save and deliver, and that this love stems from **me**, for **I** am love.

I am sufficient to meet your needs and the needs of others----and **I** will! Your love must be sufficient to break down the barriers they created to protect themselves. Go forth, shedding the love of **Christ** abroad. Many are in desperate need and will be affected.

Scriptures: Romans 5:5, II Corinthians 3:5, I John 3:16, I John 4:8, I John 5:2.

Prayer: Thank you, Father, for your love. I thank you that I am beginning to love as you do---without expecting love in return. I want to continue to grow in the knowledge of your love.

December 14

I am sending you out to minister to those who are ready to hear the *good news.* They are hungry for a way that works; **I** am the way. Those who are learning to know **me** will listen; you are blessed to tell them. **My** ways are not complicated. They are simple and sure. I made them so easy that little children can understand them----and little children will!

Just share the good news, and watch my **Holy Spirit** take control. The *Christian* walk is fruitful and full of rewards. The *Christian* walk is easy to be entreated, when your heart is pure. Keep your heart with all diligence and watch the issues of your life affect others.

Scriptures: Proverbs 4:23, Proverbs 8:32, Matthew 18:3-4, Luke 10:2-9, John 3:5, John 8:12.

Prayer: Father, I thank you that your ways are so simple that even I can understand. Help me to share with others in an uncomplicated way. You have done so much for me, and I want others to know you.

December 15

The knowing of **my** might and power is imperative before you can act on it with authority. Therefore, you must endeavor to become more

December 15

acquainted with **my word**, **my** character, **my** being----before you minister to others. Then you will truly begin to see yourself as an extension of **me**, for indeed you are. When you accepted **me** into your heart and began to let the **Holy Spirit** operate without hindrance, you became part of the kingdom of **God**, and an extension of the Godhead. In you dwells the Spirit of the **Living God.** You are my representative with might and authority in the earth.

As with any group, organization or family you represent, you must know the business in order to be effective. Therefore, you must be knowledgeable about **my** ways and power. This training is not automatic; it comes with diligence and determination to learn from the **Spirit.** An effective member must be trained or discipled, if you will, in the ways of the kingdom. Then you can operate freely, because the kingdom is inside you.

Scriptures: Deuteronomy 7:9, Psalm 25:4, Luke 17:21, John 17:21, Ephesians 1:17-23.

Prayer: Father, I know you, but I want to really know you----more every day. You have so many attributes that it will take me years to discover just some of them. If I can know and love you more each day, I will be satisfied. This is my quest. Help me, Lord.

December 16

The reality of **my** life in a believer is *the peace that passes understanding*. This is the peace that has no reason for being, but is. This is the maturation of the seed of faith that knows in whom it believes. As you dwell in **me,** you will have the deepening assurance of security, of well-being, of divine protection and sustenance that is the heart-desire of every human being. This is the reward of being in fellowship with **me**. This sense of well-being comes as you abide in **me** and **my word** abides in you. Do you not wonder why the whole earth does not actively seek this great treasure? It is because they do not believe that it is real!

Scriptures: Nahum 1:15, Haggai 2:9, John 15:7, Philippians 4:7, II Timothy 1:12.

Prayer: Father, this life I have in Christ brings such joy. I am so free! I cannot imagine wanting to live any other way. I ask that the eyes and ears of those who do not know you be opened, so they might know the truth. You are more wonderful than can be told!

December 17

When you feel that circumstances are oppressive, remember **my word**. When you have doubts about world affairs and situations that affect your life, remember **my word**. Recall that all heaven and earth will pass away, but my word will endure *forever.* **My word** does not fail. It is from everlasting to everlasting.

My prophets paid dearly for **my word**. Remember to esteem it and hold it dearly in your heart. It is the audible and visual evidence of **my** thoughts, the reality of **my** purposes. **It** is **my** gift of substance to man----a thought that he can cherish, and on which he can rely. You must also remember that *in the beginning was the word . . . . and the word was made flesh.*

Scriptures: Ezra 3:11, Psalm 41:13, Mark 13:31, John 1:1, John 1:14.

Prayer: Father, thank you for your Word. It is the answer to any problem, and just as true today as it was in Bible days. I couldn't live, Lord, without being able to count on the Word. How I wish the whole world could know you!

December 18

You have learned that *perfect love casts out fear.* This is love for the **Father** and a trust in my faithfulness. Do you believe that **I** can handle the situations you encounter in your life, that **I** can protect, save and deliver you? Do you really believe that **I** will work things to your good? that **I** will keep what you have committed unto me? All of these questions really point to the question of whether you believe in **my** love for you, of whether you love **me**

December 19

and trust **me** to take care of you. If you do, then there is no room for fear. Thus, the evil one has no room to operate in your life.

    I rely on your faith in **me** to open the way for my intervention in your life and in the lives of those you love. As you trust me, **I** can freely move on your behalf. Choose to trust **me!** Choose not to fear and you will see **my** miraculous intervention in your life. Give no place to the *devil,* and *he* will flee from you.

Scriptures: Psalm 18:2, Nahum 1:7, Zephaniah 3:17, Romans 8:28, I John 4:18.

Prayer: Lord, when I am tempted to fear, I remember that fear comes <u>not</u> from you. Fear is, in fact, the opposite of faith. Help me to keep my faith strong. I believe your promises and receive them. I thank you that the devil <u>must</u> flee. I praise and worship your name.

December 19

    When you begin to learn to worship me, you begin by thank me for the blessings I have given you. This thanksgiving then turns into praise of me. Acknowledgement of my power and might, of my creative ability and my miracles begin to well-up within you. True worship, however, comes from deep in your spirit. Thanksgiving and praise come through your mind, although prompted by the Holy Spirit. But when you enter into worship, you are hardly aware of your mind being involved at all. Your whole being becomes totally immersed in a deep spiritual experience. Your mind is hardly active, and your body is unaware of itself. Your spirit becomes the total focus and real communication takes place----from you to me, and from me to you.

This is the realm of blessing that is the highest. It refreshes and renews your spirit in a greater degree than any other form of communication. This is a state of being which is to be coveted and sought after. It is the state for which you were created, and in which you are most benefited. This happens when your spiritual man reigns.

Scriptures: I Chronicles 16:29, Psalm 100:4, Jonah 2:7, Jonah 2:9, John 4:23-24.

Prayer: Father, forgive me for often being too busy to let my spiritual man reign. The times I have entered into worship of you are so wonderful. I want this kind of worship to be the normal, not the exception. Help me, Lord.

December 20

If you will hear my voice, there is no obstacle too large to stand in your way, no mountain that cannot be moved, no pressure that can come or stay on you. I have given you victory in every area of your life, but you have to heed the leading of **my Holy Spirit.** You must submit your will to my will.

Jesus did! It means forfeiting your carnal nature for **my** nature. **Jesus** did! You will have to yield every area of your life to **me. Jesus** did! Submitting, forfeiting and yielding are the means to complete victory in **Jesus.** If you desire to live life in its fullest, reigning as a king and priest, you must take this path. You must determine to set your mind on things of the spirit, But is anything impossible with **God?**

Scriptures: Luke 1:37, John 14:15, Romans 6:13, Romans 8:7, Revelation 5:10.

Prayer: Lord, I submit myself to you. I forfeit my carnal nature and yield every area of my life to you. I know this is the only way I can live in your best. Keep me alert, so that I will not take anything back. I desire to please you, Father.

December 21

Be glad for the excellence of my word, for the integrity and wisdom in it. **My word** is the key to victorious living. The **word** is the truth, and it gives great opportunity for learners to obtain the priceless gift of life. When you put the **word** first place in your life, you are allowing your spirit to come into maturity. Your spirit yearns for the opportunity to be involved in the kingdom of God----to be loosed to rule your mind and body. Your spirit longs to come into the dominant position for which it was created.

The spirit of man is subject to the will of man,

however, just as the body of man is subject to his will. Unless your mind is renewed *with washing of the water of the* **word**, there is no "giving-in" to the Spirit. Your mind will yield to your flesh, and destruction will reign rampant. Choose to let your spirit be strengthened by the *meat* of the **word**. You will then begin to see what victorious living means.

Scriptures: Matthew 26:41, John 17:17, Romans 6:23, Ephesians 5:25-26.

Prayer: Father, your word has become so precious to me. In it I find all the answers for abundant, victorious living. I would not want to live without your life within me. Help me to stay constant, and not be governed by my flesh.

December 22

Count each day as a blessing from **God.** Look forward to the day's happenings, and when day is done, thank **me** for the blessing you have had. Each day **I** prepare good things for those who are expecting **my** blessings.

The faith of one who is yielded to me opens up possibilities that are denied to unbelievers. **I** will bless those whose hearts are pure, and **I** seek the righteous in heart. The praise you give **me** and the expectations you have are the characteristics of a heart yielded to the **Holy One of Israel.**

December 23

Scriptures: Psalm 36:1, Psalm 71:22, Psalm 97:11, Proverbs 10:22, Matthew 5:8.

Prayer: Father, as I spend time in your word, it is impossible for me not to expect blessings! I look forward to each day and the opportunities you provide. I thank you for all you have done for me in the past, and for the good things you have for me in the future. Oh Holy One of Israel, you are worthy to be praised.

December 23

Do not thwart **my** blessings by refusing to accept them. When you let doubt and fear rule your mind, you are hindering **my** flow of love to you. You are cutting off the faith action necessary to channel good things into you life. Despondency, doubt, unbelief, fear and depression are all negative devices the *enemy* looses on you to rob, kill and destroy faith. If you yield to his desires, you open the way for the evils of life to invade your domain. However, if you will resist these things, you will see positive results. Make yourself resist! You have the power and will. The **word** says that *he that is begotten of God keepeth himself, and the evil one toucheth him not.* You do not have to be touched by *Satan*. Therefore, refuse *his* worries, refuse *his* doubts, refuse *his* fears!

Let the perfect love of **me** cast out the fear and bring in hope, joy, peace and gladness. These are **my** rewards to a heart fixed on **me.** Make your heart steadfast. Trust **me**!

Scriptures: Genesis 49:25, Isaiah 35:4, Obadiah 1:17, John 10:10, I John 4:18, I John 5:18.

Prayer: Father, I trust you, and I desire each and every one of your blessings. I will refuse to think on doubt and fear, whenever they cross my mind. I will not submit to Satan's lies; because I submit to you, Satan must flee! I praise your name, Lord, which is above all names. I accept your blessings of hope, joy, peace and gladness. Glory!

December 24
The gifts of **God** are without recall or repentance. I would that all men would be holy, but that has never been a requirement for blessing. The requirement is faith. If you believe I can, I will! In the **word**, faith in me was demonstrated by great miracles. As men were obedient to my requirements, the miraculous came forth. *Without faith, it is impossible to please **me**.* Faith is acknowledgement of my presence, of my reality and power. When you lack faith in me, you actually doubt my power to perform **my word**.

I reward those who diligently seek **me**. Those who are seeking me realize that **I** can be found. They are acknowledging my reality. Those who seek, find. **My** gospel is so simple, but so misunderstood. Choose to keep it simple. I am the **I** am, and **I** change not.

What is simpler than this?

Scriptures: Exodus 3:14, Jeremiah 29:13, Malachi 3:6, Romans 11:29, Hebrews 11:6, I Peter 1:16.

Prayer: Father, I believe you can, and I believe you will! Believing you can is as natural as breathing, but believing you will requires me to stay constantly meditating in the word. From childhood I was taught that you can do anything, and now I am working at increasing my faith to the point that knowing you will will be just as natural to me. Help me to fight the good fight of faith.

December 25
   The cause of Christmas is to bring man into repentance and fellowship with me. When Christmas is abused with the dilution of commercialism, I grieve. Christmas is a time of great thanksgiving for the gift of life, given to a lost world. It is a time of expectancy for the peace and joy promised. It is a time of rejoicing and praise for the kingdom of **God** to become real to all men. It is a time of joy for **Jesus** is alive, and is soon to return to physically reign on the earth.
   Man is sick, feeble, weak and without hope in this world. I have sent **Jesus**, but so few really know the salvation **he** brings. Make **Jesus** alive in your world, and he will be received. Make **Jesus** alive in your heart, and **he** will be acknowledged. Let **Jesus**

reign supreme in your actions, and others will accept him. . . . *If I be lifted up,. . . I will draw all men unto me.* This is the real meaning of Christmas.

Scriptures: Isaiah 9:6, Jonah 2:9, Luke 2:1-16, John 12:32.

Prayer: Father, thank you for Jesus, the greatest gift of all! Help me and all of your children to keep Jesus first in our lives each day of the year. Help me to show him to a lost and dying world. I am overwhelmed to think what you gave to the world. I love you, Father; thank you for the Prince of Peace.

December 26

Take courage from **me.** Always remember my power, my might, my fierce anger, **my** loving kindness. I am the **Lord** that healeth thee, who delivers from the snare of the fowler and from the noisome pestilence. I rescue the perishing, give sight to the blind, I bind up and restore. I am the **Almighty!** Who can stand before **me?** Remember my greatness and imprint **my word** on the tables of your heart. I do not change or repent. I have said it, and shall it not come to pass? Choose to believe and act on **my word.** Choose to be stable in all your affairs, to not faint nor falter. I have given you the land. Possess it!

December 27

Scriptures: Exodus 15:26, Psalm 91:3, Joshua 1:13, Ezekiel 24:14, Luke 4:18-19, Revelation 1:8.

Prayer: Father, you are Almighty God, creator of heaven and earth. You are all powerful. I praise your holy name. I thank you for your loving kindness and that your word is true. I will rise up and possess the land you have given me!

December 27

Never grow weary in the faith. There is such a temptation to do so, because patience gets tired. Stir yourself up to remain steadfast on your confession of faith. Set you heart and mind anew to stand until you see your desire manifested. Do not lose heart before the race is won! It is the ones who finish the race who claim the prize, not the starters. I have given you the land, but only the stalwart in heart will take it!

How sweet is the victory of success. The victory of knowing that you have overcome, that you have won, gives you the strength to go on to other battles. The battle has been won, the victory given. You must go on to stand and fight again and again, until **Jesus** returns.

Scriptures: Ephesians 6:13, Philippians 3:14, I Timothy 6:12, II Timothy 1:6-7, Hebrews 12:1.

Prayer: Father, often I am tired, but I choose to stir

myself up (as you have said). I know I can stand, because you say that I can! I believe you, Lord. I am a winner, and I praise your name. You are so wonderful to provide all that I need to be more than a conqueror.

December 28

Because you have decided to place a priority on your spiritual growth, you will reap benefits you cannot imagine. I am not a beggarly God. I am not stingy with my benefits. I created the law of sowing and reaping. I give back a hundredfold and more!

The law of sowing and reaping is as unchangeable as the law of gravity. Each will not be changed, except by miraculous intervention. The law of sowing and reaping can work for you or against you, just as the law of gravity does. When you know the law is there, you can use it to its full benefit for positive results. I created all things to benefit the man I created. I have given him the choice as to how he will use my creation---for good or evil.

You have chosen the good portion. You will see good fruit from the evidence of **my** immoveable **word**. Even though heaven and earth shall pass away, **my word** shall not change. You have chosen well!

Scriptures: Job 4:8, Matthew 7:17, Matthew 7:20, Matthew 13:23, Galatians 6:7.

Prayer: Father, thank you for placing the desire in my heart to know you better, and to grow spiritually. Without knowing and understanding your word, I would live such a defeated life here on earth. I make a quality decision to learn and grow all the days of my life. I give you my thanks, my praise, and my love.

December 29

The more you grow into **my** likeness, the less you will be swayed by things of this world. Your tastes will change, as will your desires, your aspirations, your function. You will see **Jesus** manifested in your actions in ways that will amaze you; you know that in your carnal nature, these thoughts would never have originated. You will love to do the things you used to hate, and hate those things that take you spiritually away from the **Father's** good pleasure.

The truth of the **word** will become more real than the physical world, and the time you spend with me more precious than gold. You will want to spend time in prayer and meditation, above that which you now do, because of the filling of your soul that this time brings.

The love you have for others will increase, but it will also be a selfless love----loving them in spite of frailties, and because of **me.** This life **I** am giving you will make your former life seem dull and lusterless. There will be no comparison to the new richness that you will find. You will wonder how you could ever have stood being without this new injection of life.

Scriptures: I Corinthians 13:4-8, Galatians 2:20, Philippians 2:13, Colossians 1:27.

Prayer: Father, I have come such a long way in my relationship with you, but the exciting part is that I can never "arrive." I can always keep learning of you and growing. I cannot imagine my life "before you". What joy did I ever have? What enthusiasm or excitement? More important, however, I did not know how to love. When I begin to think that things cannot get better than this, I am completely overwhelmed by your generosity. I praise you and thank you, Father, with all my heart.

December 30

Prepare for the harvest, for it is coming! Would anyone plant without expecting to reap? But so many do! They plant seeds of faith, seed of giving, seeds of deliverance; then they never look for the increase. The fields should be inspected along the way, and signs of the increase should appear. As you see the crop maturing, begin to make plans for the harvest.

When you testify of me, give to **me** for the gospel, and do deeds in my name out of love of me, I am ready to reward you. You be ready to receive----

December 31

not passively, but actively! Just as salvation has been given to all men, so have my other blessings.

Unfortunately, all do not receive the blessings. They fail to receive their full inheritance. Believe for all of the blessings! They are yours. I have given them. Teach others to believe for them, too. I have given you the land. Receive it!

Scriptures: Deuteronomy 28:2; Matthew 6:1, 6:33; Luke 6:38; Galatians 6:9.

Prayer: Father, I thank you for the law of sowing and reaping. I do not give just to get, but I am so appreciative of your wonderful generosity. There are so many different areas of harvest: i.e. time, money, love, care, sharing, etc.-----and I love them all. Help me to show your loving, generous nature to others, so they may be grateful with me.

December 31

Before the beginnings of time, **I was.** I shall also be, after the end of time. Man cannot comprehend this saying, but the **Spirit** bears witness. In order to communicate with me effectively, your spiritual man must predominate. Man in his carnal nature is ruled by his mind, emotions and flesh. Therefore he is an outcast from spiritual truth. By my covenant and through the blood of **Jesus,** man has been reestablished in the spiritual kingdom. Man now has only to grow in spiritual truths to understand the concepts and precepts of the spirit life.

Man will live eternally! This may be beyond your comprehension, but it is nevertheless true. The important things of this earth are only dim reflections of spiritual values and truths. Come into fellowship with me, through **my word**, through prayer, through meditation. Learn of this realm to which you truly belong, so that you can effectively begin to rule in my kingdom now. As you walk in spiritual truth, you will never want to return to the carnal world. It will have no attractiveness for you.

Scriptures: John 1:1, John 3:16, John 17:17, Hebrews 13:20-21, Revelation 1:8.

Prayer: I really cannot comprehend, Lord, before the beginning of time. You said we would be with you eternally; this, too, is beyond me. But, **I BELIEVE YOU,** Father. Thank you for the blood of Jesus and the power in that blood. Thank you that my home is in heaven, that I am an overcomer, and more than an conqueror! I am so grateful that I will spend eternity with you!